The Men Who Made

CRYSTAL PALACE
FOOTBALL CLUB

The Men Who Made

CRYSTAL PALACE
FOOTBALL CLUB

Revd Nigel Sands

TEMPUS

Frontispiece: *Mr Arthur Wait – the man who did most to make Crystal Palace FC.*

First published 2004

Tempus Publishing Ltd
The Mill, Brimscombe Port
Stroud, Gloucestershire GL5 2QG

© Nigel Sands, 2004

British Library Cataloguing in Publication Data.
A catalogue record for this book is available from the British Library.

ISBN 0 7524 3291 5

Typesetting and origination by Tempus Publishing.
Printed and bound in Great Britain

CONTENTS

CRYSTAL PALACE ROLL OF HONOUR

FA Premiership
Best Season: Third place in 1990/91

Football League
Division One: Champions 1993/94, promoted via play-offs 1996/97, 2003/04
Second Division: Champions 1978/79, runners-up 1968/69
Third Division: Runners-up 1963/64
Third Division (South): Champions 1920/21, runners-up 1928/29, 1930/31, 1938/39
Fourth Division: Runners-up 1960/61

FA Cup
Runners-up 1989/90

Football League Cup
Semi-finalists 1992/93, 1994/95, 2000/01

Full Members' Cup
Winners 1990/91

Most Capped British Player
Eric Young 19 caps for Wales as a Crystal Palace player

Most League Appearances
Jim Cannon 571 (1973-88)

Most League Goals In Club Career
Peter Simpson 153 (1929-36)

Chairman's Foreword

I'm pleased again to be invited to preface an attractive book about Crystal Palace FC by our club historian and honorary chaplain, Revd Nigel Sands.

This book is an imposing volume, such as befits a club like ours, now that our anticipation and ambitions of securing the top-flight status which our hard work so patently deserves have been realised.

With Crystal Palace Football Club now returned to the Premiership, my intention is to continue to build and enhance our reputation; then, should 'The Rev' update this book in, say, ten years time, there should be plenty he will need to add to its contents.

Simon Jordan
Chairman, Crystal Palace FC
June 2004

AUTHOR'S PREFACE

As always, it gives me enormous pleasure to offer this latest book about Crystal Palace FC to the Club and to its legions of supporters. The pleasure this time, though, is specially poignant. This is because I have been a fan of this club since my boyhood in the early post-war years, and therefore the season 2004/05, which sees the publication of *The Men Who Made Crystal Palace FC*, will be my fifty-ninth as a follower of the Palace, and when we bring out the companion volume as part of Palace's centenary in twelve months time or so, 2005/06 will mark my own sixtieth jubilee season with The Glaziers and the Eagles. Thus, the pair of centenary works will straddle my diamond anniversary.

It won't surprise regular readers of my Palace books and articles to know that I have greatly enjoyed preparing this one for publication. In a sense this is the most prestigious book that I have written for Crystal Palace – it has certainly been the one that has taken the longest duration and greatest energy to complete! But, if the pleasure Palace folk derive from reading it and referring to it lies somewhere in proportion to my efforts then it will have been time and energy well spent!

Nigel Sands
Wickham Rectory
May 2004

Acknowledgements

No one could possibly produce a book such as this one without a great deal of assistance; some of it technical, some of it specialist.

Thus, it is only proper that I should acknowledge my gratitude for the help that was gladly provided in bringing *The Men Who Made Crystal Palace FC* to fruition.

James Howarth has become a valued friend during our association with Tempus Publishing and I should like to thank him and his team there for their involvement, encouragement and expertise from which the end product has greatly benefited.

As usual, I've received help from four Palace fans in particular: Colin Duncan has again assisted with proofreading while Tony Bowden and David Keats have added several items of fine detail which have enhanced the articles about the players. Neil Everitt's photographs are of such a high standard that it is impossible to conceive producing any Palace publication without his brilliant, unique contribution.

I was also grateful to two long-standing Palace fans, Mr Les Still and Dr Ron Cox, for information concerning Mr F.J. Nettlefold and Sir Adam Maitland, and to the family of Arthur Wait for loaning pictures of that great man.

Nigel Sands
Wickham Rectory
May 2004

Part One

PALACE OFF THE PARK

THE CHAIRMEN

It is probably worthwhile introducing this chapter about the fifteen past and present chairmen of Crystal Palace FC for two reasons. Firstly, each of these gentlemen (no ladies have held control of our club – so far at least!), must be construed to have helped to 'make' it in one way or another. 'For richer for poorer; for better for worse' as many readers will have said in a different context to their spouses – and indeed in several ways one's commitment to a football club, be it as a true, genuine fan, a director or a chairman, can be likened to a marriage. The chairman's contribution to the Club he controls must inevitably leave its mark upon it, whatever the character of that mark may be. Hence, every chairman is included here, with obviously more detailed descriptions and information supplied about the best ones.

Secondly, present-day readers and supporters (of any football club; not just of the Eagles) need to be aware of the demands upon and expectations of football club chairmen, certainly in the first half of the twentieth century. Until at least 1950 the chairmen of Football League clubs were not expected to be either the visionaries or financial wizards that they are today, although it would not be correct to assume that money did not enter into the matter, for their responsibilities usually included the provision of a guarantee securing the Club's overdraft (probably, and generally, an expanding one) at its bankers. Sometimes, too, chairmen and other directors of the Club might choose to put some of their own money towards the transfer fee of a sought-after player, although such information would never have been publicly divulged.

Equally, there is every reason to believe that most of the holders of the position of chairman at Crystal Palace FC had only the best, highest and usually unselfish motives for the Club during the periods in which they held office. Many of the early chairmen had been shareholders for long periods prior to assuming the role of club chairman: most had been members of the board of directors. Of course some grew disillusioned, or found new or existing demands too much for them to be able to retain the office, but there is no reason at all to doubt their integrity, honesty or goodwill.

Chairmen of Crystal Palace Football Club
1905-2004

Sydney Bourne	1905-30	John Dunster	1955-57
Louis Bellatti	1930-35	V.A. Ercolani	1957-58
R.S. Flew	1935	Arthur Wait	1958-72
Carey Burnett	1935-36	Raymond Bloye	1972-81
E.T. Truett	1936-39	Ron Noades	1981-98
Percy Harper	1939-50	Mark Goldburg	1998-99
David Harris	1950-53	Peter Morley	1999-2000
Arthur Wait	1953-55	Simon Jordan	2000-

Palace's first chairman was Mr **Sydney Bourne**, who was one of the original directors of Crystal Palace FC and was elected as chairman at the Club's first meeting. It was a wise decision because Mr Bourne had a great deal to do with the successful establishment and early successes of the Palace club.

Palace fans actually owe the involvement of Mr Bourne with our club to the astute work of Palace's first secretary, Mr Edmund Goodman, who invited Mr Bourne to join the newly formed company during the summer of 1905. He readily accepted and continued as chairman of the board until his death in 1930. He was the last of the original directors to remain associated with the Palace – an interesting and colourful personality.

Sydney Bourne was an all-round sportsman and played football for twenty-two years after he left school. A Londoner born and bred, he played for a team known as 'The Mosquitoes' in the early 1880s and later for Champion Hill, then Lyndhurst in Hampshire. In his early days he was an eager and aggressive forward but, as time went by, he dropped back to half-back, then to full-back and finally to goalkeeper! He had to play somewhere!

After helping Edmund Goodman in the foundation of the Crystal Palace club he was thrilled with the way the new team won the Second Division of the Southern League and gained a place in the First Division at the end of its first season. However, he always believed that Palace's greatest achievement was in the FA Cup when, in only their second season, they beat the Football League champions, Newcastle United, on their own ground, with the Magpies fielding nine internationals in their team that day.

When the Palace left the Southern League for the Football League in 1920 Mr Bourne was made a life member of the Southern League for his services since 1905, but the esteem in which he was held by Palace fans can be gathered from the great ovation they gave him when he re-took his seat for a home game with Luton on 23 March 1929 after a serious illness, which had kept him away since late the previous year.

To the end of his days Mr Bourne was to be seen at Selhurst Park with his inevitable cigar and Palace rosette. He died on Friday 19 September 1930 aged seventy-seven, at his home in Herne Hill. At the Third Division (South) match the following afternoon, the players of both Crystal Palace and Newport County wore black armbands and the

Mr Sydney Bourne.   *Mr L.T. Bellatti.*

flag was flown at half-mast – while the Palace recorded a resounding 7-1 victory to provide just the sort of farewell the chairman would have wished.

Mr Bourne's successor was Mr **Louis Bellatti**, who had been born and brought up in Upper Norwood and was the Club's vice-chairman. He was a director of twenty-one years' previous experience and one of the original shareholders of the Club.

While Mr Bellatti was sufficiently highly regarded among his Third Division (South) contemporaries to be elected by them to represent the interests of the Clubs in that division at the Football League management committee at the summer 1932 meeting, at the Palace helm he supervised a disappointing decline in the Club's standing and prospects, although it was under Mr Bellatti's chairmanship that the most successful Palace manager of the 1930s, Tom Bromilow, was appointed in 1935.

Mr Bellatti was a true supporter of Crystal Palace FC as well as its chairman. He is said never to have missed a match during his incumbency but he died suddenly in early October 1935, two days after attending our victory at Bristol Rovers and Palace's programme was fulsome in its tribute to him the following Saturday.

Eight days later Mr **R.S. Flew** was elected to follow Mr Bellatti, but astonishingly, he died within a month when complications set in following a routine operation for appendicitis.

Carey Burnett took over as Palace chairman at this difficult time, thrust into office by the sudden deaths of his two immediate predecessors. He had joined the board of directors by co-option during the 1932/33 season but, 'sensationally' as it was reported at the time, and within little more than a year, Mr Burnett resigned just before Christmas 1936 as a result of the culmination of differences between factions on the board and turmoil at the Club.

Mr **E.T. Truett**, a prominent Thornton Heath businessman and part-owner of the builders Truett and Steele, was a former chairman of the pre-war Crystal Palace Supporters' Club. He had joined the board during the reorganisation necessitated by the deaths of Messrs Bellatti and Flew and he took over as chairman immediately after the resignation of Carey Burnett.

Clearly approved of by football followers in general, Mr Truett became president of the national federation of football supporters' clubs in the summer of 1937. It was under Mr Truett that Palace again began to look like possible champions of the Third Division (South) – and that Palace first changed from our traditional colours of claret and blue to black and white for season 1938/39, the term in which we so nearly earned a return to the Second Division, finishing as runners-up to Newport County.

However, boardroom controversy was never far away from Selhurst Park at this time and in December 1939 Mr Truett and three other directors were suspended by a joint FA and Football League commission over irregular payments that had been made to two players. To modern-day readers this decision may sound absurd, and certainly at the time it was made discerning followers of the game knew very well that such payments

Mr R.S. Flew.

Mr Carey Burnett.

Mr Percy Harper is second from the right in this 1949 group.

were commonplace, even if never spoken of and made with discretion in discreet circumstances. The mistake made by Mr Truett and his colleagues was to be discovered!

Succeeding Mr Truett was **Percy Harper**, the owner of an early automatic-washing-machine company in Waddon, who had joined the board of directors earlier in 1939. It fell to Mr Harper to chair Crystal Palace FC throughout the long remaining years of the Second World War. Inevitably, these were extremely tough times for all football clubs, but Palace enjoyed welcome if perhaps surprising levels of success during them, winning wartime competitions in 1940, 1940/41 and 1945. However, by the end of the hostilities, the Club was not at all well-placed to progress from the Third Division (South) upon the resumption of fully competitive football, and partly due to two calamitous managerial appointments, the early post-war years at Selhurst Park were among the most disappointing in the Club's history.

However, it should be added that Mr Harper was held in high regard by his successors at Crystal Palace, who expressed regret at his decision to leave the directorate and voiced appreciation for the 'valuable' work he had done for the Club.

It was on Saturday 21 January 1950, prior to Palace's home game against Southend, that Percy Harper announced to a Palace board meeting that a group of seven local businessmen had approached him with a view to becoming directors of the Club. The existing directors approved such a course of action and the men were co-opted five days later. Among them were no fewer than four future chairmen of Crystal Palace FC.

The first member of the new directorate to become Palace's chairman was Mr **David Harris**, and he did so immediately upon his co-option. However, Palace's fortunes immediately subsided even further for, as another new director and the one who would become the most prominent at Crystal Palace, Mr Arthur Wait, later admitted, the new board initially 'made a real mess of things through our inexperience even though we were full of enthusiasm'. Thus, after grossly over-investing in new players and publishing grandiose plans to turn Selhurst Park into the Highbury of South London with a capacity of some 130,000, Palace had their worst-ever season in 1950/51 and had to seek re-election for the second time in three years.

The most significant achievement at Crystal Palace during Mr Harris' tenure as chairman was the installation of our club's original floodlighting system in the autumn of 1953, and the inaugural pair of games, against top-flight clubs Chelsea and Cardiff City, netted a profit of £1,400.

Arthur Wait had an initial two-year stint as Palace's chairman following Mr Harris' resignation in November 1953 but this was an undistinguished period for the Club to say the least, although during it the appointment was made of Cyril Spiers as our manager in October 1954 with the completely new remit here to cultivate a youth policy. Under Mr Spiers several key youngsters were secured and their development put in hand.

Four Palace chairmen are in this picture. Front left is Arthur Wait, front centre David Harris, front right is Victor Ercolani, while back right is John Dunster. Completing this group which comprised the new 1950 board, are, from left to right, back row: Guy Robson, Ralph Shrager and Colonel Jack Trevor. Behind the group hangs the picture of club president, Mr F.J. Nettlefold, referred to in the next chapter.

Mr Wait's friend **John Dunster** became chairman in 1955. His biggest contribution to the game was on a wider canvas because it was he who put the case on behalf of the lower division clubs at the 1956 annual meeting of the Football League for the introduction of national Third and Fourth Divisions. It was agreed that the proposal should be implemented at the end of the 1957/58 season and, while Mr Dunster was not chairman of Crystal Palace for very long, his advocacy on behalf of the smaller clubs obviously enhanced the name and reputation of his own – and it did it when its status was at a distressingly low ebb.

By the time the national divisions were coming into being, Mr Dunster had himself been succeeded under an agreed rotation system by Mr **Victor Ercolani**. His tenure at our helm was brief and, as is well known among Palace fans, by the time we came to the first season of life in the Fourth Division, Arthur Wait had resumed the chairmanship.

Arthur Wait first watched Crystal Palace play when he was a little lad perched upon his brother's shoulders in order to see over the heads of the crowds that thronged the rudimentary Selhurst Park terraces. After he left school, Wait's building concern flourished wonderfully and at the same time a friendship was forged with David Harris – it was a partnership which was to provide Crystal Palace with a new lease of life in the early 1950s and then, ultimately, the impetus to seek and grasp a place in glory nearly twenty years later.

Arthur Wait was no ordinary chairman. Not only did he rarely miss a home match, but he was to be found at the most distant and unglamorous venues too so that fans of the late 1950s will recall meeting him at such unlikely outposts as Barrow or Gateshead, from where he would give some of us a lift home in his car to save us having to hang around for the night trains to London.

Mr Wait never lost his vision of a much-improved stadium here at Selhurst Park and, even if the earlier plans could now be seen to have been a pipe dream, Mr Wait nevertheless brought about the erection of the stand that bears his name today. It was erected during the spring and summer of 1969 under his own personal direction (and personal involvement!) for he was determined that it should be ready in time for Palace's top-flight debut against Manchester United on 9 August 1969. The stand is 270 feet long, 33 feet high and had a depth of 137 feet so that, certainly at the time of its erection, its roof had the largest span of any stand at any Football League ground, although until 1990 only its upper two tiers provided seating accommodation, the lower part remaining as a standing enclosure. It was officially opened on Wednesday 26 November 1969 by Sir Alf Ramsey, prior to Arthur Rowe's testimonial match and remains a fine and lasting memorial to a remarkable man.

Of course it was under Mr Wait's chairmanship that the appointment was made of Arthur Rowe as Palace's manager in April 1960 and these two men formed a brilliant working partnership for the benefit of our club. Mr Wait also appointed Dick Graham and then Bert Head to the post – and each took the Club to a higher level. No other chairman has ever been able to claim that he supervised the rise of Crystal Palace from the League basement to the top flight, and all in a single decade at that!

Of course, to lead our club from a place with the nonentities in the Fourth Division to a position among the elite in the toughest Football League in the world was Arthur

Wait's greatest triumph, but there was one particular Palace occasion which had nothing whatever to do with League progress which showed him at his very best – the visit of Real Madrid to Selhurst Park in April 1962.

Early that year the Palace directors were discussing the possible clubs who might be invited to come to formally open the new, improved floodlighting. A big, really big outfit was wanted. It turned out to be the Spanish and European champions themselves – Real Madrid! Real had appeared in five consecutive European Cup finals (and won them all!) and were on their way to another one. And Arthur Wait, chairman of a modest Third Division club, persuaded these acknowledged kings of European football to make their first visit to London! The Spaniards agreed to play for £10,000. Palace put up their prices – the ticket stubs remain among the most treasured keepsakes of our fans – took over £15,000 despite the most awful weather, banked a profit of some £3,000 on the night and provided their loyal supporters with a totally unforgettable evening.

In October 1972 Crystal Palace were taken over by a new consortium and Mr Wait was appointed as president here, though he seldom came to Selhurst Park again and never in that capacity. He died in June 1981 and the Club printed a moving obituary to him in the programme for the first match of the ensuing season while Palace supporters who knew him are pleased and thankful that members of his family are now among the regulars at our matches here.

Raymond Bloye took over as Palace's chairman in October 1972 when a Matthews Holdings consortium gained control at Selhurst Park, but the season proceeded on a knife-edge and the collective nerve of the new board failed as the climax of the term approached. Bert Head was moved upstairs to be general manager, though he left soon afterwards, with Malcolm Allison appointed in his stead. The following afternoon, Saturday 31 March 1973, Palace fans were treated to a rare sight of the chairman for those days as Mr Bloye and Bert Head flanked Malcolm as he strode out to the centre spot like a matador before our First Division game against Chelsea.

Palace won that match, but were relegated at the end of the following month – and twelve months later down we went again. Under Mr Bloye, Palace then appeared in the 1976 FA Cup semi-finals as a Third Division club. Terry Venables was appointed to succeed Malcolm Allison that summer to set in train progress to two promotions in three years and a return to the top flight before Venables' eventual defection to Queens Park Rangers and the Club's takeover by Ron Noades' consortium.

One is left with the impression of Raymond Bloye as a somewhat ineffectual figure at the Palace helm, at the whim of circumstances, events and stronger personalities around him, and one who was unaware (or careless) of the financial burdens implicit in expensive purchases sanctioned in sometimes frenzied and certainly futile attempts to prevent relegation.

Thus, while there is a relative parity in League status between the 1972 club that Mr Bloye took over and the 1981 one he bequeathed, few would argue that the reality was of a club that had lost much of its direction, credibility, dynamism and vigour under his chairmanship while also becoming heavily indebted.

Ron Noades became the chairman of Crystal Palace FC when he headed a consortium that took over the Club in January 1981. Ron was and still is very much a 'hands-on'

Mr Ron Noades.   *Mr Mark Goldberg.*

chairman and he was the first one to hold the post at Crystal Palace having previously done so elsewhere in the League because he had been in charge at Wimbledon and, before that, at Southall.

Within considerably less than a decade Ron had revitalised the Club from an ailing, fading institution that lacked momentum, finance or direction, into a positive and successful outfit that was strong enough to reclaim its top-flight status in 1989 and to reach the 1990 FA Cup final. These achievements and other subsequent ones were brought about by a great amount of hard work and by the necessary imposition of severe financial restraints upon the Club, particularly during his early years in control (for, after all, the Palace that Ron had taken over had debts of some £1.75 million), and by the inspired installation of Steve Coppell as the Eagles' manager in the summer of 1984. Although Ron's earlier and subsequent appointments of Palace managers were generally of dubious value (the exception being that of Alan Smith in 1993), it was probably his splendid working relationship with Steve Coppell that was of the greatest worth and influence to our Club during his years as its chairman.

Mr Noades became only Palace's second-ever member of the Football League Management Committee in 1986 and he was involved in the introduction of the now familiar and hugely popular play-offs which were originally instituted to assist in the restructuring of the top divisions of the Football League between 1986 and 1988. Ron also initiated the first-ever Football League ground-sharing arrangement when Charlton Athletic became tenants at Selhurst Park in 1985 – a deal that was subsequently extended to Wimbledon.

Under Mr Noades' control, Crystal Palace became a dynamic club once more, although this did not happen immediately, but ultimately the Eagles reached levels of success far beyond those which we had experienced previously. After reaching the 1990 FA Cup final against Manchester United, which itself went to a replay, the Eagles returned to Wembley to win the Full Members' Cup (in whose establishment Ron himself had been instrumental), then again in 1996 and 1997 for First Division play-off finals, being successful on the latter occasion. The Club also achieved its highest-ever finishing position in a season, third in the top flight in 1990/91, while it was under Ron's control that the imposing 8,500-seat Holmesdale Road Stand was built over a sixteen-month period during his time in charge, at a cost of some £6 million, and was opened by Ron and Steve Coppell on 26 August 1995.

By the time Mr Noades sold control of Crystal Palace in June 1998 the Club had become one of the largest employers in the Croydon area and Ron himself had become the longest-serving chairman of it since and apart from the original holder of the office Mr Sydney Bourne.

Although his direct style had not always endeared Mr Noades to our fans, all of us would acknowledge that he provided new and much-needed dignity and status for Crystal Palace FC and that is something of which every supporter of the Club approved. As such, Mr Noades is certainly among the most significant of 'the men who made Crystal Palace FC' but, as Eagles' fans know very well, he is also the owner of the freehold of Selhurst Park. This was secured via a holding company in the mid-to-late 1980s for something over £1 million in a deal which was favourably received by Palace folk of that time. The money the Club received bought us our freedom from our substantial debts, inherited from the previous administration, and from the implicit (and at that time of high rates) crippling interest payments they incurred. In this capacity Ron is not merely a key figure in Palace's past, but in our future too.

The succeeding chairman of the Eagles was Mr **Mark Goldberg**, who completed a protracted £22 million takeover from Ron Noades in June 1998 and brought new and additional finance as well as an infectious verve and enthusiasm to the club... along with former boss Terry Venables to again become our manager. Mark's stated ambitions for Crystal Palace were lofty ones, including involvement in major European competitions, with all the domestic success that that would imply, and every Palace fan wished him success in bringing them to fruition.

However, and as is also all too well-known among Palace people, Mark was not only quite unable to deliver any of his objectives but actually created a situation which was to threaten the very existence of the Club itself. Perhaps blinded by the prospect of owning and leading a major football club (Mark claimed to have supported Palace since he was a boy, but this is dubious to say the least), Mr Goldberg had hugely overreached himself in what he had paid to secure the club and in what it was costing him to run it. It became necessary for the Club to pass into administration on 31 March 1999 and during the first week of the following season Mark Goldberg resigned as chairman with his reputation at Selhurst Park in tatters.

Taking over as Palace chairman in those most demanding of circumstances was long-time supporter of the Club, director and company secretary **Peter Morley**. Peter was the ideal man for the situation at the Palace at that time: known, respected and liked in the football industry, a fine ambassador for Crystal Palace over several decades, a CBE, and renowned for financial integrity.

Mr Simon Jordan.

Of course, and as Mr Morley acknowledged, all decisions affecting the Club were in the hands of the Administrator – and they were to remain so for another eleven months! But Peter brought much-needed dignity, openness and probity to the recently sullied position of the chairman of Selhurst Park and for that the Club itself and all its followers were grateful at the time and remain so today.

By the summer of 2000 the agonies and embarrassments suffered virtually daily by Palace people everywhere were almost commonplace, but astutely judging the timing of his entry, a serious bidder for Crystal Palace emerged in the person of genuine Eagles fan and former schoolboy player **Simon Jordan**, the Pocket Phone Shop tycoon, who had been born and brought up in Whitehorse Lane. Simon certainly seemed to Palace fans to have only the best interests of the Club at heart, so that late in the afternoon of Wednesday 5 July 2000 there arrived the news that every Eagle had longed for months to hear. The Club was out of administration! It had been bought by a new company called Crystal Palace 2000 under the chairmanship of Mr Jordan and at a cost thought to have been in the region of £10.5 million. By that single act Simon immediately became one of the most important figures in the entire history of Crystal Palace FC.

Mr Jordan's early appointments to the managerial post at the Palace were less successful than he (or we) would have wished, but there can be no doubt that his installation of Iain Dowie in December 2003 was quite outstanding. The entire club was revolutionised, its credibility entirely regained and the First Division stormed. From being among the relegation candidates Palace became the best team in the section, gained a place in the 2004 play-offs, beat Sunderland over two legs on penalties on Wearside, then were simply superior in every respect to West Ham at the Millennium Stadium in Cardiff. Simon Jordan's transformation of Crystal Palace FC was complete – within four years of assuming control of an evidently ailing (even, perhaps, dying) club, he had taken the Eagles back to the Premier League!

THE PRESIDENTS

For similar reasons to those expressed at the beginning of the previous section concerning the chairmen of our club, I've deemed it proper to include all our presidents in this short part of our book. In total the Palace have had only six presidents: two had formerly served the Club with distinction as our chairmen; two appear to have been little more than figureheads (probably for a generous consideration!) while two more were local men of outstanding calibre who would unquestionably qualify among the 'men who made Crystal Palace FC' in a much more brief analysis than this volume is able to offer.

Our first president was the Rt Hon. the **Earl of Plymouth**, who was announced as such in the Club's 1914/15 yearbook, but at this distance in time it is impossible to deduce the reasons which lay behind his association with the Club, though any information on the matter would be welcomed, and a picture of him in profile, wearing a fur-collared and lapelled overcoat and a top hat appears in the aforementioned yearbook. He died during the 1922/23 season and his passing was mentioned, 'with regret' by the directors in their annual report.

Mr **Frederick John Nettlefold** was a member of a greatly respected local family who had spent most of his life in Upper Norwood and was known to possess a keen interest and to take a large role in community matters. He became Palace's president in late October 1923.

Mr Nettlefold's support for Crystal Palace was always recognised as being generous; so much so in fact that not only was he the major contributor towards the cost of building Selhurst Park in 1924, but he also surrendered nearly £24,000 (a huge sum at that time) that was due to him by the Club some ten years later. Thus, it would clearly not have been inappropriate if our beloved ground had been renamed Nettlefold Park, although the president himself would never have wished it so.

Mr Nettlefold remained as our president until 1939 but relinquished the position (along with its financial responsibilities) during a period of convoluted and thoroughly unedifying boardroom politics. He was presented with a lifelong pass to the directors'

Above: *Sir Adam Maitland MP.*

Right: *Mr Stanley Stephenson.*

box and boardroom the following year and, at the directors' request, donated a large photograph of himself which hung in the boardroom for many years.

Mr Nettlefold died at the end of November 1949 and was remembered with gratitude in a silent tribute at the Club's 1950 annual meeting.

Sir **Adam Maitland** was elected as president of Crystal Palace FC in 1940 by the recently established board of directors under Percy Harper.

Although Sir Adam was a member of parliament (he represented Faversham in Kent for seventeen years from 1928) and lived locally in Purley from 1919, his contribution to and involvement with the Palace is unclear, but probably modest. Sturdy, genial, straightforward and with extensive sporting interests, it seems likely that he was acquainted with Percy Harper and, because of his political eminence, which extended to serving on the county council and local urban district council, was invited to fill the position of president at the football club which had fallen vacant upon the resignation of his illustrious predecessor.

Little or nothing is heard of Sir Adam and the presidency seems to have virtually fallen vacant by default, probably after the 1945 general election. Sir Adam died in October 1949.

Arthur Wait became the president of Crystal Palace FC upon the completion of the 1972 takeover of the Club, but Mr Wait chose not to associate with Crystal Palace after he ceased to be our chairman. A full appreciation of his work in that role is to be found in the preceding section of this book.

Stanley Stephenson was probably the first president of Crystal Palace FC of whom readers were ever aware, but such was the quiet, self-effacing nature of this man it is quite likely that his time in office passed with relatively few Eagles fans being aware of it.

Mr Stephenson accepted the position of club president in 1981 following the death of Arthur Wait and he held it with distinction until his own passing in May 1994. Unlike many presidents of major football clubs, Stanley had had a continuous association with Crystal Palace and had served it in various capacities, including those of a director and a lifelong supporter. He was almost certainly the last surviving Palace fan who had been present at the Club's first-ever match at the Crystal Palace in September 1905 and even towards the end of his long life he could recall incidents from Palace games and personalities from our initial season, having attended the matches and seen the men in question with his father from their family home in Upper Norwood.

It was typical of this modest, gracious, retiring gentleman that in 1989 he should donate a solid silver, late-Victorian cup to Crystal Palace to be known as the President's Trophy, and to be awarded to the person considered to have made the greatest contribution to the benefit of the Club over the year. The first winner was Alan Pardew, the second Joanne O'Donnell, but the trophy appears to have fallen into disuse after that.

Mr **Peter Morley** is the present-day president of Crystal Palace FC, having been appointed early in the 2000/01 season after the Club's takeover during the summer. Peter had held several important posts at Selhurst Park, but none more so than that of chairman during the major part of the period in which we were in administration. An appreciation of him therefore appears in the last chapter while the fact that Simon Jordan swiftly made him our president is a further acknowledgement of Peter's contribution as his predecessor.

Mr Peter Morley CBE.

THE MANAGERS

It seems to the author that the proper course in this part of our book is to include reference to every manager of Crystal Palace FC. As with the chairmen previously, the contribution of each of them, whether it be great or small, positive or negative, has been instrumental in some way in bringing about the Club that exists today: each one helped to 'make' it. It is also hoped that in the case of some of the more obscure, little known, previous managers, some of the detail provided here will be of help and interest to Palace fans of course, but also to other football folk who, for any one of a whole spectrum of reasons, find themselves reading this volume.

Managers of Crystal Palace Football Club
1905-2004

1905-07	John Robson	1958-60	George Smith	1995-96	Steve Coppell
1907-25	Edmund Goodman	1960-62	Arthur Rowe		(Technical Director)
1925-27	Alec Maley	1962-66	Dick Graham	1996-97	Dave Bassett
1927-30	Fred Mavin	1966	Arthur Rowe	1997-98	Steve Coppell
1930-35	Jack Tresadern	1966-73	Bert Head	1998	Attilio Lombardo
1935-36	Tom Bromilow	1973-76	Malcolm Allison	1998-99	Terry Venables
1936	R.S. Moyes	1976-80	Terry Venables	1999-00	Steve Coppell
1937-39	Tom Bromilow	1980	Ernie Walley	2000-01	Alan Smith
1939-47	George Irwin	1980-81	Malcolm Allison	2001	Steve Kember
1947-49	Jack Butler	1981	Dario Gradi	2001	Steve Bruce
1949-50	Ronnie Rooke	1981-82	Steve Kember	2001-03	Trevor Francis
1950-51	Fred Dawes &	1982-84	Alan Mullery	2003	Steve Kember
	Charlie Slade	1984-93	Steve Coppell	2003	Kit Symons
1951-54	Laurie Scott	1993-95	Alan Smith	2003-	Iain Dowie
1954-58	Cyril Spiers				

John ROBSON
1905-07

Mr Robson was Palace's first manager. He joined us from Middlesbrough, who he had taken into the First Division of the Football League in 1902, and he brought several fine players from the North-East with him when he came to South London.

Under Mr Robson the Palace won the Second Division of the Southern League in our inaugural season, 1905/06, but we found the First Division the following season a real struggle and as soon as the 1906/07 season had ended Mr Robson joined Croydon Common.

Unquestionably, the high spot of Mr Robson's term as our manager was our run to the FA Cup quarter-finals in 1906/07, which included the fabulous victory over the Football League Champions and FA Cup finalists the previous year Newcastle United, at Gallowgate where the Magpies were unbeaten for more than a year! Small wonder then that there are Palace pundits who join this author in believing that, given the relative status of the two outfits, that victory must, still, be regarded as Palace's greatest of all – and it was achieved under the management of Mr John Robson.

Edmund GOODMAN
1907-25

It was the end of a promising football career when a young man, then aged just nineteen, suffered a bad knee injury. Today he would have responded to treatment and surgery, but the injury was sustained over 100 years ago and it was necessary for the leg to be amputated.

The injured lad was Edmund Goodman. He became assistant secretary to his club, Aston Villa, instead, and when the founders of Crystal Palace FC turned to Villa for direction and help in the formation of the new club they were offered the services of this same fellow. He came to Crystal Palace FC in the summer of 1905 before a ball had been kicked by the new club, and he stayed for over twenty-eight years! It must rank as *the* transfer deal which 'made' Crystal Palace! For the first two seasons Mr Goodman was too deeply involved in the hard graft of administration to be able to spend sufficient time with the players to act as manager, but Mr John Robson was appointed under his guidance, and he found the Club's superb first chairman, Mr Sydney Bourne, who has already been introduced to readers in a previous chapter.

After the first two seasons Mr Goodman added to his secretarial tasks the responsibility of team management and held this job until 1925. He remains the longest-serving manager in the Club's history and seems likely to continue so forever. Under him the Palace immediately climbed to fourth place in the Southern League's First Division in 1907/08. We just missed out on the Southern League Championship itself immediately before the First World War, conceding the 1913/14 title to Swindon Town on goal average alone, but we gained entry to the Football League in 1920 and became the first Champions of the newly formed Third Division the following year before enjoying four seasons in the Second Division – the most successful period in Palace's history until nearly fifty years later.

It was also under Mr Goodman's stewardship that Crystal Palace secured some thoroughly notable and prestigious victories in the FA Cup – for example over Cup holders Wolves in 1908, an incredible 6-0 rout of distinguished Everton at their own headquarters in 1922 and over pedigree Tottenham in 1924. Then, after the Club had moved into its present headquarters at Selhurst Park, what was ostensibly Mr Goodman's Palace beat Chelsea in the fourth round to establish a ground record attendance which stood for nearly forty years!

In October 1925 Mr Goodman relinquished managerial control of the club and reverted to his original post as our secretary. He retired in 1933.

Clearly, if Crystal Palace can be said to have had a founding father, that person is most certainly Mr Edmund Goodman, and few of the men whose biographies appear in this book can be argued to have a claim better than his.

Alec MALEY
1925-27

Mr Alec Maley joined Crystal Palace from Hibernian in Edinburgh in December 1925 to succeed Mr Edmund Goodman as our manager and began a policy of recruiting men from north of the border. Probably Mr Maley's most successful signing for our Club was that of the highly rated full-back Bobby Orr from Greenock Morton, who joined Palace for 1926/27 and went on to make 70 league appearances for us over the next two seasons.

Mr Maley's team of 1927/27 was certainly more consistent than its recent predecessors – for the first time in five years we won the opening game of the season, a Percy Cherrett header and a Cecil Blakemore overhead bicycle kick in

the last minute proving too much for Queens Park Rangers at Selhurst Park, although the visitors had netted within thirty seconds of the first whistle! Palace finished 1926/27 in sixth place, but that was as good as nowhere in the old Third Division (South) and we were 17 points adrift of the champions Bristol City.

Under Mr Maley Palace began 1927/28 poorly, including 1-6 defeats at Southend in mid-September and at Luton a month later, so that when we were knocked out of the London Challenge Cup by our old amateur rivals, Leyton, on 12 October there was nothing for it but for Mr Maley to resign later that day and return to his homeland.

Fred MAVIN
1927-30

It was in late November 1927 that Mr Fred Mavin, formerly the manager at Exeter City and a player with Fulham, Bradford and New Brompton, took up the responsibilities at Selhurst Park and, if at least the worst of the tide had been turned by then, the new manager inspired the team to a much-improved performance for the remainder of that season so that we were able to finish 1927/28 in fifth place.

Mr Mavin then spent a busy summer in the transfer market on our behalf. It was from his former club, Exeter City, that he secured the skipper of his restructured Palace side, full-back Stan Charlton, who had already earned the respect of Palace fans with his displays against us for The Grecians and was to go on to become a top-class defender for us over the next four seasons. Alongside Stan was another new boy, Tom Crilly, who joined us from Derby and became a lynchpin Palace defender for five years. The partnership between Charlton and Crilly was an appealing feature of Palace line-ups and it is certainly significant that during the period they were together at Selhurst Park we were able to make two serious assaults on the single promotion place available from the regional Third Division.

Mr Mavin made several other astute captures too. Suave little Welsh goal-poacher Lewis Griffiths arrived from Torquay and netted on his debut, but he sustained an early injury which made his three-month absence crucial in the last analysis. Another goalscorer, Hubert Butler, came from Chorley, although in 1928/29 he was more of a provider for Griffiths and Harry Havelock, then in the autumn Mr Mavin augmented our defence with centre half 'Jimmy' Wilde. Thus our 1928/29 side was the best one we had between our return to the Third Division and the outbreak of the Second World War, and, many would argue, for long afterwards too: Palace came within an ace of gaining promotion! A crowd of over 22,000 flocked to Selhurst Park for the last game of the season only to dis-cover that our 1-0 victory over Brighton (secured by a Stan Charlton penalty) could not prevent neighbours Charlton taking the title on goal average.

Mr Mavin made further interesting and invaluable signings towards the end of 1928/29 and during the summer recess, most significant of which was that of Palace's most prolific striker of all time – Peter Simpson. Peter's record with Crystal Palace is exceptional, but in the present context the point is that we owed his presence and his goals in our colours to manager Fred Mavin.

It was with great disappointment that Palace accepted Mr Mavin's resignation, because of the ill-health of his wife, in mid-October 1930. Although perhaps the team he crafted for 1930/31 was not quite the equal of the 1928/29 one, it was still powerful enough to finish as runners-up again in the Third Division (South) – and for that fact too, much credit is due to Fred Mavin.

Jack TRESADERN
1930-35

Jack Tresadern joined Crystal Palace from Northampton Town. He was a former England international wing half and had played for West Ham (appearing in the first Wembley cup final), Burnley and the Cobblers.

Probably, Mr Tresadern's best signing for the Palace was that of brilliant striker Albert Dawes from his former club in January 1934, but not even Albert's 16 goals from 22 League appearances could rescue another lacklustre season. Another fine acquisition for Palace was full-back Ted Owens, but Palace under Mr Tresadern were never more than one of the better sides in the Third Division (South) and could not make a serious promotion challenge during his tenure. Given the quality of some of the players he had available to him, that must be con-sidered a serious indictment, so that most folk connected with our Club were surprised if not altogether disappointed when he moved across London to take charge at Tottenham in July 1935, but his subsequent career in management at White Hart Lane and elsewhere was uneventful.

Tom BROMILOW
1935-36, 1937-39

England international wing half Tom Bromilow had enjoyed a fine inter-war playing career with Liverpool, where he won two League Championship medals. He then coached in Amsterdam and managed Burnley and it was from The Clarets that he moved to Selhurst Park to take charge of Crystal Palace in July 1935. Tom remained our manager until the summer of 1939 except for a few months in 1936 when he left over a matter of principle in a shake-up in our board-room, but returned when things had settled down.

Like many men before and since, at Selhurst Park and elsewhere, Tom Bromilow found that the rigours of play-ing top-flight football are as nothing when compared to managing a team in one of the lower divisions, However, a glimpse at the record book alone shows us that it was Mr Bromilow who brought Palace nearest to regaining the Second Division place that had been forfeited in 1925 since we had missed out on goal average in 1928/29. Bromilow's Palace chased Newport County so hard that we finished up in second place in the last inter-war season with just a three-point deficit.

History judges Tom Bromilow as one of Palace's better managers – and that verdict was secured in difficult times for the Club. Not only did he bring us nearer to the Second Division than any other manager in a span of thirty-five years, but he made some thoroughly adroit sign-ings of established players while at the same time bringing on a crop of fine young protégés.

Among the former were Albert Wilson, a raiding left-winger from Mansfield; Les Lievesley, a towering wing half from Torquay; and, best of all, Fred Dawes from Northampton Town who went on to complete over a century of appear-ances for us on either side of the Second World War.

Palace fans of the 1930s and 1940s will recall with pleasure the names of some of the grand young footballers who came to maturity under Tom Bromilow: Arthur Hudgell, who became the costliest Third Division defender when he moved to Sunderland early in 1947, Nick Collins, Jack Lewis, Tommy Reece, Albert Robson and Ernie Waldron who at times kept even the great Albert Dawes in the reserves.

From Palace's point of view it was the greatest pity that the Second World War should largely dissipate the contribution these men could make towards the Club's playing fortunes, but before the hostilities got underway Tom Bromilow left us in the summer of 1939 to manage Leicester City. He did so on good terms and with the knowledge that he had done his job well at the Palace.

R.S. MOYES
1936

If astonishment characterised the gen-eral reaction to Tom Bromilow's June 1936 resignation at Crystal Palace, prob-ably bemusement is the best description of the response to the appointment of club director Mr R.S. Moyes as his suc-cessor.

Mr Moyes did perform one excellent piece of business on Palace's behalf when he obtained Scottish international centre half George Walker from Notts County, a model professional and a fine leader whose absence in the second half of

1938/39 could be argued to have cost Palace promotion.

In fairness to Mr Moyes, his problems began even before the 1936/37 season got under way because Albert Dawes fractured his jaw in a trial match – but Palace were unable to challenge for the top places with or without Albert and we went out of the FA Cup at the first hurdle in a replay at Southend.

Then, disapproving of certain dealings in relation to a couple of incoming transfers, Mr Moyes resigned in early December, little more than five months after becoming the manager, and chaos erupted at Selhurst Park! A week or so later the chairman also resigned and while all this was happening Albert Dawes was allowed to move to Luton Town and Tom Bromilow was reinstalled with effect from 1 January 1937.

George IRWIN
1939-47

George Irwin was the popular manager of Crystal Palace FC throughout the years of the Second World War. He was a former Palace goalkeeper and prior to his appointment in the summer of 1939 had served for a couple of seasons as our trainer under our previous boss, Mr Tom Bromilow.

As a former professional George knew the game thoroughly and he was well respected by the players, management and fans at Selhurst Park. He was a genial, humorous personality, though he had a streak of iron in his make up that enabled him to drive himself and his players when that was required. Certainly the war years demanded much from everyone in every walk of life and it was as well for Crystal

Palace FC that our fortunes were in the hands of such a capable and well-equipped person.

As events turned our George had as testing a time at the helm of a football club as any manager has ever had, but he achieved no little success for the Palace during the years of the war and certainly enhanced our reputation as a club of integrity both on and off the field. The only pity is that George's successes at Crystal Palace were achieved while the Football League was in suspension so that the club did not benefit greatly in the long term from his undoubted talent and he left us after we had performed very moderately in the first post-war season of 1946/47.

Jack BUTLER
1947-49

Jack Butler, formerly a distinguished player with Arsenal and an England international, came to Selhurst Park to manage Crystal Palace for the last three matches of the extended, but disappointing, 1946/47 season. He arrived with an impressive coaching and managerial pedigree, having coached the Belgian national side, the Denmark FA and Leicester City, and been in charge at Torquay United.

But Jack Butler's tenure of the manager's chair at the Palace came at an extremely difficult time. The Club was in the doldrums, and there was little or no money available to strengthen the playing squad, so that Jack's two seasons at Selhurst Park were thoroughly depressing ones for everyone connected with the Club. In 1947/48 we were never more than a mid-table outfit, and, always finding goals hard to come by, we finished in thirteenth place. However, 1948/49 was nothing short of disastrous. Mr Butler put out no fewer than thirty-three different players but could never field a settled side. We were always in the lower reaches of the Third Division (South), hit rock-bottom after Christmas and were never able to get off it, thus having to apply for re-election for the first time in the club's history.

Jack Butler himself was bitterly disappointed by it all and he insisted that his letter of resignation be accepted. He later returned to coaching in Belgium, then had a spell as manager of Colchester United. He died in January 1961 at the age of sixty-six.

(With grateful acknowledgements to Des Beamish)

Ronnie ROOKE
1949-50

The story of Ronnie Rooke, of the distinctive rugged features, the Latin nose, thunderous shot and rolling gait, who became an outstanding top-flight marksman, is, regrettably, only one of frustration and bitter disappointment at Crystal Palace FC.

In the Palace reserve side of the mid-1930s he was quite remarkable, with 160 goals to his name in just three-and-a-half seasons, but he was never able to reproduce even a glimmer of such form in our first team. He then moved to Fulham in October 1936 where he played with great success and gained a wartime international cap. In 1946 Arsenal sought his services and he helped them to the 1948 League Championship as the League's top scorer with 33 goals.

Rooke then returned to Selhurst Park as our player-manager in the summer of 1949 and Palace rose from last place in 1948/49 to seventh in 1949/50 – our best post-war season in the Third Division (South). Rooke hit 21 League goals himself and some big crowds came along to Selhurst Park to watch and support 'The Rooke Regiment' as our side was briefly dubbed by the press.

But, with the approval of the new board of directors it must be said, Rooke then proceeded to bring a spate of highly priced veteran players to the Palace. The outcome was nothing short of disastrous, the playing record at the start of 1950/51 was abysmal, the Palace finances were in penury and Rooke himself was relieved of his post at the end of November.

Thus, as far as Crystal Palace FC is concerned, Ronnie Rooke was the complete enigma. His proven goalscoring prowess paid small dividend for us and his managerial tenure was nothing short of calamitous.

Fred DAWES
1950-51 (Joint Manager)

Fred Dawes had become a great favourite among Palace fans in a long and distinguished playing career and he had been assistant manager to Ronnie Rooke, so everyone at Selhurst Park knew that our Club was in a strong and loyal pair of hands at a particularly troubled time for it when Fred was appointed to manage it in tandem with Charlie Slade.

However, anyone with any discernment realised that the situation Fred and his colleague had inherited was a dreadfully difficult one: the Club was bottom of the League with only nine points from eighteen matches and we were already out of the FA Cup, having crashed 1-4 at home to Millwall in the first round, for our seventh consecutive defeat.

There was not to be an heroic, story-book recovery – how could there possibly have been? Palace faced re-election at the end of our worst-ever season with the most dismal playing record; once again we had utilised thirty-three different players but this time that was also the number of goals we were able to score which was not only our lowest ever total but the worst in the entire history of the Third Division (South). With a swollen overdraft there could be no out-lay on new players – it was actually a case of salvaging some small return from the huge expenditure of summer 1950. Inevitably, the first two months of 1951/52 produced little or no improve-ment and the directors decided that Fred and his colleague would have to go. It was a shabby finale for a grand and loyal Palace servant – quite unworthy of him, or of the men who made it.

Charlie SLADE
1950-51 (Joint Manager)

Charlie Slade had played a lot of League football for northern clubs between the wars but he was probably little more than a name to most Crystal Palace fans when he was installed as our joint-manager with Fred Dawes in November 1950, although he had been a useful scout on Palace's behalf and was respected in the game as a coach.

Without doubt, Charlie's best contri-bution to Palace's fortunes was his knowledge of Chester striker Cam

Burgess, whom he and Fred Dawes signed, upon the recommendation of another former Chester player, Les Devonshire, in September 1951 to boost our goals tally. Cam went on to become the Club's sharpest goalscorer – for a short while at least – since Albert Dawes and Peter Simpson, but by the time he did so the managers responsible for bringing him to Selhurst Park had both been replaced.

Laurie SCOTT
1951-54

Laurie Scott was Palace's third post-war manager to have played with distinction for Arsenal, yet, like Ronnie Rooke and Jack Butler before him, Laurie's period in charge of our club did nothing to advance its prospects.

Laurie arrived at Selhurst Park with 17 full England caps and a 1948 League Championship medal. He was our player-manager and certainly things began brightly enough as the Palace secured a 3-1 victory over Ipswich Town on Laurie's debut on 20 October 1951.

However, the honeymoon was short-lived! Palace were knocked out of the FA Cup at Great Yarmouth in the first round the following month and we finished the 1951/52 season down in nineteenth place, which was precisely where we had been when Mr Scott had joined us!

An injury incurred at Bristol City early in the following season meant that Laurie could play only one more game for us and 1952/53 then saw the disappointing, dreadful FA Cup defeat at Finchley, although it must be admitted that Palace's League form did improve con-siderably in the last third of that season, but 1953/54 saw us in real trouble yet again and Mr Scott was dismissed at the end of September.

Cyril SPIERS
1954-58

Cyril Spiers was appointed as secretary-manager at Crystal Palace FC on 13 October 1954. He had had a grand career as a top-class goalkeeper with Tottenham and Aston Villa before turning to management. He served at Wolves under Major Frank Buckley and then had spells in charge of Cardiff and Norwich City, but where his sometimes illustrious predecessors at Selhurst Park had failed, so too, eventually, did the kindly, avuncular Spiers.

Admittedly, his task at the Palace was enormous. He inherited an ageing, ailing team which had settled in the lower reaches of the old Third Division (South), but rang the changes and tried to groom his own youngsters. In this Spiers was at least partially successful, for it was under his guidance that Vic Rouse came to the fore while the mercurial Johnny Byrne came through his ranks, as did striker Mike Deakin, who set a post-war scoring record with 23 League goals for Palace in 1958/59, although by this time we were a Fourth Division outfit and Mr Spiers had departed from us.

Mr Spiers' first season saw us finish twentieth, then in his first full term in charge Palace had to seek re-election. In 1956/57 Palace were twentieth again but the acid test came in 1957/58 when Mr Spiers was unable to lift Palace into the top half of the divisional table and thus we became founder members of the new League basement.

Cyril Spiers.

George SMITH
1958-60

George Smith came to Selhurst Park as the Crystal Palace manager in the summer of 1958, charged with the task of lifting Palace out of the newly formed Fourth Division of the Football League. George was a tough disciplinarian who had gained a reputation as a player and coach, having previously been in charge of Eastbourne and Sutton United before accepting the position at the Palace. Upon taking up his appointment George stated that, should he not achieve his and the club's objective within two years, he would leave, but, while we gained some local credibility by reaching the final of the Southern Floodlit Cup in 1958/59 (against Arsenal 1-2), and despite gaining the Club's record victory, the 9-0 annihilation of hapless Barrow on 10 October

1959, Palace never seriously challenged for promotion while George was with us and, true to his word, he left the Club in April 1960.

Arthur ROWE
1960-62, 1966

When Arthur Rowe arrived at Crystal Palace in November 1958, as assistant manager to George Smith, he did so as a legend in London's footballing circles. A distinguished and highly successful playing career with Tottenham, cut short prematurely by injury, had been followed after the war by a dazzling spell as Spurs' manager with promotion then a League Championship in successive seasons,

achieved by a brilliantly evolved and attractive style of play which became popularly known as 'push and run'.

In April 1960, when he took charge at Selhurst Park, Palace were a Fourth Division outfit with a sizeable overdraft and in real danger of sinking into oblivion. But Arthur adapted the Palace – who had no shortage of skilful players on their staff at that time, all well known to the new manager of course and with Johnny Byrne paramount among them – to his proven style of play and, augmented by some astute signings, led his new charge to immediate promotion with crisp, delightful football which created Palace's post-war goalscoring record and drew some huge crowds to watch us play, including the 37,774 record Fourth

Arthur Rowe (left) with chairman Arthur Wait.

Division attendance for our derby against Millwall on 31 March 1961.

It was under Mr Rowe's skilled and experienced guidance that Johnny Byrne came to maturity, to international recognition, and to the attentions of West Ham, who paid a record £60,000 fee for the chirpy, confident Palace youngster.

But Arthur was never a robust man: he was often plagued by ill health and he had to surrender control in the winter of 1962/63, although he returned to assist Dick Graham as Palace climbed into the Second Division and then assumed temporary full charge again in 1966 after Dick left us. Arthur then reverted to a background role once more under Bert Head as we drove towards the top flight for the first time, and the Club awarded him a testimonial against an International XI in November 1969 when the Arthur Wait Stand was formally opened.

Inevitably then, Palace fans of the 1960s never forgot Arthur Rowe and, while everyone at Crystal Palace was saddened to hear of his death in November 1993, those of us who knew him or watched his Palace teams with delight, will always remain grateful for his marvellous contribution to our club.

Dick GRAHAM
1962-66

Dick Graham, Palace's popular former goalkeeper, rejoined our Club as assistant manager in 1961 after a spell as coach at West Bromwich Albion, and if his playing career with Palace was never crowned with success, his later time with us more than compensated for that.

Promoted to full charge at Selhurst Park in November 1962, Dick's first task

was to avert the looming spectre of possible relegation back into the League basement. He immediately made two perceptive signings, those of proven strikers Dickie Dowsett and Cliff Holton, and changed our style to a much more direct and forceful one. Palace improved beyond all recognition, had an excellent second half to the season, climbed away from trouble and eventually finished the protracted 1962/63 season in a creditable eleventh place.

The following season, Dick's Palace side was always among the promotion contenders from the early days of autumn. We took over at the top of the table when matters reached the crucial closing stages and looked every inch the likely champions of the Third Division, only to be denied that prize by a quarter of an hour's aberration in our final match, which allowed a 1-0 lead over visiting Oldham to become a 1-3 defeat.

In 1964/65 Dick took Palace to a place in the FA Cup quarter-finals for the first time in nearly sixty years and to a most praiseworthy seventh place in the Second Division but, by this time, some of his team selections were becoming contentious while his decision to transfer-list the supremely popular Cliff Holton in the summer of 1965 caused ferment among our fans. It also became apparent that there were disagreements between the manager and some of his players so that the inevitable end could not long be delayed. Early in January 1966 Dick left and thus wrote 'finis' to a tremendous contribution to Crystal Palace FC.

Sporting a fashionable crew-cut hairstyle, Dick was a tough character and something of a disciplinarian, although he was anything but rigid in his approach to the game and was one of the earliest

Dick Graham.

Bert Head.

managers to deploy a defence which incorporated the duo of central defenders considered mandatory today. Equally Dick was among the first managers to use a 'squad' system, drafting players in and out of the side when there was a particular job to do, or to promote or counter a favoured tactic. Dick also refused, to the consternation of many opponents, to be bound by the traditional use of the numbers which identify a player in the programme and, in order to puzzle or unsettle the opposition, would frequently put a defender into a winger's shirt or ask a striker to wear the old number four or five, so that he became quite a controversial figure for his audacity. In those hide-bound days, Dick provided something of a challenge to current thinking, so there was no chance of his managing a top-rank club, but he had a flair with the smaller outfits, and while Palace were the first to benefit from it he subsequently had a further successful spell in charge of Colchester.

Bert HEAD
1966-73

Bert Head had been a player with Torquay long before he joined Bury as assistant manager in 1951 and he became the boss at Swindon Town in 1956. His time at the County Ground was most successful, he took charge back at Bury in 1965 then joined Crystal Palace on 14 April 1966 to begin a wonderful partnership with the man who became his close friend as well as his chairman, Mr Arthur Wait.

After two seasons in the Second Division, when Bert gained precisely the same finishing positions as his predecessor, seventh then eleventh, he managed our Club into the top flight for the first time. This was achieved with the rousing and passionate crescendo of a superb run of sixteen undefeated matches in the spring of 1969 (the best such sequence in a single season at the Palace since the Second World War and only once improved upon here) to gain the Palace a status that appeared to even our most fanatical of supporters to be totally impossible only a few years earlier.

Bert's task was by no means finished – having led the Club to the top flight, he now had to keep it there. That is a much more difficult matter, but Bert demonstrated that he possessed the ability to do so. Partly with the benefit of adroit manipulation of the transfer market, Bert shaped and reshaped our side so that, three times, possible relegation was averted. Then in March 1973, with another cliffhanger in the offing, a new administration brought in Malcolm Allison and Bert was moved upstairs. He left quietly soon afterwards, joined Bath City and steered them to a Southern League promotion in 1975.

One feature of Bert Head's management at Crystal Palace was his astute signing of players at bargain transfer fees. Bert always regarded the £1,500 he paid Aberdeen for John McCormick as the best deal he ever struck and certainly McCormick, along with another bargain signing, Mel Blyth, became magnificent players with us, gaining promotion from the Second Division, and then in the top flight, while Bert's promotion-winning team of 1968/69 cost a bare £80,000.

Bert Head's achievements at Selhurst Park will always be unique and are warmly remembered. He took the Palace to the elite for the first time; he kept us there, against the odds, for nearly four seasons and he was, unquestionably, one of the most likeable men ever to be associated with Crystal Palace FC.

Malcolm ALLISON
1973-76, 1980-81

Malcolm Allison is possibly the most complex and controversial character to have been associated with Crystal Palace FC. He had played for Charlton and West Ham, then managed Bath City and Plymouth but he came to prominence when he joined Joe Mercer at Manchester City and helped lead that club to top honours in domestic and European competitions.

Malcolm arrived with typical flamboyance at Selhurst Park on 31 March 1973 for Palace's home game against Chelsea and quickened the side to record its first and only victory over London opponents in thirty-two top-flight games between 1969 and 1973! However, he was unable to prevent Palace from falling out of the First Division – we lost five of the next seven games. Then we had a terrible time in 1973/74 when Malcolm virtually restructured the side in a vain attempt to arrest our decline. The changes he made included several highly controversial decisions, chief among which was to replace John Jackson with Paul Hammond in goal and some fans never forgave him for this. Relegated for the second year running, Malcolm's larger than life image was a mixed blessing in the Third Division for it prematurely raised the hopes and aspirations of Palace fans while also serving to motivate every other club to raise their game against us!

The 1975/76 season was Malcolm's most successful at the Palace. We finally began to warrant some of the plaudits he showered upon his team and in the FA Cup he spurred us to fabulous victories at Leeds, Chelsea and Sunderland to earn

Malcolm Allison.

a first-ever place in the cup semi-finals. But Malcolm took our failure to reach Wembley really hard and when Palace then contrived to throw away the promotion that had seemed so certain throughout most of that season it became all too much for him. He left us on 19 May 1976 – only to return as our manager for two months in midwinter 1980/81 when Palace were desperately seeking to halt another decline.

Assessing Malcolm's contribution to Crystal Palace is not a simple matter. The only honour he won with us was the semi-final place, while he was unable to prevent our relegations of 1973 and 1974. He also paid out several large sums of money for players which were never recouped while his decisions to part with established favourites were highly controversial and cannot really be justified in any critical assessment.

Thus, even though the mid-1970s will always be remembered by Palace fans of the era for the famous FA Cup run which Malcolm and his fedora inspired, it is difficult to regard his period in control of Crystal Palace as having been a successful one, even though in fairness it should be acknowledged that the seeds of some later progress were sown.

Terry VENABLES
1976-80, 1998-99

Terry Venables holds a unique and distinguished place in the annals of Crystal Palace FC for he was, after all, the first man to lead our Club to two promotions and to the honour of gaining promotion to the top flight as Champions in 1979. Yet Terry was regarded by Palace fans with far from universal enthusiasm at the time

he left us in the autumn of 1980, while today most Eagles folk feel as if they and our Club have been badly let down by him.

This is in such contrast to the manner in which Terry was acclaimed at Selhurst Park at the height of his first term as our manager that the question must be asked as to why that is. It is a tantalising query but few could deny that Terry was an enigma with Crystal Palace in both his management tenures or that both times he left us he did so with our Club in dire straits from which it would take a long time to recover.

In 1976/77, his first season in football management, Terry took the Palace up from the old Third Division after bringing in George Graham and then Jeff Bourne. The latter was a brilliant coup; for Jeff hit nine vital goals in the last fifteen games and the season ended with a brilliant, incredible 4-2 victory over Wrexham when, with barely ninety seconds remaining, we were only drawing 2-2 and doomed, so it seemed, to at least one more term in the Third Division.

Two years later a different, highly talented and extremely youthful side fashioned by Venables, augmented by the return of experienced and popular Steve Kember, finally won the old Second Division title with a rampant 2-0 win over Burnley here at Selhurst Park in front of the ground's biggest-ever crowd of 51,482 having carried the look of Champions from early in the season. Palace's progress under Terry continued – briefly. We took the senior section by storm, headed the League at the end of September 1979, only to begin to fall away and were a club in decline by the end of the season. Early in 1980/81 it was apparent that, while the deterioration was continuing, Terry was either unable or unwilling to arrest it and he then left us when we were at the foot of the table to take over at London rivals Queens Park Rangers. At this, Terry's once splendid relationship with Palace fans was, at best, soured.

Thus, Terry's appointment as the Palace manager by our new chairman Mark Goldberg in the summer of 1998 was not greeted with delight by everyone with our Club's interests at heart, although he received a rapturous welcome at Palace's opening League game of 1998/99. Alas, for a number of reasons, including some that were not of his own making, Terry was quite unable to bring any success to Selhurst Park.

Early doubts as to Terry's commitment to us were expressed when he was to be seen almost every night on the nation's television screens as a member of the ITV panel viewing the 1998 World Cup in France. This did little to allay the doubts of the older fans about him while supporters of every age group found it difficult to understand his absence from his new club which was in considerable turmoil after a disastrous relegation and a controversial boardroom takeover.

Then Terry sold several of the supporters' favourite players; men who could have been expected to play a key role in any attempt to regain our Premiership status at the first attempt. Stars like Neil Shipperley and 1998 Player of the Year Marc Edworthy were despatched, only to be replaced all too often with nonentities or less-able men. Thus, Palace seldom even graduated to the upper half of the First Division table under Terry's stewardship and several of our away performances were little or nothing short of disgraceful.

Terry Venables.

In the end, in mid-January 1999 Terry moved aside in a series of cost-cutting moves by the chairman, leaving those fans who had feared the worst at the time of his re-appointment now thoroughly disillusioned by him and gaining no satisfaction whatever upon having their doubts as to the wisdom of his return fulfilled in the worst possible manner.

Ernie WALLEY
1980

Caernarvon-born Ernie Walley had been Palace's youth and then reserve team coach and so, since many of the senior team in 1980 had matured under Ernie's guidance, he was certainly the choice of many of our players to succeed Terry Venables.

Tough, open and a former Football League professional with Tottenham and Middlesbrough, Ernie immediately led the Palace to two home wins in four days, then gained a draw at Norwich which was followed by another victory at Selhurst Park, over Manchester United on 1 November. Regrettably though, this progress was not maintained, but, since several senior members of the Palace side were now eagerly intent upon following their former manager to Loftus Road, Ernie's task had become an impossible one.

At the end of November, after a 2-3 home defeat by Manchester City, it was decided to bring Malcolm Allison back to Selhurst Park. Soon, Ernie was acting as Malcolm's assistant and he served in that capacity too under Dario Gradi.

Dario GRADI
1981

Crystal Palace FC was taken over on 26 January 1981 by a consortium headed by Wimbledon chairman Ron Noades. Malcolm Allison was dismissed that very morning and replaced by Dario Gradi, a former England amateur international and successful manager at Plough Lane, who thus became Palace's fourth boss in little more than three turbulent months.

But Dario was favoured with little luck at the Palace helm. Top players left us, either by desire or in order to raise funds to bring some sanity to the Club's hugely overstretched finances. We lost our first seven games under the new administration, a clutch of newly arrived players proved unable to turn the tide and Palace were doomed to relegation a full month before the end of the season. Seeking to

ease the pressure on his beleaguered men, Dario went on record to assert that it was not part of his task to keep Palace in the First Division, but that statement only served to alienate the Eagles' bewildered and demoralised fans.

The early months of 1981/82 provided little relief and with Palace languishing in fifteenth place in the old Second Division, Dario left us in mid-November.

Steve KEMBER
1981-82, 2001, 2003

The man chosen to step into the breach left by Dario Gradi's departure was youth team coach Steve Kember. Steve has always been highly popular with Palace folk and his appointment was welcomed by our supporters.

Initially it appeared that Steve would indeed be able to quicken the Palace side to a better showing – he immediately led us to an impressive victory at First Division Sunderland in a League Cup tie and early results in the Second Division were encouraging. However, Steve's first managerial tenure at Selhurst Park is best remembered for the run he inspired in the FA Cup in the spring of 1982, when victories over Enfield, Bolton and Orient took us to the sixth round, where we were cruelly unlucky to lose to a late goal by our former player Clive Allen when the last-eight draw pitted us against Queens Park Rangers on their plastic pitch at Loftus Road.

Whether any manager could have stimulated Palace to a better showing in the league in 1981/82 is doubtful. Lacking goal-power we were always going to struggle and we eventually finished in fifteenth place, having avoided a second successive relegation only in the penulti-mate match when we beat Wrexham 2-1 at Selhurst Park. Thus, Palace fans were shocked and disappointed when Steve was dismissed during the close season: if Steve lacked anything at that time it was only managerial experience at this level and to axe him appeared at that time to have been extremely harsh treatment for a loyal Club servant – and the sequel to it showed that it had been a hugely mis-taken folly.

Steve's second term in charge of the Palace team was more brief – but even more effective! In April 2001 the Eagles were sliding inexorably towards relega-tion and after a dreadful showing in our final home game, against Wolves (0-2), the then-current management team was axed and Steve given the responsibility for maintaining our First Division status from the two remaining games, both away and against similarly threatened sides. It was essential for Palace to win both matches and trust that one of the other strugglers slipped up. The first task, at Portsmouth on 2 May 2001, was accomplished in brilliant style, plus our 4-2 win took us ahead of Pompey on goal difference. Everything hung on the final game, at Stockport four days later. We left it late: because of other scorelines a draw would have seen us go down, but Dougie Freedman netted a fine solo goal with three minutes of normal time remaining.

Two years (and two more departed managers) later, Steve was again put in temporary charge of Crystal Palace, though now for the final four matches after Trevor Francis had left Selhurst Park. But this time Steve was only able to inspire one (home) victory, understand-ably finding it difficult to provide momentum to our fading, mid-table side.

Then, towards the end of May 2003 and at a Fans' Forum, chairman Simon Jordan announced that Steve had been appointed as the Palace manager. Most fans were delighted and simply hoped that this most loyal of club servants could bring the success to Crystal Palace for which we all craved.

Steve started in quite brilliant style and Palace topped an early First Division table after three victories from our first three outings, but injuries and sometimes dubious dismissals cost us dearly while his adventurous playing style and forma-tions were turned to our disadvantage by other thinking managers. Thus, after just one more League success from the next twelve games the Eagles travelled to Wigan Athletic for our first-ever meeting with Latics and were crushed 0-5. Steve's departure was inevitable after that, and he left forty-eight hours later on Monday 3 November 2003.

Alan MULLERY
1982-84

Alan Mullery had been an inspirational midfielder with Fulham, Tottenham and England. He was awarded the MBE and voted Footballer of the Year in 1975 and his subsequent time in management had been equally impressive at Brighton and at Charlton, from whom he joined us in June 1982. However, his appointment was a highly controversial one because he had been a fierce opponent and critic of our Club, especially in his time on the South Coast, and there had been several emotive clashes between him and our managers and supporters. Thus it is cer-tainly true to say that his appointment was the one most opposed by our fans in

Alan Mullery.

Steve COPPELL
1984-93, 1995-96, 1997-98, 1999-00

Steve Coppell is Palace's longest-serving post-war manager and the most successful in the entire history of our Club. At the time of his initial appointment in June 1984 he was the youngest manager in the Football League and to have taken the Palace to the heights that he did, with no previous managerial experience, represented a magnificent achievement.

The Palace Steve inherited was in a poor state but, by astute manipulation of the transfer market and benefitting from a healthy relationship with chairman Ron Noades, Steve built a team that was able to stave off the spectre of possible relegation and then showed real character by finishing the season with our best sequence of that term. Then, during that autumn of 1984, Steve revealed a talent which was to be deployed greatly to Palace's advantage several times in the coming years. Steve was able to discern true footballing potential, even when it was in a raw state, and his successful recruitment of men from the lower divisions of the League, reserve-team football or non-league teams, then the nurturing of them into quality players, was a feature of his management at our Club. Andy Gray was the first such signing and he was followed in the summer of 1985 by Ian Wright.

the whole Club history, and equally that his two years with Crystal Palace were bitterly disappointing ones and quite ineffectual.

The fact was that Alan's previously attested ploy of securing proven, experienced players who were nearing the end of their careers for modest fees or on free transfers simply failed to produce any cohesion or even the beginnings of an effective side, so that for many of our fans of the mid-1980s the lasting memory of his management remains our humiliating dismissal from the League Cup at Peterborough in a penalty shoot-out, after we had surrendered a 3-0 lead from the first leg in the 1983/84 competition.

After a season in which we finished eighteenth it came as no surprise to anyone at the Palace that Alan was dismissed at the end of the term for the first time in his long and previously so successful playing and managing career.

Steve's Palace matured greatly over the ensuing seasons and, with an increasingly attractive style which almost invariably involved the use of wingers, Palace were barely denied promotion or play-off places for three years running. But by 1988/89 Steve's chosen pair of strikers, Ian Wright and Mark Bright, were scoring so freely that they established new Club records for the higher divisions and the Eagles were able to finish in third position. The momentum never faltered in spite of defeats in the away legs of the play-offs and Palace's power in the Selhurst Park returns was awesome to see.

Palace fans knew from previous bitter experience that maintaining a top-flight status is even more difficult than gaining it. Nevertheless, Steve ensured our immediate survival in 1989/90 when, to finish fifteenth in the wake of a 0-9 hiding at Liverpool was most praiseworthy, but he also led us to a wonderful revenge victory over the Reds in the FA Cup semi-final which is regarded by many contemporary fans as the finest single performance by their favourites that they have ever seen. It was certainly tactically brilliant and Steve thus became the only man to have led our Club to an FA Cup final. Indeed, with the benefit of two top-class signings in defenders John Humphrey and Eric Young, the 1990/91 Palace side was the best, by a distance that our Club has ever had. It finished third in the old First Division and, to the huge delight of our fans, won a Wembley final by gaining the Full Members' Cup at the expense of Everton.

What followed under Steve Coppell was disappointing to be sure, but it should not be taken out of context. Ian Wright left us for Arsenal in September 1991 and injuries and loss of form by established players cost both the manager and the Club dearly, yet this was the season in which the Eagles did the double over Liverpool and our youth team reached the FA Youth Cup final.

Steve was desperately unlucky to see Palace relegated at the end of 1992/93, for the Eagles would have survived under

Steve Coppell.

the old system of two points for a win and only one other club has ever gone down from the top flight with our tally of 49 points, and everyone at Selhurst Park was saddened when Steve resigned towards the end of May 1993.

After an absence of two years Steve Coppell returned to Crystal Palace under a new management regime with the enigmatic title of 'director of football' but in February 1997 he resumed full responsibility, and maintained Palace's latest drive for promotion to a successful conclusion, achieved with a stunning victory secured in the last minute of a tense, tight Wembley play-off final with a fabulous strike from skipper David Hopkin. Thus, Steve became the only manager of Crystal Palace to have twice taken our Club to promotion to the top flight!

Steve remained in charge of the Eagles for the first seven months of 1997/98, which were characterised by several brilliantly achieved away victories in the

Premier League, but unquestionably there remains still much to be told about that traumatic season during which the club was increasingly overshadowed by the prospect of a major boardroom takeover, with the prospective chairman repeatedly asserting that he would be employing Terry Venables as our manager when he assumed control. Ultimately, and correctly, with his own managerial authority all but completely eroded thereby, Steve moved aside from his post in mid-March after his most miserable and least successful three months at our helm.

However, the deteriorating position of Crystal Palace under its newest administration saw Steve Coppell installed as our boss once again. Few men can have faced such footballing traumas as Steve did then, as a whole series of key players and men of real talent were sold merely to raise funds to keep a string of creditors at bay. More and more, Steve was forced to rely upon lads from Palace's Youth team – yet he inspired them, with tremendous professional help from youth-team coach, former Palace star Peter Nicholas (and, let it be added, the wonderful support of the Eagles' ever-faithful fans), to secure some of our best results of the season in the spring of 1999 to achieve a fourteenth-place finish for this club in the throes of administration.

A chaotic opening to 1999/2000 saw chairman Mark Goldberg resign from the Club as the financial crisis dominated everything at Selhurst Park, but Steve Coppell maintained both morale and the League position by shrewd use of incoming loan transfers and brilliant motivation to achieve outstanding playing results from our depleted resources. And when a group of Palace fans established The

Crystal Palace Supporters Trust in the spring of 2000, Steve placed himself firmly at the head of this magnificent initiative.

The midsummer 2000 takeover of Crystal Palace by new chairman Simon Jordan was welcomed by everyone at Selhurst Park in the hope that it would be the precursor of more stable times here, but with just eleven days to go before the opening of 2000/01, there occurred an event which Eagles fans have rued ever since, for, in circumstances which remain unclear, Steve chose to leave our Club for the fourth time.

There are plenty of Eagles fans who find it difficult if not impossible to believe that the association of Steve Coppell with Crystal Palace has finally come to an end, but regardless of what the future may hold for either of them, there can be no doubting the fact that Steve has been the best, the most successful and the most popular manager our Club has ever had and Palace supporters will for ever be grateful to him for his amazing contribution here.

Alan SMITH
1993-95, 2000-01

It was to tall, stylish, urbane Alan Smith that Crystal Palace turned to lead our Club after the 1993 relegation. Alan was a footballing man through and through and a splendid communicator. He had joined the Eagles in November 1983 to take charge of our resurrected youth team, became our reserve-team manager and was assistant manager when Palace reached the FA Cup final, won the Full Members' Cup and gained our best final placing of third in the old Football League.

Taking on a relegated side is always onerous, but, ultimately in an imperious manner, Alan secured Palace's immediate return to the Premier League as the outright and acclaimed champions of the First Division, playing an attractive brand of 'pass and move'. Alan was also an astute manipulator of the transfer market and arguably his best signing for us was that of Liverpool's Paul Stewart on loan in January 1994 – Paul became brilliantly effective and proved the catalyst that inspired Palace to triumph.

The 1994/95 season saw Alan Smith take Palace to two major Cup semi-finals with some glorious victories over Premiership sides – we were the only Club this term to reach the last four of the FA Cup and the League Cup and in both we were only narrowly defeated by Manchester United and Liverpool respectively. But in the League we were always in danger of falling foul of the decision to relegate four clubs in order to reduce the size of the League and we succumbed on the last day of the season, at Newcastle.

That Alan would leave at this point had become inevitable after he had been at loggerheads with the chairman for several months, but Palace fans held Alan in high regard so his reappointment in August 2000 was received by us with pleasure.

Intriguingly, Alan's second term as Palace manager followed much the same pattern as the first: in the League Cup Alan led us to stunning victories over Premiership opponents, at Leicester, then Sunderland at Selhurst Park, to set up the fixture which supporters will long recall as the highlight of Alan's second tenure as our boss – at home to Liverpool in the first leg of the semi-final of the League Cup when the Reds were made

Alan Smith.

to pay heavily for some profligate finishing and were fortunate to escape with merely a 2-1 beating after Palace had netted magnificent second-half goals from Andrejs Rubins and Clinton Morrison.

However, Palace were annihilated at Anfield in the return and our League position, never healthy, deteriorated further and further. Thus, following the 0-2 defeat by Wolves in our last home game of the season, chairman Simon Jordan dismissed Alan Smith and his team of coaches, leaving Palace fans with just the nights of the League Cup triumphs to savour from his Selhurst Park return.

Dave BASSETT
1996-97

Chirpy, perky Dave Bassett was installed as Palace's manager in early February 1996. His remit was starkly simple: to revitalise and remotivate the Palace team into serious promotion contenders.

Dave's impact was almost immediate for, within a month, Palace had surged thirteen places up the table, established themselves firmly among the clutch of leading clubs and won five consecutive matches at Selhurst Park in the process with an aggregate goal difference of 15-3!

In fact Palace's progress at that stage under Dave Bassett was quite relentless. Certainly, it was all but unstoppable by First Division opponents. The home sequence was extended to six consecutive victories, 'Harry' was named Manager of the Month for March 1996 virtually without opposition and the run-in provided irresistible entertainment for Palace fans, culminating in the drama and tension of the play-offs and our fourth visit to Wembley in six years, but Palace fell to an injury-time fluke goal at the end of extra time when our former reserve striker Steve Claridge volleyed past Nigel Martyn off his shin to put Leicester into the Premiership.

But nine months later, with Palace in the play-off places and again looking serious promotion candidates, Eagles folk were astonished to learn that Dave Bassett was leaving Selhurst Park to become general manager at Nottingham Forest. Chairman Ron Noades expressed himself as 'left reeling' by the departure of his protégé and some fans were openly angry, but the Club moved swiftly to redress the situation and the following day, Friday 28 February 1997, announced that Steve Coppell would return to the Palace helm.

Attilio LOMBARDO
1998

Two days after the Eagles had suffered a demoralising 2-6 midweek Premiership defeat at Chelsea on 11 March 1998 Attilio Lombardo replaced Steve Coppell as the Palace manager, but this was a bizarre appointment because, however wonderfully skilled and vastly experienced the Italian international star was as a player, he was quite unproven in coaching or management and he was unable to speak more than a few words of English! The situation invited confusion and certainly received a measure of ridicule from sections of the media.

Attilio's major contribution as our boss was to inspire and open the scoring in a morale-raising 2-1 victory over Newcastle at St James' Park and he also led us to our overdue first home League victory of that season, against Derby in mid-April – but Attilio was relieved to relinquish the post of manager at the end of that month after Palace had been statistically relegated following a home defeat by Manchester United.

Steve BRUCE
2001

Although many Palace fans would have welcomed the appointment of Steve Kember as the Club's manager for 2001/02 after the manner in which he had contrived the Eagles' First Division survival against all the odds the previous spring, it was the former Norwich City and Manchester United skipper and centre half Steve Bruce whom chairman Simon Jordan installed on the last day of May. As a player at club level Steve's career had been distinguished, but as a manager at Sheffield United, Huddersfield and (as a co-manager) at Wigan, success had eluded him while his loyalty to his clubs had appeared suspect.

Thus, in mid-October, with Palace comfortably within the play-off zone and playing some pleasing and effective football, there occurred one of the less edifying sagas in our history when Steve sought to resign in order to manage Birmingham City. Simon Jordan initially refused to accept the resignation and much rancour was expressed, but a measure of decorum eventually prevailed, until Steve Bruce returned to Selhurst Park with his Birmingham side on Easter Monday to a hostile reception and a torrent of abuse throughout from Palace fans. The game finished goal-less with Bruce sprinting to the sanctuary of the dressing-room from his dugout to avoid any further humiliation.

Trevor FRANCIS
2001-03

Trevor Francis became Palace's second manager for 2001/02 on 30 November. He had had a brilliantly successful playing career during which he had become the game's first £1 million player and gained 52 full international caps for England.

Trevor was a vastly experienced manager and his best years were with Sheffield Wednesday, whom he took to the finals of both the FA and the Football League Cups in 1993 following a third-place League finish upon their return to the top flight the previous year. Later, at Birmingham, he led The Blues to the 1999 and 2000 play-offs, but without

Steve Bruce.

reaching the finals, and to within a penalty kick of winning the League Cup in 2001.

Trevor was also a popular football pundit on Sky TV: he was erudite, well-spoken, equable and conscientious.

Much of the remainder of 2001/02 was spent in securing players who Francis believed could blend into an effective unit capable of winning promotion, beginning with his first signing, former Manchester City, Fulham and Portsmouth centre half and Welsh international Kit Symons, and Palace finished tenth in the table. Some football scribes called his first year or so at Selhurst Park 'a revolution' because no fewer than twenty-five players left the club during a period of some fourteen months with nine new signings arriving.

A slow opening to 2002/03 was kick-started by a fine autumn run of nine undefeated League matches and Palace

Trevor Francis.

fans began to believe that their latest manager might indeed have moulded a side which could at last fulfil their hopes, not to mention the chairman's demands of a play-off place as a minimum requirement. But this ultimately proved to be way beyond the capabilities of Trevor's Palace side so that the highlight of his seventeen-month spell in charge was our dismissal of Liverpool from the FA Cup in a fourth round Anfield replay and, to the relief of most of our fans, he left the Eagles 'by mutual consent' on 18 April 2003 with Palace becalmed in mid-table.

Kit SYMONS
2003

Kit Symons became Palace's sixth manager in little more than three years when club chairman Simon Jordan installed him as Palace's caretaker boss after Steve Kember's dismissal in November 2003.

At thirty-two years of age Kit was Palace's youngest manager since Steve Coppell's initial appointment and our first player-manager since Laurie Scott. But, although Kit was very experienced at international level with 36 full caps for Wales and had played over 400 League games for four different clubs, his management task with Palace was a hugely difficult one.

Kit's efforts at the Palace helm were praiseworthy, his eight League matches in charge yielding three victories and three draws while his tenure climaxed in a 3-0 success at Reading, managed by Steve Coppell, but a couple of disappointing performances were sufficient to cause the club's chairman to look for a more experienced candidate.

Iain DOWIE
2003-present

Iain Dowie had been the Palace manager for some five months when this book went to print and has been the most successful Eagles boss to serve under chairman Simon Jordan. He had proved himself in management at Oldham, whom he led to the Second Division play-offs in 2002/03.

Kit Symons.

Although he opened his Palace management career with a home defeat on Boxing Day by Millwall, Iain has completely transformed the Eagles, so that within three months of his appointment Palace were within sight of the play-off places themselves while Selhurst Park was again full of optimism and expectations for the future.

If the turnaround was not quite immediate, it was unquestionably profound. Dowie's strong work ethic and intense training regime helped to produce a run of six victories and a draw as Palace drove into the top third of the First Division table, and included a 6-3 win over Stoke (who had been in even better form than us to that point!).

Table-topping champions-elect Norwich were comfortably disposed of, as were West Ham and Sunderland to secure a play-off place. Pitted against the Mackems again, Palace won the home leg 3-2 then progressed to the final by winning an intense penalty shoot-out at The Stadium of Light to take on West Ham at the Millennium Stadium at Cardiff. The Eagles proved superior in every way and secured a narrow but conclusive 1-0 victory to return to the Premiership after an absence of six years.

Iain Dowie thus led Palace to the top flight for the sixth time in our history, though the third via the play-offs, and thereby ensured that the Eagles' 100th season was to be spent among the game's current elite. Dowie is very much a player's manager. He is always keen to deflect praise for his team's achievements towards the men concerned; so obviously emotionally involved in the action yet without ever losing his composure. His adjustments to the Palace line-up proved completely successful: his

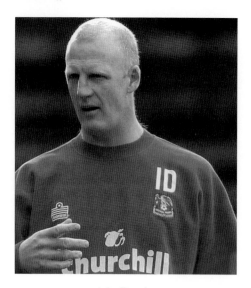

Iain Dowie.

use of loan signings was marvellously astute; his nurturing of precocious or inexperienced talent and of long-term injuries showed discerning intelligence and understanding of the professional footballer's psyche. Accordingly, the Eagles owe their manager a huge amount of appreciation and our fans recognise that Iain Dowie is a master-manager whom we are privileged to have in charge of team matters at our club.

The manager's trademark celebration!

THE CLUB OFFICERS

As well as the presidents, chairmen and managers of Crystal Palace FC there have been a number of employees of the Club, past and present, whose contributions to it have emphatically bettered it while also helping to mould its character and ethos. They, too, are men (and women) who have 'made' Crystal Palace.

Most notable among these folk must surely be the Palace's secretaries. Secretaries' responsibilities are onerous and extensive, but include all aspects of football administration. Thus, they take in all the arrangements of the fixtures, for all the Club's teams, together with the potentially fraught and demanding task of rearrangements necessitated by a postponement or abandonment. Traditionally, the Secretary used effectively to edit the match-day programme but this role has now passed to the control of commercial or marketing staff at most clubs or been delegated to independent but trusted sports writers.

Supporters are all too fully aware that the negotiations of players' transfers and the renewal of their contracts have become an extremely complex matter and it is the club secretary who must be aware of the regulations that govern these, in order that everything about them may be settled in a proper manner. There are also strict FA rules concerning the day to day running of a major football club and it is to its secretary that a club will look for guidance and instruction concerning every aspect of its administration.

It will surely come as no surprise to any Palace reader that Mr **Edmund Goodman** still retains his position as our longest-serving secretary, having held that post from the Club's foundation in 1905 until 1933, but Mr **Alan Leather** was in office from 1973 to 1989 and in terms of years in the post is second only to the great man. Alan's successor, Mr **Mike Hurst**, served the Club initially as assistant to Mr Leather then as secretary in his own right for almost thirty years and recognition of the first twenty-five of them was made in the match-day programme in September 1998. But with the greatest respect to these gentlemen our most attractive secretary was undoubtedly Miss **Mary Montague** who served in this capacity from 1958 to 1964. It may be commonplace now

Above: *Edmund Goodman.*

Right: *Alan Leather.*

for ladies to hold executive positions at leading football clubs, but in those days it was extremely rare to say the least, and if Mary was (just possibly) not unique in the Football League in doing so, she was certainly the first such at Crystal Palace.

Mary was followed as Palace's secretary by Mr **Chris Hassell**, who moved on to Everton in 1973 and with whom occasional contact is retained, but an earlier secretary who served the Club faithfully and well in particularly testing circumstances was Mr **F.E. Burrell** whose full decade with Crystal Palace from 1933 included the chaotic early years of the Second World War, but Mr Burrell died suddenly on Christmas Day 1943 at Norwood Junction station as the Palace team and officials were setting off for our match at Brighton.

If Crystal Palace have been exceptionally well served by their secretaries then the same may be said of their groundsmen. In fact the longest-serving member of all at the Club is former groundsman **Charlie Catlett** who tended the Palace pitch for thirty-eight years. His years in that position actually spanned even longer, from the opening of Selhurst Park in 1924 to 1966, but there was a break in them, presumably for War service. Charlie, with Kate his mare, who pulled the pitch roller – and helped with grass-cutting at strategic periods! – but bolted on one occasion with Charlie on her back and then produced what must have been the fastest ever run down the flank ever to be seen at Selhurst Park, were a familiar scene during the inter-war period and for twenty years after the end of hostilities. Perhaps his most difficult task was readying the Selhurst Park pitch for Palace's game against Watford on Saturday 15 February 1947. One of the cruellest winters of the century was just about to carve a huge gap in the football fixture list but with the aid of some German prisoners of war the snow was sufficiently cleared for the match to take place, with the pitch marked out in a blue dye. Charlie was the first member of Palace's non-playing staff ever to receive a testimonial – or benefit match as they were called in those days – Queens Park Rangers providing the opposition on the evening of the 1959 FA Cup final on his behalf.

Charlie's successor as groundsman at Selhurst Park in 1966 was **Len Chatterton** and Len nurtured the Palace pitch for more than twenty years, but, while no one who ever knew him in that role, particularly with his inventive, unique 'Flatterer', will ever forget him there, this was in fact simply the latest of several tasks he undertook for the club. Len originated as a talented young amateur winger in Palace's 'A' team, – the name given at that time to the Club's third eleven and referring not in the least to the imported 1980s television extravaganza of the same designation! – at the outset of 1941/42. After wartime military service with the Royal Marines for which he won the distinguished Burma Star, Len returned to Crystal Palace at the invitation of then manager George Smith in 1958 to assist with the schoolboys and run the reserve team with Dick Graham.

Nor did Len's contribution to the Eagles end when he retired from the pitch. He has always demonstrated huge compassion for the disabled and underprivileged members of the community and for many years took a leading role in raising money for local charities, while as his other persona 'Leo the Clown' he was the star attraction at the annual Christmas Party run by members of Palace's backroom staff every year at Selhurst Park since 1970. Thus it was thoroughly deserved when Len was nominated to the Football League in 1985 for a loyalty award which was presented to him by League president Mr Jack Dunnett at our match against Mr Dunnett's own club, Notts County, on Easter Monday 8 April 1985. Then, on Saturday 9 August 1987, Palace played a testimonial for Len against Watford, but this remarkable fellow continues to serve the Club on match days in his capacity as liaison officer in the family lounges . He also conducts tours of the Selhurst Park complex both on match days and sometimes during the week.

If Len was a footballer whose major contribution to Crystal Palace lay behind the scenes, the reverse was true of two other men who ultimately became valued members of Palace's back-room staff after their superb playing careers with us were over. **Bobby Greener** made 317 senior appearances for us between 1922 and 1932 as a tough, sturdy, driving wing half with a ferocious tackle who is remembered as playing with an eternal smile on his face for his opponents and the referee. After a single season with York City Bob rejoined the Palace as assistant trainer. He later became the senior trainer, served the Club under ten managers and was one of a tiny staff left at Selhurst Park during the Second World War. He left the Club in a financial purge at the end of 1954/55 but was invited back in 1969 to help out with the groundstaff. Gladly, willingly, he accepted and again became a familiar figure at our ground as he had been all those years before. Bob died in February 1970 and the Club he loved and had served so well printed a moving obituary in the programme for 21 February 1970.

Another grand servant of the Palace was **Johnny McNichol** who, after skippering our Fourth Division promotion side of 1960/61 and playing 205 League and Cup matches for us, turned to the commercial side of the game. He set up Palace's first weekly pools and bingo competitions and it is from those humble beginnings that the Club's massively productive present-day marketing enterprise has grown. By the time Johnny finally retired from Selhurst Park he had spent over twenty years here, making an invaluable contribution to the Club both on and off the field.

Popular, likeable **Beryl Whitfield** was another extremely long-established Palace employee and at the time of her retirement at the end of March 2000 she was certainly

Len Chatterton.

the longest-serving member of the post-war full-time staff. In fact, Beryl completed thirty-one years at Selhurst Park, working in a variety of positions, initially supervising the match-day refreshment arrangements at the kiosks around the ground then taking responsibility for the catering in the executive areas as the corporate hospitality aspect at Selhurst Park began to increase in momentum. However, Beryl probably became best known at the Palace as the former manageress of the Club Shop, then, later, of the ticket office which was, originally, part of the wider merchandising operation.

Having held these posts for so long it seems probable that Beryl's actually became the best-known face of all at Selhurst Park over the final three decades of the twentieth century so that no book about the people who 'made' our club what it is today could possibly be considered to be complete without proper reference to and appreciation of her many roles.

There now follows mention of three men whose off-the-park contribution to Crystal Palace FC has been highly significant and whom it would be improper to omit from a book with the wide-ranging remit carried by this volume.

John Cartwright

John's inclusion in this book may be a mystery to some readers! After all, his playing career with West Ham and Crystal Palace in the late 1950s and early 1960s was quite undistinguished, though he was a former England Youth international. Certainly, his time with the Palace produced but one memorable occasion and that was our third-round FA Cup tie at Aston Villa in January 1962 when Palace lost 3-4 in the dying moments of the match, having surprised the home side with a level of sophistication seldom encountered anywhere in the game.

However, John subsequently made an enormous contribution to Crystal Palace FC. It came in the mid- to late 1970s, was hugely influential and for it alone he would have to appear in this book. Appointed as Palace's youth team coach by Malcolm Allison and in conjunction with reserve team manager Alan Harris and chief scout Arnie Warren, John brought to Selhurst Park the cream of junior footballing talent from England and Wales, then nurtured and developed it into young men of supreme ability who would take the country by storm by winning the FA Youth Cup twice in succession, and then, usually, go on to distinguished playing careers at League (and sometimes, international) level. Well over a dozen played in the old Divisions One and Two for Crystal Palace: some half of them remain household names among our fans to this day and feature large in this book.

Such was John's coaching ability with young footballers that he subsequently became the highly successful manager of the England Youth team, and in 1998 he returned to Crystal Palace to take charge of our Academy for three seasons.

A 'man who made Crystal Palace FC' to be sure!

Simon Paterson.

Simon Paterson

Simon Paterson was in the employ of accountants Moore Stephens Booth White, whom Crystal Palace used as the Club's Administrator from 31 March 1999 to 5 July 2000. As such, Simon's primary function was to ensure the survival of Crystal Palace FC.

Unquestionably, Mr Paterson behaved with complete integrity during the period of administration, yet, equally, Palace fans and some employees and Club officials found his actions and statements difficult to approve, while, in common with so many modern-day business leaders, he often came across poorly in the media.

Given that Simon's remit was to ensure the continuance of Crystal Palace FC, he was ultimately successful, but it is entirely legitimate to question whether, had it not been for the most welcome but eleventh hour intervention of Simon Jordan, he would have been able to fulfil that charge. Indeed, he did express the view that there was 'no point in carrying on if no exit from administration had been agreed by the transfer deadline' in March 2000. Though perhaps that statement simply reflected his frustration and exasperation with the whole protracted saga.

In the end Simon Paterson held sway at Crystal Palace FC for a few days in excess of fifteen months and as such was at Palace's helm for longer than several chairmen, including the one who had called upon his services, Mark Goldberg. While his task was virtually an impossible one, his lasting impression is that, even if his judgement at times appeared to demonstrate a measure of partiality, it is doubtful if any other appointment would have done the job any better. Thus, while everyone at Selhurst Park remembers Simon Paterson as a man who helped to shape the destiny of Crystal Palace, he was also one whom the fans of the Club were extremely relieved to see depart from its portals.

John Harbin

John Harbin is Palace's no-nonsense fitness coach and it is difficult to overestimate his contribution to the club's promotion at the end of 2003/04. His sporting roots lie in Rugby League and after a hugely successful extended period as the coach of Australian club sides in that sport he was the boss of Wakefield, then Oldham Roughyeds.

John was introduced to Iain Dowie by former Oldham manager Mick Wadsworth. Their friendship was immediately forged, based upon mutual respect – so much so that John was Dowie's first signing after the latter became the manager of Crystal Palace in December 2003. The pair share a conviction in a strong link between physical fitness, discipline and mental toughness – that each need to be nurtured and developed so the other areas respond as well.

John's effect upon the Palace players was plain for the fans to witness. In Palace matches, injuries became much reduced, the manager thus had almost a full squad of players available for each fixture, the team's performances were considerably enhanced and, of course, inevitably, so were the all-important results. By the time John's charges had triumphed in the play-off final at Cardiff's Millennium Stadium, he had not been at the Palace much more than five months. But in that short time he had helped to fashion a revolution at our club and as such, however brief his contribution has been, it has already been more than enough for him to be included in this book.

Terry Byfield. Terry is the longest-serving member of the club's current full-time staff and by the time fans are reading this book will have been with the Eagles for over twenty years, having served Palace brilliantly in a wide variety of responsible positions.

THE CHAPLAIN

The publisher of this special volume about Crystal Palace FC deemed it only proper that a book concerning key personnel at the football club should certainly include at least some reference to its honorary chaplain and historian Revd Nigel Sands.

Nigel is the author of this book, along with a whole clutch of others, about the football club he loves, but the piece which follows has been compiled by reference to a similar, shorter article about him in the first book he wrote for publication about Crystal Palace, to several of his friends who work for or are involved with the club and to the Football Chaplains' Association.

Nigel's contribution to Crystal Palace is both considerable and unique, so it is right that it should be acknowledged before the Club's contemporary supporters and officials along with those of future generations who will not have the pleasure of knowing him for themselves but whom he obviously has in mind when he is compiling his Crystal Palace books.

Crystal Palace was among the earliest football clubs to experience the benefits of a chaplain's services and the Revd Nigel Sands has served the Eagles in that capacity since the 1974/75 season. While football chaplains were once a rarity in the Football League they are now much on the increase and with over half the Premier and Football League clubs now profiting from their involvement, voices of appreciation for the ministry are to be heard frequently in our sport, although these notable gentlemen do not actively seek publicity let alone acclaim for their office. Interestingly too, Nigel was instrumental in the early advance of chaplaincy, being involved in the appointment of several of his colleagues.

Some third-millennium readers may find unusual the idea of the close association of a clergyman with a major football club, but, as Nigel himself has pointed out several times, although the Palace are not among them, the fact is that about a fifth of all Premier and Football League clubs were either founded by a parson (e.g. Barnsley and Swindon Town) or owe their origins to a church or Sunday School (e.g. Queens Park Rangers,

Here's two aspects of our chaplain's work. In the Palace dressing room prior to a game, he engages with some of the players while, overleaf...

Southampton and Aston Villa), so a clergyman's presence is actually perfectly natural. In fact it was at the very first national conference of Football Chaplains that Palace's then manager Steve Coppell spoke appreciatively of the chaplain's involvement at Crystal Palace, and even then, back in the mid-1980s, there were plenty of other folk concerned with the Club who endorsed Steve's view.

The role of the chaplain, as epitomised by Nigel Sands, is a supportive (as against a supporting) one. The injured or out-of-form star player; the bereaved club official or supporter; the bitterly disappointed former member of the youth team who has learnt that his club are releasing him; the promising midfielder facing a career-threatening operation; the lonely new signing who is living away from home and family – these are all simply examples of folk connected with a big football club who have been glad of the availability of a chaplain. Equally, there are Christian footballers, administrators, stewards, directors, referees and their assistants, as well as supporters, who are pleased to have the presence of a minister at their place of work or recreation and to use him as a focus for and demonstration of their own Christian allegiance.

But chaplaincy is only one area in which Nigel Sands has been involved with Crystal Palace: his association with it is much wider and even longer established than his chaplain's involvement. Nigel is a Croydon boy and he has supported his local team since the immediate post-war years. He is a third-generation Palace man. He celebrated the fiftieth anniversary of his first match at Selhurst Park, to which, like so many fans of the period, he was taken by his father, in September 1996 with the Eagles playing at Reading's

... after baptising baby son Jake, he poses with proud father and lifelong Palace fan Simon Blackwell. Incidentally, are those badges at the bottom of 'The Rev's' preaching scarf what they appear to be?!

Elm Park, the ground closest to Nigel's West Berkshire home, where Palace romped to a 6-1 win on a warm, sunlit afternoon. Understandably, 'The Rev', having taken something of a hammering from the undertakers in his neighbourhood who had avidly soaked up their local newspapers' repeated references and reminiscences of Palace's 2-10 defeat at that self-same ground just fifty years plus two-and-a-half weeks earlier (which had reduced the young Nigel to tears!), returned home in jubilant mood. However, it is perhaps as well that his comments to the directors of his next funeral remain unrecorded!

And all this despite the fact that Nigel hasn't lived any closer to Selhurst Park than the Lambourn Valley since he was ordained in Liverpool diocese in 1967! His University degrees were gained at Durham between 1961 and 1965 which he once memorably likened to 'seeming to be as far away from South London and Selhurst Park then as Greenland would be today!' But Nigel's loyalty and devotion to Crystal Palace have never wavered, despite the difficulties imposed by distance, professional responsibilities or, as he himself has sometimes amusingly described, referring to the Palace teams of earlier days, 'the evident lack of any quality except enthusiasm in our side'. Thus, today he seldom misses a Palace home game and travels away whenever he can even if this is not as frequently as it used to be or as he would like.

It has also been during the last decade or so that Nigel's other major contribution to Crystal Palace FC has reached a wider public and gained more fitting recognition, through the publication of his books about the Club. He has actually contributed to every Palace match-day programme for over thirty years (indeed, he edited it for the Club for several years) and during that time has offered properly researched historical articles and information about the Eagles to several publications, but inevitably his books, initially published by Sporting and Leisure Press, and more recently by Tempus have helped to maintain a profile for the Club on the shelves of local bookshops and to create a considerable enthusiasm for historical and statistical data about the Club. This series of books perhaps reached its zenith with his Club history, *Crystal Palace FC 1905-95*, which went to a second impression and was then expanded and republished after Palace's promotion in 1997.

Nor is Nigel's enthusiasm for and on behalf of Crystal Palace a narrow, uninformed thing. He has attended major football games at considerably more than 110 different venues, he is among the three longest-standing members of football's prestigious '92 Club' for which he qualified in 1966; he has followed the Palace at a full century of opponents' grounds, while his views and comments on wider football issues as well as those connected with Crystal Palace are sought by sections of the media.

The Supporters

Clearly, obviously, no football club can exist without its supporters, be they the mums and dads, other relatives and admirers who stand unprotected in all weathers on the touchlines of matches taking place on park pitches and in Leagues which few football followers have ever heard of, perhaps having previously assisted with the essential preliminaries like putting up the goalposts (not always with goal netting!) or having washed and ironed the kit in which their loved one(s) will parade; or the fans of the Premiership and Football League clubs who pay considerable sums of money to throng the stands (and, still, in some places, it is good to be able to state, the terraces) of their teams' stadia in their tens of thousands for game after game.

And Crystal Palace FC is no different. The club depends upon its fans: that is how it always has been and, presumably, always will be.

Our original fans were the football followers from around the vicinity of the old Crystal Palace whose interest in the sport had been kindled, then captured by the cup finals and occasional England international staged at the famous venue. However, there is an intriguing and extraordinary feature of those original Palace supporters: given that they had flocked to the big – and I do mean 'big' because the Crystal Palace FA Cup finals drew the greatest throngs of football supporters to any matches, anywhere in our country, ever – high-profile spectaculars, and on gentle spring afternoons at that, the amazing fact is that the ones who gave their allegiance to Crystal Palace were content to do so in the obscure reaches of the Second Division of the Southern League, the soon to be defunct and usually midweek United League, and in friendly games!

Probably, two reasons can be advanced for the bond between the earliest Palace fans and the new club. Firstly, we scored goals in profusion (an incredible 172 of them in our first season!), an ability which inevitably steered us to the divisional title of the more significant competition in which we were involved. The other reason lies in the thrilling FA Cup runs of the embryonic Crystal Palace club which saw major Football and Southern League clubs embarrassed and sometimes humbled by our more modest favourites.

PALACE

your official Crystal Palace Football Club matchday programme

£2.50

Nationwide 1
FOOTBALL LEAGUE

vs BRADFORD CITY

Tuesday 16th September 2003
Kick Off 8:00pm

Matchday Sponsor

citigroup

Above: *John Richard's wonderfully evocative picture shows Palace fans about to leave for the away game at Reading on 21 August 1948. A youthful John is in the middle of the back row, under the 'Up the Palace' sign. His father, Robert, is in front of him, wearing a fashionable cap.*

Previous page: *The front cover of Palace's match-day programme has featured pictures of fans for the last two seasons (2002-04). Here's a typical example.*

And that relationship between the club and its supporters has remained for almost 100 years. Sometimes the attitude or decisions of the club's leaders has broken the bond between it and individual fans; sometimes the playing performances and/or playing record of the club has been so dismal that it caused the desertion of some (occasionally, even many) more; but the club has continued throughout bad times and good to have a loyal kernel of support upon which it can rely, come what may.

Thus, the supporters in general are most certainly among the men (and women) who have made Crystal Palace FC. Barring only the presidents and chairmen from our ranks who have previously been mentioned, few if any of us, through all the generations, could claim to have made an individually decisive contribution to Palace's standing or status – but collectively, together, present-day followers of the club together with our forebears and predecessors have emphatically helped to make Crystal Palace FC what it is. Some of us may swagger round our localities in our duplicate Eagles' strips or wear pithy

Palace T-shirts on holiday; some of us may have been season-ticket holders for decades and still seldom miss a match at Selhurst Park, while some travel to away matches on a regular basis in addition; for some of us life, family, business, commitments, or simply circumstances have taken us to live at a distance from South London – some, I know, at huge distances even across oceans or continents – but, whether we can attend four or five or forty to fifty Palace matches in a season, we are all Palace supporters who have made our football club what it has become.

Actually, there have even been occasions when the supporters were the club, as against the players, or those who control its finances. Probably the best examples of this took place in the 1998/99 season when, during some awful months for anyone who cared about the Palace, our travelling fans in particular witnessed several abysmal performances where the display of the men wearing our colours – at times they could not remotely have been described as a 'team' – made it evident that they cared much less about the match in which they were taking part, or its result or its implications, than any of our supporters. It was clear on those occasions that the supporters were the club: usually the players are too, but they may be nothing more than mercenaries, plying their trade for a consideration but without any loyalty whatever to the cause they represent.

So let no one doubt that, although the principle is true at every football club, the Palace supporters are emphatically among those folk who have made Crystal Palace FC. And to conclude this section, there's the rare opportunity to recognise the sheer effort, devotion, energy and expense to which some of our number go, and have gone for years, in demonstration of the fact. The few mentioned here should not (nor would they want to) be regarded as particularly outstanding. Rather their exceptional support is mentioned to highlight our point.

Among the relatively local supporters who seldom miss a Palace fixture here at Selhurst Park and who are rightly proud of their impressive sequences is the foremost of them all. David Keats is also a regular traveller to away games and possesses an astonishing memory for all things to do with our club, but his record of attendances at Selhurst Park is nothing short of awe-inspiring because he has not missed a Palace League, Cup or Friendly fixture here for approaching fifty years! David has been featured several times in the Palace programme when particular anniversaries have come round and we have usually invited readers from our own or opposing clubs to challenge his wonderful record, but, unsurprisingly, none have ever been able to do so!

Among the long-distance supporters who come regularly to Selhurst Park three season-ticket holders stand out to highlight our main point. Paul Firmage lives in Downham Market in Norfolk. He has followed the Palace since 1978 and wasn't going to allow a move to somewhere, say, 140 miles away to affect his attendance at our games more than marginally! Paul openly admits that he cannot get to every single match here, but his record of doing so is impressive by any standard and readers won't complain if some fixtures are inevitably beyond him. Then there are Pam and Lynne Kyle, who are mother and daughter season-ticket holders in the Holmesdale Stand. Nothing unusual about that? No... at least not until you learn that they live at St Lawrence, close to the southernmost point of the Isle of Wight! It's almost exactly 100 miles from Selhurst Park, but that distance includes the little matter of The Solent! Yet Pam and Lynne seldom miss a

Chairman of the Crystal Palace Supporters' Trust, Paul Newman (back left), with then-manager Steve Kember, Youth Academy director Paul Holden MBE and Under-15 player Tyrone Berry.

Palace game here and regard as normal a journey that can take up to three-and-a-half hours and includes the vagaries of a sometimes uncertain ferry crossing! Wonderful!

Now, consider a different sort of exceptional record of support for Crystal Palace. This one is the Pudney dynasty of Norbury, where support spans five generations and reaches unbroken all the way back to the earliest days of Crystal Palace FC. Eric Pudney and his wife Pat are well known among Eagles fans: Eric has seldom missed a Palace game, home or away, even in wartime since the mid-1930s! He originally attended and travelled with his father Alf who himself has an exemplary record of Palace support having seen his first game at Newcastle in January 1907 as a small boy with his father when Palace knocked the mighty Magpies out of the FA Cup. Today, Eric and Pat's three sons, Ian, Andrew and Michael all join their parents at Palace games all over the country on a regular basis, and that's despite the fact that Michael lives in Herefordshire! Meanwhile, their daughter Christine, who is married to a distinguished local clergyman, is allowed occasional relief from her duties at the Vicarage and frequently comes to Palace games, bringing her son Luke with her!

Incidentally, just in case any readers think that such supporting dynasties are a thing of the past, others like the Rourkes and the Butlers were mentioned in 2003 Palace programmes with four generations of them attending Eagles matches!

Programme sales manager and lifelong Palace fan Brian Simpson provides a magnificent example of a Palace follower who has worked for the Club on match days – he has done this job for fifty-four years! It's a task that gains few plaudits and little appreciation but one upon which Brian has stamped his own cheery personality as well as his organisational flair.

But finally, here at Crystal Palace we had a recent, brilliant, demonstration which proved that the supporters' contribution may be greater even than helping to make their club. It is heart-warming to recall the group of Palace fans who, eager to assist towards the Club's survival at a time when its continued existence appeared to be increasingly unlikely, established The Crystal Palace Supporters' Trust in the spring of 2000 following months of intense, detailed legal and financial preparation. The men who brought the Trust into being were Richard House, Paul Newman, Jim Piddock and Ray Bateup. It was one of the first supporters' trusts in the country and its constitution has been a blueprint for dozens of others.

The Trust was launched on Saturday 4 March 2000 when Palace had a home game against Manchester City (1-1). Its initial aim was to raise a useful, possibly even a substantial sum of money to help to rescue the Club and to publicise its plight. Nearly 4,000 Palace fans paid £20 each to join the trust – a public demonstration that, even if our club had been brought to the verge of extinction and (so it seemed) that no one was interested enough or willing to save it, then the supporters would go to any lengths in order to try to do so. In addition, more than 1,000 supporters lent £1,000 each to the Trust to take its fighting fund to well over £1 million.

Of course, ultimately, it proved unnecessary for such an investment to be made and the loans were all repaid, but the scale of the response to the initiative in terms of interest (which extended to several other similarly troubled League outfits), the numbers of fans involved and the sum raised, allied to the original initiative, amply demonstrate that here at Crystal Palace there are actually thousands of supporters who are prepared to become the Club, not merely to assist in making it!

Part Two

A PALACE PLAYERS' DIRECTORY

THE PLAYERS

There now follows, in strict alphabetical order, a directory of those men who have made sufficient contribution as players representing Crystal Palace FC to be considered as having helped to 'make' our club. It is acknowledged that in some respects every player could be argued to have contributed in this way – indeed, the earliest books in this particular series from Tempus do simply interpret the title in such a manner, but realistically, that is not so. A player who made an appearance which lasted only a few minutes and did not influence the outcome of the game in question cannot seriously be claimed to have helped to 'make' his club!

Indeed, although we are probably not alone among football fans, Palace followers could readily – possibly, even enjoyably, in a macabre sort of way – provide an extensive list of men who played for the club without contributing anything whatever to the benefit of our cause! Why, some of them even have appearance-records here that are considerably into double figures!

Thus, for that reason as well as for practical ones to limit the extent of this volume, some criteria must be established to determine reasons for inclusion in the following pages. Few readers would argue that a playing career with our club which embraced 100 or more appearances would demonstrate a man who certainly had helped to make Crystal Palace, as would anyone who had scored a minimum of fifty senior goals for us. So, all such men are included in this chapter, but the author has added many others whom he considers also affected Palace's progress, status or dignity for the better and who thus also warrant inclusion among such a prestigious assembly of stars of Crystal Palace.

Club and international appearances for current players are correct to the end of the 2003/04 League season.

ALDERSON, Jack
Goalkeeper 1919-24

Appearances: 205
Born: 28 November 1891 Crook, Co.
  Durham
Previous clubs: Middlesbrough 1912,
  Newcastle 1913
Subsequent League clubs: Sheffield
  United 1925, Exeter City 1929
International honours: 1 full cap for
  England

Jack Alderson is one of a number of excellent goalkeepers to have served Crystal Palace FC. He played a few wartime games for us at The Nest, signed professional forms upon leaving the forces and went on to become the first Palace goalkeeper to gain full England honours while with the club.

Jack's first-class debut for the Palace was the opening Southern League match when soccer started again after the war, against Northampton at The Nest on 30 August 1919 (2-2). He played in all forty-two League games that season and helped the club to finish in a respectable third position. Statistically however, his best term with the Palace was 1920/21 when, along with all the other Southern League clubs, Palace were admitted to the Football League – then won the newly formed Third Division at the first time of asking!

Jack appeared in every League fixture and his record of conceding only 34 goals in a full League season was to remain easily the best by a Palace goalkeeper for over half a century. But Palace found the Second Division tough going in the early 1920s. The fact that we stayed in it for four seasons was not a little due to the presence of Jack Alderson between the posts. He gained applause and admiration at many grounds when keeping Palace in matches which opposing forwards should have won and actually improved as he went along so that, in his final season with the club, 1923/24, he became a wonderful and renowned penalty saver, to enormous acclaim!

There can be little doubt that, had Jack Alderson been with a more glamorous or more successful club he would have gained many more international caps than the single honour awarded to him when he played for England against France in Paris on 10 May 1923. England triumphed 4-1 and Jack was only beaten in the last ninety seconds when the game was well won.

ALLEN, Ronnie
Forward 1961-65

Appearances: 109
Goals: 37
Born: 15 January 1929, Fenton,
  Staffordshire
Previous clubs: Port Vale 1946, West
  Bromwich Albion 1950
Managerial appointments: Wolves 1966
  and 1968, Walsall 1973, West Bromwich
  Albion 1977 and 1981 (general manager
  1983)
International honours: 5 full caps for
  England

Ronnie was approaching the end of a career at the highest level with West Bromwich Albion and England when he signed for Crystal Palace in May 1961 following our club's promotion to the Third Division.

Although he was rather small for a striker at just 5ft 8in Ronnie immediately struck up an exciting and productive partnership with Johnny Byrne that delighted Palace fans and confounded most opponents. But, it was actually later in his Palace career that he was seen at his vintage best, as he played the passes and plied the crosses from which Cliff Holton, Dickie Dowsett and then Peter Burridge scored the goals which first kept the club in the Third Division, then took it into the Second Division in 1963/64.

Ronnie was also Palace's captain for that promotion season, although injuries restricted his contribution as the campaign drew towards its climax. He then completed a century of League appearances for us before moving back to the Black Country to take up a coaching position with Wolves. Before doing so, however, he performed delightfully in the Second Division with a particular highlight being a hat-trick against Charlton in one of his last games in our colours in September 1961. An almost 30,000 crowd gave Ronnie a rousing ovation at the final whistle to show their appreciation of his masterful skills!

ANDREWS, Cecil ('Archie')
Wing half/Striker 1952-56

Appearances: 105
Goals: 12
Born: 1 November 1930, Alton, Hants
Previous clubs: Portsmouth 1949
Subsequent League clubs: Queens Park
  Rangers 1956

Archie Andrews' real name was Cecil, but this good-natured footballer was inevitably nicknamed after the ventriloquist's famous dummy of the time.

Archie usually performed as a combative left half for the Palace, but he was also occasionally drafted into the front line to play as a makeshift centre forward to useful effect, because his considerable height gave him a distinct advantage in that department and he scored on his first two outings for Palace in the role.

Archie always gave 100 per cent for the Palace and was a firm favourite with the fans of the mid-1950s. New manager Cyril Spiers regarded him as surplus to requirements, but the left half position was never satisfactorily filled after Archie's departure until it was taken over by Johnny McNichol some five or six years later.

ARMSTRONG, Chris
Forward 1992-95

Appearances: 136
Goals: 58
Born: 19 June 1971, Newcastle upon Tyne
Previous clubs: Wrexham 1988, Millwall
  1991
Subsequent League clubs: Tottenham
  Hotspur 1995, Bolton Wanderers 2002,
  Wrexham 2003

Chris Armstrong joined Crystal Palace in September 1992 as a £1 million striker. He was quiet and withdrawn off the park, but he made an immediate impact before our fans with a brace of goals on his home debut against Oldham, then scored another one to secure our first Premier League victory in the following match at Everton. His tally of 15 goals that term was easily Palace's best and, in a struggling side and without the assistance of a regular and proven partner, represented a splendid haul.

Chris again performed in most praiseworthy fashion in 1993/94, helping Palace

Chris Armstrong at Grimsby in February 1994.

to the First Division Championship with 23 league goals, including some highly spectacular affairs and a fabulous hat-trick against Portsmouth in an early season game, but his performances back in the Premiership the following season were one key to our failure to retain top-flight status, so that few Eagles fans rued his £4.5 million departure to White Hart Lane in June 1995.

ASTLEY, Horace
Half-back/Centre forward 1905-07

Appearances: 46*
Goals: 16*

Previous clubs: Middlesbrough
Subsequent League clubs: Bury 1907
Note: including appearances and goals in Southern League Second Division 1905/06

Horace Astley would deserve inclusion in this gallery of Palace players for just one of his games for Crystal Palace, because it was he who netted the forty-first-minute goal in Palace's old first-round FA Cup tie to beat Newcastle United, League Champions and finalists of 1906, fielding several current internationals, favourites to win by the biggest margin of the round and on their own Gallowgate ground!

But Horace was a powerful, driving and resourceful wing half too, and his value may be measured by the fact that when he left the Palace he went to a leading top-flight Football League club of the period, Bury.

AUSTIN, Dean
Defender 1998-2002

Appearances: 168
Goals: 6
Born: 26 April 1970 Hemel Hempstead
Previous clubs: Southend United 1990,
    Tottenham Hotspur 1992

Full-back and central defender Dean Austin arrived at Crystal Palace from Tottenham Hotspur in July 1998 but had the misfortune to be with the Eagles during some of the most difficult times in the club's history. However, showing great character and resilience, Dean became a huge asset and a real favourite at Selhurst Park. His willingness to take a pay cut in the early spring of 1999 when acute financial problems hit the Palace certainly helped to gain the approval of our fans, then, upon his reappearance in the side, our team immediately secured several excellent results in those trying times.

In fact Dean was made Palace's captain during the critical weeks of the run-in to 1999/2000. He missed only one game in that entire season and was a keystone of the club's successful survival bid, during which his experience proved an invaluable steadying influence among the young players upon whom we were forced to depend more and more during the time we were in administration.

Palace relied heavily upon Dean again in 2000/01 when several other senior players failed to show either resolve or loyalty, but not even the most demanding supporter could have asked for more from Dean Austin. He made more appearances for us than any other Palace defender, his bloodstained, heavily bandaged head at Portsmouth in the critical penultimate game symbolised his and the club's defiance at the very real threat of relegation, and if ever a player has been the man for the moment at Crystal Palace FC that player was Dean Austin.

BAILEY, Roy
Goalkeeper 1949-56

Appearances: 119
Born: 26 May 1932, Epsom, Surrey
Subsequent League clubs: Ipswich Town 1956

Roy Bailey made his Palace debut at the age of just seventeen, but he became our regular goalkeeper after his spell of national service had ended early in 1953, and then it soon became clear that Roy was a goalkeeper of the highest quality, even though he was performing in a Palace side that was almost invariably a struggling one.

A tremendous favourite with the fans of that time, Roy was both handsome and spectacular, and a most worthy member of the gallery of fine goalkeepers who have served Crystal Palace down the years. He was awarded a benefit match with Jack Edwards in October 1955, when Leyton Orient were our visitors but in March 1956 he inevitably left us to play for a club where the immediate prospects were considerably brighter than our own. He signed for aspiring Ipswich Town, then still of the Third Division (South), but helped them to the Second Division the next season and then on to the First Division Championship.

Curiously, perhaps Roy's finest goalkeeping feat with the Palace was in a reserve match at Luton in 1950 when he saved a thrice-taken penalty magnificently each time!

BANNISTER, Jack
Midfield/Defender 1965-69

Appearances: 129
Goals: 7
Born: 26 January 1942, Chesterfield
Previous League clubs: West Bromwich Albion 1959, Scunthorpe United 1964
Subsequent League clubs: Luton Town 1968, Cambridge United 1971

Manager Dick Graham brought Jackie Bannister to Selhurst Park on a free transfer from Scunthorpe United in July 1965, having assessed this combative wing half or full-back at close quarters when they were at The Hawthorns together in the early 1960s, and Jackie certainly became a valued member of Palace's Second Division defences under Mr Graham in the second half of the decade, missing only one match in two seasons between August 1966 and May 1968. He also developed a penchant for scoring goals against Second Division rivals Plymouth – he did so home and away in 1965/66 and then hit another one when the Pilgrims were at Selhurst Park in February 1967!

A hard tackler and a great distributor of the ball, Jackie was strong in the air too, while he stood out in our defence with his shock of black hair. But to the disappointment of many Palace fans he left us for Luton Town in October 1968.

BARBER, Phil
Forward/Midfield 1983-91

Appearances: 288
Goals: 41
Born: 10 June 1965, Tring
Subsequent League clubs: Millwall 1991, Bristol City 1995.

Phil Barber was secured for Crystal Palace by manager Alan Mullery from Aylesbury and was probably the latter's best signing for the Eagles, for Phil went on to a distinguished Palace career as a valuable and effective member of several Palace teams. He came to be known as 'Fizzer' to his colleagues and the club's fans. He could always be relied upon to give his utmost in the Palace cause; his career record keeps him well to the fore in our all-time charts and he made a major contribution at the time of Palace's most substantial achievements.

Phil began as a striker but increasingly featured on the left side of midfield and it was there that he started in every game of Palace's 1988/89 promotion season. Phil's efforts in that success are sometimes underrated but knowledgeable fans of the period never make that mistake. Not only could no one have played in more matches during that campaign than Phil, but he also scored some extremely useful goals, of which a gem of a strike to win the Good Friday fixture at Watford was probably the most significant and best remembered. He was involved in the build-up to Ian Wright's early goal at Selhurst Park in the play-off final against Blackburn, while his two goals in three minutes at Leicester earlier in the season had turned that match in our favour after The Foxes had taken the lead.

Only the misfortune of an injury sustained in Palace's first match upon returning to the top flight prevented Phil from making a full number of appearances in 1989/90, although he was an ever-present member of the team that reached the 1990 FA Cup final and came so close to snatching the trophy – indeed, it was Phil's goal that enabled the Eagles to overcome defiant Rochdale in the fifth round of that cup run and prevented the embarrassment (or worse) of a Spotland replay.

BARRIE, George
Defender 1929-34

Appearances: 80
Born: Markinch, Fifeshire
Subsequent League clubs: Gillingham 1934

Defender George Barrie first played at Selhurst Park in the Kettering Town side which included Peter Simpson and three further men who subsequently joined Crystal Palace, in a first-round FA Cup tie in November 1928 which Palace won 2-0. But Peter apart, none of the others made such an impression for Palace as George did – he moved to us the following summer and stayed for nearly five seasons.

Most of that time George was a steady, secure deputy centre half, though he also played in both full-back positions. He made 17 appearances in Palace's defence in 1930/31 when we finished as Third Division (South) runners-up to Notts County, but his best sequence was from November 1932 when he held the centre half berth in his own right but, with Peter Simpson out for most of the second half of the season, Palace just lacked sufficient goal-power to push higher than a creditable fifth place.

However, it was back to a deputy's role for 1933/34, so George was pleased enough to move to Gillingham who were managed by Fred Mavin, the boss who had originally signed him for Crystal Palace, but, while it ensured him a first-team place (and the captain's role) his new club lost both the Easter fixtures with the Palace a few weeks later!

BARRON, Paul
Goalkeeper 1980-83

Appearances: 108
Born: 16 September 1953, Woolwich
Previous clubs: Plymouth Argyle 1976, Arsenal 1979
Subsequent League clubs: West Bromwich Albion 1982, Queens Park Rangers 1985

Paul Barron.

Paul Barron was a more than capable goalkeeper who joined the Palace in the summer of 1980, as part of the complex deal which also brought Clive Allen to Selhurst Park and took Kenny Sansom to Highbury, but, for the £400,000-rated Barron, along with everyone at Crystal Palace at the time, 1980/81 was a miserable season.

Managers came and went at an alarming rate, there was a boardroom takeover; gates began to dwindle and the Palace were candidates for relegation from the First Division from well before Christmas.

However, the following season Paul did justify his large transfer fee and had an excellent run of performances, missing only two games, so that the big, blond goalkeeper was virtually unchallenged as our Player of the Year for 1981/82. Thus, many Eagles fans were disappointed when Paul left us just before Christmas 1982, in a sudden transfer to West Bromwich Albion, having appeared in all seventeen League fixtures of 1982/83 to that date.

BASSETT, Bill
Defender 1942-49

Appearances: 74
Born: 8 June 1912, Brithdir, South Wales
Previous clubs: Wolverhampton Wanderers
   1934, Cardiff City 1935

At six foot and twelve stone Bill Bassett was ideally built for the centre half berth in wartime and 1940s defences although, by the time he was with the Palace his sparse hair had deteriorated into a bald dome. Nevertheless, Bill was a magnificent header of the ball and on the heavy grounds that usually existed throughout the second half of the season in those times, he would leave the field with his pate covered in mud and present a fearsome sight to all the spectators!

Bill joined the Palace in September 1942 and made his debut in an 8-1 win at Brighton, but because of the war he didn't really become known or appreciated by many of the Palace fans.

While Bill was on war service with the Welsh Guards he was wounded in Italy, but he recovered sufficiently to appear in several Army representative sides and to play regularly for the Palace in the second part of the last wartime season, 1945/46. He became Palace's first post-war captain in 1946/47.

His experience meant that Bill was unhurried and unruffled even during the fiercest moments of a match and he was a model centre half of the post-war era but, as an intelligent and creative defender, one might suggest that Bill was actually half a century ahead of his time for he would have made a fabulous modern-day 'sweeper'.

BATEMAN, Ben
Outside right 1913-24

Appearances: 180
Goals: 11
Born: 20 November 1892 Shepherds Bush

For the first twenty or so years of our existence, most of the Crystal Palace players were Midlanders or came from the North. Ben Bateman was a popular and welcome exception as a Londoner born and bred. He was unusual too in the fact that he played as an amateur. Indeed, during 1913/14 he gained amateur international honours and toured Denmark and Sweden with the England Amateur XI.

Powerfully built for a winger at 5ft 10ins and 13 stone Ben made a strong impact for Palace in his initial season with us. He made 29 Southern League appearances in our 1913/14 side which only conceded the Southern League Championship to Swindon Town on goal average, but Ben was among the first to respond to the call to the colours in the First World War.

After the war Bateman made 37 League appearances in our final Southern League season, but his fine turn of speed and immaculate crosses were seen at their best after Palace had joined the Football League. During the drive to promotion from the Third Division he laid on centres galore from which Ted Smith then John Conner netted the all-important goals. Then in the Second Division in 1921/22 Ben had his best season. Not only did he prove himself to be the master of a number of accredited and experienced Second Division full-backs, but he was in Palace's glorious FA Cup victory when we walloped Everton 6-0 at Goodison Park on 7 January 1922, during which he laid on the first goal for John Whibley after only four minutes, hit the bar himself, then made Palace's fourth goal, netted by Bert Menlove, during the second half.

BATES, Phil
Defender 1919-21

Appearances: 68
Goals: 3
Born: Beckenham, Kent

Phil Bates was a superb attacking centre half of the old school from before the 'stopper' idea had been conceived, and he played a major role in Palace's early progress in the days immediately after the First World War. Palace finished third in our last Southern League season, 1919/20, then won the new Third Division Championship in 1920/21 when Phil was part of one of the best defences Palace had ever had. He scored a couple of important goals in vital games against promotion rivals towards the end of the season!

But, Phil was, quite simply, one of the bravest players ever to appear in the League. He had suffered a nasty injury to his right arm while on active service in the war, and it had become limp and withered, hanging at his side. Just before Palace's Second Division debut the limb required an urgent operation and six weeks later it was announced that Phil could never risk playing again because a blow to it could have disastrous results.

Crystal Palace FC and our fans rallied to their stricken stalwart and two well-supported benefit matches were subsequently staged for him.

BELCHER, Jimmy
Midfield 1954-58

Appearances: 137
Goals: 22
Born: 31 October 1932, Stepney
Previous League clubs: Leyton Orient 1950, West Ham United 1952
Subsequent League clubs: Ipswich Town 1958, Brentford 1961

Jimmy Belcher was a cultured wing half or inside forward from the West Ham academy. Upon signing for Palace he immediately became a pillar of our side and was leading scorer in 1954/55 with 12 goals. He was creative in attack, as you would expect from any protégé nurtured at Upton Park, and he possessed a fierce shot. In defence he was steady and reliable even if, in a way, his sophisticated, refined play was out of its element in the hurly burly of Third Division (South) football. In fact, hindsight leads one to suggest that Jimmy came to the Palace twenty years too soon – he could have become an inspiration in Malcolm Allison's footballing teams of the mid-1970s.

It was a mark of the respect Jimmy earned here at Crystal Palace that, when we ran an article about him in the spring of 1977 in the Palace programme, it evoked a larger response from our fans than any other in that series.

BERRY, Peter
Forward 1953-58

Appearances: 161
Goals: 28
Born: 20 September 1933, Aldershot
Subsequent League clubs: Ipswich Town 1958

Fleet-footed Peter Berry joined the Palace as a junior straight from school in 1949 and he became a versatile forward, appearing in four different front line positions during five seasons at Selhurst Park once he had graduated to the League side. Normally Peter played at outside right, but a combination of events led him to have several useful and productive spells at centre forward and he also played at inside right and outside left for us.

Peter's older brother, Johnny, was also a right-winger. He was one of the Busby Babes at Manchester United. He was badly injured in the 1958 Munich air disaster, but Peter bravely played for the Palace at Reading on the Saturday after the crash even though Johnny's life was still in danger.

A resourceful and pacy winger, with a strong shot, Peter deservedly earned the affection of all the Palace clientele in the mid-1950s, but these were troubled days at Selhurst Park and fans of the period are left with the feeling that we never really saw Peter Berry consistently produce the level of football of which he was undoubtedly capable.

BERTHELIN, Cedric
Goalkeeper 2002-

Appearances: 33
Born: 25 December 1976, Courières, France
Previous club: Luton Town 2002

Cedric was originally signed to be the Eagles' second-choice goalkeeper, but, in both the seasons he has been at Selhurst Park, injuries to the senior custodian have given him his opportunity and he has become a huge favourite with our fans, for when Cedric has been called into action he has proved his worth with solid performances – and never more so than in the first hour at Anfield in Palace's wonderful FA Cup replay victory in January 2003.

Cedric initially replaced Alex Kolinko as Palace's 'keeper in January 2003 but had to leave the action himself with a thigh strain in the match at Reading in mid-March. In 2003/04 Matt Clarke was unable to play after the first four games so that Cedric took over responsibility between the posts and despite Thomas Myhre and Nico Vaesen coming in on loan from more senior clubs, Cedric played more games for the Eagles last term than any other 'keeper.

BIGG, Bob
Forward 1934-1939

Appearances: 114
Goals: 41
Born: Croydon

The Palace had never been able to fill the outside left berth adequately after George Clarke's long reign had come to an end, but there was no doubt that a worthy successor had at last been found when Bob Bigg made his Palace debut. It was in the opening match of the 1934/35 season, at Aldershot, where the young amateur capped an impressive display by scoring our first goal of the term with a header after half an hour.

Like his illustrious predecessor, Bob was a powerful raider in his own right – he finished his first season as second-highest Palace scorer to the great Albert

Cedric Berthelin.

Dawes – and he supplied plenty of openings for his colleagues. Partly, no doubt, because Bob had been brought up in Thornton Heath, he was hugely popular with our fans, but that also stemmed from the fact that he made or scored vital goals precisely when they were needed, though none delighted the Palace fans more than the hat-trick he scored on the opening day of 1935/36, to enable us to beat Cardiff City 3-2.

Sadly, Bob's Palace career was greatly diminished by a badly broken leg sustained at Newport County in February 1937 which kept him out of first-team action for a full twenty-one months, and some of the contemporary pundits reckoned that his absence cost us the single promotion place from the Third Division (South) in 1938/39.

BIRCHENALL, Alan
Forward 1970-71

Appearances: 52
Goals: 15
Born: 22 August 1945, East Ham
Previous clubs: Sheffield United 1963, Chelsea 1967
Subsequent League clubs: Leicester City 1971, Notts County 1976, Blackburn Rovers 1978, Luton Town 1978, Hereford United 1979

Alan Birchenall was an experienced and refined striker, effective both on the ground and in the air, who joined the Palace for top-flight duty in the summer of 1970. His 10 goals in 1970/71 made him our leading scorer in the League and helped us to our best season during the Palace's first spell at the highest level of domestic football.

Alan Birchenall.

Strongly built and with a mane of blond hair, Alan was idolised by the young fans of the period, but he left us in the autumn of 1971 as Bert Head sought to raise funds in order to augment his resources for survival in the senior section. However, such was Alan's popularity at the Palace that he was always accorded a great reception from our supporters when he returned to Selhurst Park with his later clubs.

BIRNIE, Ted
Centre half 1905-06

Appearances: 29*
Goals: 3*
Previous clubs: Newcastle United
Subsequent League clubs: Chelsea 1906, Tottenham Hotspur
These are appearances and goals in Southern League Second Division 1905/06

Ted Birnie was the captain and pivot of the Palace side in our inaugural season. He was an exemplary skipper and just the sort of onfield inspiration the new Crystal Palace club would require.

It was Ted who uttered the famous rallying call to the club and its players when it was learned, to everyone's dismay, that we were going to have to play in the Southern League's Second Division, which comprised just thirteen clubs, mainly the reserve teams of First Division sides together with some lesser-known outfits: 'We must win nearly every Southern League match' Ted declared, 'then they will have to have us in the First Division.'

That was almost exactly what Ted Birnie and his boys achieved, and Ted's prowess was soon recognised throughout the capital, so it was little surprise when he moved across to Football League club Chelsea in the summer.

BIRTLEY, Bob
Midfield 1935-39

Appearances: 69
Goals: 16
Born: 1908, Easington, County Durham
Previous League clubs: Everton, Coventry
   City 1934
Subsequent League clubs: Gateshead
   1939

Bob Birtley came to Crystal Palace late in October 1935 when manager Tom Bromilow was involved in a major flurry of transfer activity during which Frank Manders left Selhurst Park for Norwich. Bob was an experienced and hard-working forward and quickly demonstrated that he was a more than useful signing.

He made a goalscoring start for us the Monday afternoon after he joined the club when Palace beat Exeter 4-2 in a Southern Section cup tie, then, more importantly, netted again with a header on his League debut to help Palace rout Millwall 5-0.

Stocky and well-built, Bob could be depended upon to perform well in whatever position he was placed, although he usually operated somewhere on the right. It was perhaps his misfortune to come to the Palace just when there was about to be a series of managerial and administrative upsets and in such an unsettling atmosphere it is doubtful if many Palace fans really witnessed the best of him.

Season 1936/37 was probably the one Bob would regard as his best at Selhurst Park: he played 30 League and FA Cup matches and netted 9 goals, but, once Albert Dawes had left us for Luton, there simply were not enough regular scorers around and Palace slipped to their lowest position (fourteenth) since joining the League.

BLACK, Tommy
Midfield/Forward 2000-

Appearances: 146
Goals: 17
Born: 26 November 1979 Chigwell
Previous clubs: Arsenal 1998, Carlisle
   United (loan) 1999, Bristol City (loan)
   1999

Tommy Black has been exciting the Palace faithful since his arrival from Arsenal for a bargain £500,000 fee in the summer of 2000. His tenacious, zestful style, his mazy, incisive dribbles on or

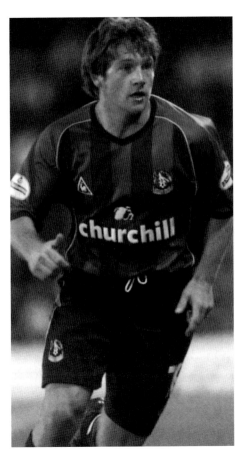

Tommy Black.

from the flank, not to mention his constantly changing hairstyle, have all delighted Palace supporters and become increasingly frequent and more productive, with season 2002/03 yielding Tommy's peak for the Eagles with 43 appearances and 10 goals.

Equally, Tommy's strikes include an exciting sequence of nine goals from as many League and Cup games in midwinter that term, although his last-gasp, sizzling equaliser at Watford in April 2001 which proved crucial in the final analysis might be considered to have been his most important one.

BLACKMAN, Jack
Forward 1935-39

Appearances: 106
Goals: 55
Born: January 1911, Bermondsey
Previous clubs: Queens Park Rangers

Jack Blackman was a strong, aggressive, bustling centre forward who joined the Palace from Queens Park Rangers at the end of October 1935, during a flurry of transfer activity at Selhurst Park.

Jack was an astute purchase for he came to us as a proven goalscorer and immediately proved the point by netting on his debut against Millwall and going on to hit 19 League goals from 27 outings for us in the remainder of the season. Then, after Albert Dawes moved to Luton Town, Jack became our leading goalscorer and he topped Palace's scoring charts in 1936/37 and 1937/38. Ultimately, Jack hit 52 League goals for the Palace from 99 outings before the Second World War, but he continued with us during the makeshift wartime arrangements and again produced a steady supply of goals, including a hat-trick in our first official wartime fixture at West Ham.

After a short spell with Guildford City, after the war, Jack returned to Selhurst Park in 1947 as our assistant trainer. In 1950 he became trainer to Palace's senior side and was twice nominated in that capacity to the Third Division (South) team against their Northern counterparts.

BLAKEMORE, Cecil
Forward 1922-27

Appearances: 141
Goals: 56
Born: 8 December 1897, Stourbridge,
   Worcestershire
Subsequent League clubs: Bristol City
   1927, Brentford, Norwich City 1931,
   Swindon Town

Cec Blakemore joined the Palace in December 1922 as a clever goalscoring inside or centre forward although he took some time to come to terms with the standard required in the Second Division of the Football League. However, with Palace back in the Third Division (South) in 1925, Cec had what was certainly his best season with us and hit two hat-tricks among his tally of 19 League goals which made him our second-highest scorer that term. The following season Cec was again our second-best scorer and his partnership with Percy Cherrett produced 48 goals in the Third Division (South) and helped Palace rise to sixth place in the final table.

Cec refused the terms that were offered to him in the summer of 1927 but his 54 League goals for the Palace still keep him among the top twenty goalscorers in the history of our club.

BLYTH, Mel
Midfield/Defender 1968-75, 1978

Appearances: 254
Goals: 12
Born: 28 July 1944, Norwich
Previous club: Scunthorpe United
   1967

Subsequent League clubs: Southampton
   1974, Millwall 1978

Mel Blyth bestrode the Palace scene like a colossus. A tall, strong, fair-haired Adonis, he came to the club in the summer of 1968 as an old-style wing half, but developed into a magnificent back-four man where his height and stature made him a natural central defender.

Mel immediately became a regular member of Palace's 1968/69 promotion side from the old Second Division and, in our first ever match in the top flight, gained a permanent niche in all Palace record books by securing our first goal there with a controlled, dipping header which put us in the lead and on the way to a creditable 2-2 draw against illustrious visitors Manchester United.

As Palace came under pressure in the top flight so Mel became a permanent

Mel Blyth.

feature of our defensive line-ups and, alongside John McCormick, made twin pillars around which so much of the action centred. Over the four seasons Palace were in the First Division between 1969 and 1973 only John Jackson played more games than Mel – he was a stalwart defender who could be relied upon at all times.

Mel moved to Southampton early in 1974/75, but he came back to the Palace, briefly, in the winter of 1977/78 to play on loan for us as we sought to adjust after Ian Evans' leg had been broken. Mel's half-dozen extra games in our colours took him into the elite company of men who have played over 250 top-class League and cup matches for us since our club's foundation.

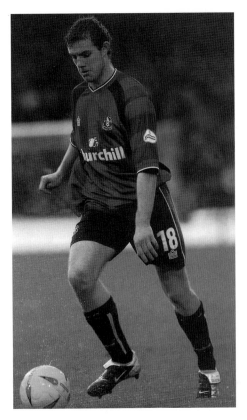

Gary Borrowdale.

BORROWDALE, Gary
Defender 2002-

Appearances: 43
Born: 16 July 1985 Carshalton

Not every seventeen-year-old Football League debutant goes on to a successful career... but be sure that Gary Borrowdale will! Sixteen appearances at left-back in 2002/03 provided the foundation, and he built on that in 2003/04 so that, despite the return to first-team action of Danny Granville, Gary has worn a Palace shirt in approaching fifty games.

Gary always looks at ease with his responsibilities despite his lack of years and, while there is no doubt his career will flourish at higher levels than he has graced so far, few Palace fans would argue that it has already qualified him for inclusion in this book.

BOURNE, Jeff
Forward 1977-78

Appearances: 37 appearances
Goals: 10
Born: 19 June 1948, Linton, Derbyshire
Previous clubs: Derby County 1971
Subsequent League clubs: Sheffield
   United 1979

Jeff was the absolutely superb signing made by Terry Venables as the transfer deadline of 1977 approached. Palace's sights were on promotion from the Third Division but they were seemingly unable to forge their way into the top places for want of sufficient goal-power. Jeff's tally

Jeff Bourne.

Languid, quiet and thoughtful in the dressing room, hard-working midfielder Bobby Bowry packed considerable power in his slight frame and provided a useful contribution to the Palace over some three years. His temperament was ideally suited to the big occasion – he made an outstanding debut at Liverpool in a December 1992 League Cup tie when a youthful Palace side gained a most praiseworthy draw, while the highlight of his Palace career was his seventh-minute goal, lashed in from the edge of the penalty area, which proved sufficient to expose the pretensions of Aston Villa and inspire the Eagles to a splendid and memorable victory over a team that was aspiring to the Premier League title in March 1993.

of 9 goals from 15 outings remedied that deficiency and enabled the Eagles to snatch third place at the last gasp, in a truly thrilling run-in to the season and a fabulous victory in our last match of the season at Wrexham, who were our close rivals, where Jeff scored twice.

Curiously, though, Jeff could not continue in such style and he left us for Dallas less than twelve months after he joined us, but his contribution was both hugely significant and totally unforgettable.

BOWRY, Bobby
Midfield 1992-95

Appearances: 61
Goals: 1
Born: 19 May 1971, London
Subsequent League clubs: Millwall 1995, Colchester United 2001

BRIGGS, Harry
Central defender 1948-55

Appearances: 157
Goals: 4
Born: 27 February 1923, Shotton, Co. Durham

Harry Briggs was a burly centre half who came late into Football League soccer, but he developed into a pillar of our defence in the early 1950s as well as becoming the Club captain at Crystal Palace FC.

Commanding in the air, a great header of the ball and a strong tackler, Harry was the epitome of the 'stopper' centre half, and in spite of playing for a struggling club he was always loyal to the Palace. He could be relied upon in all circumstances to give of his best for us, even though in all honesty we were seldom more than a pretty poor bunch throughout the period he was with us. Harry led our team by

*The incomparable Mark Bright
scored twice in this fixture
against Norwich (3-4) on
29 February 1992.*

example – although perhaps what some
of his colleagues needed was a skipper
who could also drive or cajole them to
better levels of performance – but it was
a mark of the respect in which he was
held by Palace fans that his well-deserved
benefit in 1953/54 was so well supported.

BRIGHT, Mark
Forward 1986-92

Appearances: 286
Goals: 113
Born: 6 June 1962 Stoke-on-Trent

Previous clubs: Port Vale 1981, Leicester
City 1984
Subsequent League clubs: Sheffield
Wednesday 1992, Millwall (loan) 1996,
Charlton Athletic 1997

Mark Bright was Palace's supreme
goalscorer throughout the most successful years our club has ever known. It was
his goals, along with those from his partner Ian Wright, which took the Eagles
back to the old First Division in 1989
while 'Brighty' earned the Golden Boot
for the division's highest scorer the previous term with 24 strikes.

Mark hit 12 goals in the top flight in 1989/90 as part of our creditable showing that season, while our supporters will always remember that it was Mark's crashing drive at the start of the second half that began the club's recovery against Liverpool in the FA Cup semi-final, and, ultimately, helped to take us to Wembley. He gained further national recognition when he scored the decisive goal against Liverpool in a televised League match at Selhurst Park on 30 December 1990, and with a sequence of seven strikes in just ten games during midwinter, he ensured that Palace pursued the might of Arsenal and Liverpool at the top of the table to finish in third place, easily the highest final placing our club has ever attained.

Even after Ian Wright had left Selhurst Park, Mark continued his sparkling form for the Eagles and many fans from that period will agree that 1991/92 was actually his best one of all for us. Not only did he captain the side for a few games in early winter but he netted a remarkable 17 top-flight goals – Palace's best ever at that level – and was our only player to make full appearances in every competition in which the club was engaged.

Mark remains a huge favourite among everyone connected with Crystal Palace and he is one of just six men to have netted over 100 Palace goals in the entire history of our club, while, curiously, his 92 League goals is exactly the same number as those scored for the club by his partner Ian Wright.

BROOKS, Shaun
Midfield 1980-83

Appearances: 66
Goals: 5
Born: 9 October 1962, London
Subsequent League clubs: Orient 1983, Bournemouth 1987, Leyton Orient 1994

Shaun Brooks is the son of Johnny Brooks and the pair are the only father and son duo ever to have both played in the League for Palace. Shaun was a skilful, resourceful midfield player who had gained England schoolboy and youth honours as a lad. Regrettably though, he was just approaching maturity at one of the most volatile periods in the Palace annals and thus, with repeated changes of management and a side constantly in decline, he was never seen at anything approaching his best for the Palace, though discerning fans appreciated his talent and recognised his potential.

BROUGHTON, Ted
Forward 1948-53

Appearances: 100
Goals: 6
Born: 9 February 1925, Bradford
Previous clubs: New Brighton 1947

Ted Broughton joined the Palace in the summer of 1948 to occupy the outside right position which had never been satisfactorily filled since the Second World War.

Ted was a clever, tricky player with neat ball-control. He was difficult to dispossess and he liked to beat his man and create space for his crosses by craft rather than by sheer pace. His skill on the ball meant that he was occasionally useful in an inside berth too, but the Palace were seldom more than a struggling outfit while he was with us and it is doubtful if many Palace fans ever saw Ted at his best.

Ted's career ended abruptly with a badly broken leg sustained in a Football Combination match and he joined his home-town club, Bradford Park Avenue, as assistant trainer in 1954.

BRUSH, Paul
Defender 1985-87

Appearances: 56
Goals: 3
Born: 22 February 1958, Plaistow
Previous clubs: West Ham United 1977
Subsequent League clubs: Southend United 1987
Managerial appointments: Leyton Orient 2001

Paul Brush was an intelligent and proven left-back or occasional central defender whom manager Steve Coppell secured to add craft and experience when our defence had developed unwanted leaks early in the 1985/86 season. For some two years 'Brushy' was a considerable asset. He was a thinking defender, cultured, and possessed a real measure of the sophistication football fans expect to see in a product of the West Ham soccer academy.

BULCOCK, Joe
Full-back 1909-14

Appearances: 146
Goals: 2
Born: unknown

Previous clubs: Bury, Exeter City
Subsequent League clubs: Swansea Town 1914

Joe Bulcock joined the Palace in the summer of 1909 and made an immediate impact here, missing just three Southern League matches in his first season and being selected to represent the Southern League against the Football League at Stamford Bridge in April. He then went out to South Africa with the FA summer touring side and played for the national team in one of the representative games.

Joe was strong and sturdy and thus ideally suited to the tough demands of the Southern League. He was Palace's first-choice left-back for four full seasons and had become a firm favourite with Palace's pre-First World War supporters before injury offered talented Horace Colclough the chance to succeed him. Joe thus moved to Swansea Town in February 1914, but he was killed in France on active service during the First World War.

BURGESS, 'Cam'
Forward 1951-53

Appearances: 50
Goals: 40
Born: 21 September 1919, Birkenhead
Previous clubs: Bolton Wanderers 1946, Chester City 1948
Subsequent League clubs: York City 1953

Cam Burgess was not a very big fellow – but his goals-to-appearances ratio for Crystal Palace is higher than that of anyone else in this book!

Cam was signed for the Palace in September 1951 by Charlie Slade and Fred Dawes and he netted a hat-trick in only his second game for us, at Leyton Orient (4-0), totalled 21 strikes from 22 appearances that season, then hit another 19 in 1952/53! It was during the latter term that he registered an amazing sequence of goalscoring, accumulating three hat-tricks in four games and ten goals from five outings! To modern readers it sounds astonishing – to the long-suffering Palace fans of the early 1950s it was quite wonderfully an adventure in dreamland!

BURKE, David
Defender 1987-90

Appearances: 97
Born: 6 August 1960, Liverpool
Previous clubs: Bolton Wanderers 1978, Huddersfield Town 1981
Subsequent League clubs: Bolton Wanderers 1990, Blackpool 1994

Calm and authoritative, David Burke brought experience and stability to Palace's left-back position after Paul Brush's long-term hamstring injury had left us somewhat depleted there, and for two seasons he was our regular number three. 'Burkey' had actually played against the Palace for his previous club, Huddersfield Town, in the opening match of the 1987/88 season, two months before he joined us! Assured and capable throughout Palace's promotion season of 1988/89 and occasional captain of it, David's previous top-flight knowledge, gained with Bolton, stood the Eagles in good stead as we advanced upon the senior section and it was to The Trotters that he returned when he left Selhurst Park in the summer of 1990.

BURNS, Tony
Goalkeeper 1974-78

Appearances: 98
Born: 27 March 1934, Edenbridge
Previous clubs: Arsenal 1964, Brighton & Hove Albion 1966, Charlton Athletic 1969
Subsequent League clubs: Brentford (loan) 1976, Plymouth Argyle 1978

Tony Burns was brought back to England from Durban City by Palace manager Malcolm Allison as the latter revamped virtually our entire playing staff after his appointment in March 1973, although it was Terry Venables who benefited most from the availability of this secure, steady, undemonstrative professional.

Tony was initially purchased to be an experienced reserve to Paul Hammond, but he had two valuable spells as our senior 'keeper, acquitting himself most ably for the Eagles, particularly in our surge to promotion in the spring of 1977, although a self-inflicted injury prevented him from playing in the final, crucial game. We impressed in the Second Division the following term, during which he played 29 consecutive League games before flying out to play for Memphis Rogues as he made way for John Burridge.

BURNSIDE, David
Midfield 1964-66

Appearances: 64
Goals: 10
Born: 10 December 1939, Bristol
Previous clubs: West Bromwich Albion 1957, Southampton 1962

Subsequent League clubs:
Wolverhampton Wanderers 1966,
Plymouth Argyle 1968, Bristol City 1971,
Colchester United 1971
Managerial appointments: England
Youth 1990

David Burnside was a supremely skilled inside forward-cum-early midfielder who joined the Palace on Christmas Eve 1964 for a club-record fee of £14,000. He immediately enthralled Palace fans with a splendid display on his Boxing Day debut when we romped to a 4-2 victory over Portsmouth on a tricky, icy surface. He netted two delightful goals in that success and in the early months of 1965 assisted Palace to heights the club had not scaled for decades.

Most memorable among these was the FA Cup run to the quarter-finals, where he scored the opening goals in Palace's 5-1 demolition of Bury (this, with only ten men after the departure of Brian Wood with a broken leg!) and the 3-1 triumph over First Division Nottingham Forest in front of a record crowd, in rounds three and five respectively.

Possessed of amazing ball control – as a youngster he had entertained and astonished half-time crowds by keeping the ball off the ground for the entire interval! – David provided the complete rebuttal to the charge that Dick Graham's Palace of the mid-1960s were merely a physical bunch. His departure from our club was interesting and possibly unique too, for he featured in our line-up in the match programme for our visit to Wolves in September 1966, yet appeared for the Molineux side after a speedily arranged transfer!

David Burnside.

BURRIDGE, John
Goalkeeper 1978-80

Appearances: 102
Born: 3 December 1951, Workington
Previous clubs: Workington 1970,
Blackpool 1971, Aston Villa 1975
Subsequent League clubs: Numerous!

In terms of sheer goalkeeping ability, most post-war Palace fans would probably agree that John Burridge has only John Jackson and Nigel Martyn standing ahead of him. Certainly, Palace supporters of the late 1970s will never forget this amiable extrovert, gymnast, joker and goalkeeper supreme, who was an ever-present member of the club's 1978/79 promotion side and starred in what is statistically the Eagles' best ever defence.

But glorious though his playing record for Palace was, it reveals only part of

'Budgie's' contribution to the club. His imposing presence exuded confidence which spread to teammates and supporters alike. He used his voice to great advantage in a manner few goalkeepers have ever done, to help, direct and encourage his colleagues, and he simply refused to allow an opponent to even consider that he might, just, have a chance of beating him – with the result that very few ever did!

Palace fans immediately took John to their hearts after his arrival from Aston Villa, and would throng the terraces (in those days!) of Selhurst Park long before kick-off to witness his extraordinary pre-match warm-up sessions, in which he entertained and amused the supporters before returning to the dressing room as mud-stained as if he had played a full game! A mark of the esteem in which John was held at the Palace was noticeable whenever he returned with his later clubs, for he was invariably accorded a warm welcome both from our fans and from his former playing colleagues.

BURRIDGE, Peter
Forward 1962-65

Appearances: 124
Goals: 49
Born: 30 December 1933, Harlow, Essex
Previous clubs: Leyton Orient 1958,
   Millwall 1960
Subsequent League clubs: Charlton
   Athletic 1965

Peter Burridge was naturally left-footed but possessed a venomous shot in both feet, plus the ability to head the ball with great power and accuracy, so that it was surprising that Palace had no rivals when

Peter Burridge.

manager Arthur Rowe prised the former Millwall skipper away from The Den in the summer of 1962.

Peter immediately demonstrated his worth by becoming Palace's top goalscorer in 1962/63 with 14 strikes including a hat-trick in the Easter Monday 5-0 rout of Wrexham. He then managed to net 20 goals in the 1963/64 promotion season and thereby finished as joint-top scorer with Cliff Holton.

However, the goal for Crystal Palace for which all our fans of the period will always remember Peter was the one which he later described as the best one of his entire career. Palace were enjoying a fine FA Cup run in the winter of 1964/65 and were pitted in the fifth round against sophisticated Nottingham Forest from the top flight. The score was 1-1 but with a little more than an hour played Cliff Holton swung over a cross from the Palace left for Peter to volley left-footed, and from some twenty-five yards and it crashed into the top corner of the net to an explosion of sound from the packed Palace crowd!

BUTLER, Hubert
Forward 1928-32

Appearances: 124
Goals: 39
Born: 11 July 1906, Atherton, Manchester

Hubert Butler came to Crystal Palace in the summer of 1928 with an established reputation as a goalscorer from the inside left position, even if he did have the misfortune to make his Palace debut in a disastrous 1-8 defeat at Northampton the following October.

It is significant that the Palace were able to make two serious challenges for the Third Division (South) title during the four seasons that Hubert was with us. In 1928/29 he was an ideal supplier of chances for Len Griffiths and Harry Havelock, while also providing 10 League goals himself from 26 appearances (including a glorious hat-trick at Brighton just before Christmas) and helped the Palace to their best run in the FA Cup for years. In 1930/31 Butler netted 14 goals in 39 games to reinforce the efforts of Peter Simpson and George Clarke. Butler's role at Crystal Palace was thus a largely supportive one and he seldom gained much publicity, but knowledgeable fans of the time recognised him as a most useful contributor to the Palace cause.

BUTTERFIELD, Danny
Midfield/Defender 2002-

Appearances: 108
Goals: 6
Born: 21 November 1979, Boston, Lincolnshire
Previous clubs: Grimsby Town 1997

Danny Butterfield was an excellent free acquisition from Grimsby Town in the summer of 2002, so much so that the former England Youth international had an outstanding opening season with the Eagles, playing in every game, demonstrating consistency, reliability, flair and adaptability as he did so. He was a strong contender for the Player of the Year award.

Tall, quiet and studious, while possessing considerable vision and versatility, Danny has been absolutely invaluable to the Palace, for he has appeared as a right-winger, right-back, wing-back and central defender while in our colours. His intelligence and dependability have made him a huge asset here.

He also scores glorious goals! Few supporters will need reminding of his screaming half-volley against Wimbledon in August 2003, his edge-of-the-box strike at home to Derby in October or his far-top-corner effort against Crewe two months later. But surely Danny's best goal of all was his lashing volleyed strike which arrowed into the top right corner of Gillingham's goal from the edge of the penalty area and brought the Holmesdale Road stand to its feet as one man as it did so!

Danny Butterfield shields the ball from a Wolves defender in Palace's 4-2 win on 14 September 2002.

BYRNE, Johnny
Forward 1956-62 and 1967-68

Appearances: 259
Goals: 101
Born: 13 May 1939 West Horsley, Surrey
Subsequent League clubs: West Ham
  United 1962, Fulham 1968
International honours: 11 full caps for
  England
Managerial appointments: Several in
  South Africa 1971-1998

Johnny Byrne.

Stylish, skilful and confident, the chirpy, goalscoring and versatile Johnny Byrne signed for Crystal Palace on the day after his seventeenth birthday and progressed to become one of the greatest players ever to grace Selhurst Park.

Byrne had the prototype nickname 'Budgie' on account of his ceaseless chatter on the pitch and was very much the prime reason for Palace's success in climbing out of the Fourth Division in 1960/61. His 30 League goals that term remains Palace's post-war scoring record for a single season. Certainly his silky talent, deft touches and ball-playing skills, nurtured and refined by Arthur Rowe, drew huge admiration from Palace fans, but it became quickly evident that he would soon be a target for the bigger clubs, although he was still with the Palace when he gained his first full England international cap, against Northern Ireland at Wembley on 22 November 1961 – our club's first such honour in thirty-eight years!

When Johnny moved to West Ham in March 1962 the fee of £60,000 plus the return of Ron Brett was the biggest between British clubs at that time and his career flourished amid the glamour of the top flight. However, in the spring of

1967, to the delight of everyone at the Palace, Johnny came back to Selhurst Park and was given an emotional reception by our fans at a friendly against Leicester City, played on the evening after he had re-signed. Byrne hit Palace's thirty-sixth minute goal in a 1-1 draw that night, but overall Johnny's return to us was not a success and little more than a year later he moved on to struggling Fulham.

In retrospect it is quite evident that, at his peak, Johnny Byrne was one of the most gifted footballers that Crystal Palace FC has ever known. Accordingly it was a great pleasure for Palace fans from Johnny's era when he was invited back to the club on a couple of occasions in the 1990s and the rapturous welcome he was given indicated the permanence of his reputation here. A much sadder occasion, following Johnny's untimely death in South Africa, was the reception and reunion staged in his memory in the Selhurst Park suite that bears his name in November 2002, but the attendance and reminiscences by his contemporaries and the memorabilia produced by Palace supporters simply confirmed the enormous respect in which he continues to be held here.

Billy Callender.

CALLENDER, Billy
Goalkeeper 1923-32

Appearances: 225
Born: 5 January 1904 Prudhoe,
  Northumberland

Billy Callender joined the Palace in October 1923 as a nineteen-year-old and saved a penalty against West Ham reserves in his first match here. He gained unchallenged possession of the goalkeeper's jersey in January 1926 and earned a place in a Football League representative side later that year. He was only ever missing from Palace line-ups as a result of injuries or illness, but his playing record demonstrates that he was prone to neither.

It was while Palace had Billy in goal that the club came closest to returning to the Second Division in 1928/29 when we finished as runners-up to Charlton on goal-average alone. Billy was awarded a benefit match on 15 April 1931 against the Combined Universities, but a knock in the League match the previous Saturday prevented him from playing – so he appeared as a linesman instead!

This was typical behaviour from Billy Callender and his popularity at Selhurst Park knew no bounds, but, sadly his career and his life ended in tragedy. In the summer of 1932 Billy's polio-stricken fiancée died. He took her death very hard and committed suicide. Those who knew Billy were still speaking of him with great affection some sixty years after – a measure of the standing and ability of the Palace goalkeeper who, but for one of life's tragedies, might have reached the highest honours in the game.

CANNON, Jim
Defender 1973-88

Appearances: 663
Goals: 36

Born: 2 October 1953, Glasgow
Subsequent League clubs: Bristol Rovers
  1988

Palace's strong, tough central defender or left-back throughout most of the 1970s and 1980s, Jim Cannon, is one of those rarities in the modern game – a one-club footballer – and it is thus the judgement of many Palace fans that Jim's contribution to the Eagles ranks head and shoulders above all the rest.

Jim joined Palace from Glasgow Amateurs as an apprentice in February 1970 and turned professional on 3 May 1971. Everyone connected with the club knows that he made his senior debut in the London derby against Chelsea at Selhurst Park on 31 March two years later and that, with Chelsea desperately seeking an equaliser, Jim headed a fine goal from a Don Rogers far-post cross to ensure a Palace success.

By 1975/76 Jim was appearing regularly for Palace's Third Division side at left-back. This was the season when the club made its first really impressive impact upon the FA Cup and reached the semi-final – the following term, with Jim now alongside Ian Evans at the heart of our back four, Palace won promotion, both men being ever-present.

A new central defensive partnership was required after Ian Evans' leg was broken and Jim and Billy Gilbert became hugely effective, but by mid-December Jim had also been appointed captain, a position he held for the rest of his career.

In 1978/79 Palace's defence, with Jim at its heart, was absolutely superb, remaining, statistically at least, the club's best-ever with only twenty-four goals

Jim Cannon going for goal against Oldham in 1986/87.

conceded all season and the primary reason why Palace won the Second Division Championship, thus making Jim Cannon the first man to captain the club into the top flight as champions.

An analysis of Jim's career also shows him to be the scorer of many crucial goals but probably the one for which he will longest be remembered was his spectacular final strike in the 4-1 victory over Ipswich on 29 September 1979, a win that took the Eagles to the top of the entire Football League. Jim received a first testimonial in the 1980/81 season with an interesting match against a Vince Hilaire XI, but he then went on to capture every appearance record at the club and in 1988 became the only post-war Palace player to have been awarded a second testimonial when Tottenham provided the opposition. Jim is also the only man to have been Palace's Player of the Year on three occasions and he has earned the undying admiration and gratitude of all Palace fans.

CASWELL, Peter
Goalkeeper 1977

Appearances: 3
Born: 16 January 1957, Leatherhead
Subsequent League clubs: Crewe
  Alexandra 1978

It might be thought absurd that a player with only three senior games should appear in this book, but anyone from Crystal Palace who saw him play his first match for us would disagree!

Because of a self-inflicted injury incurred by senior goalkeeper Tony Burns in the penultimate match of 1976/77, twenty-year-old Peter Caswell

was drafted in for the vital, final fixture at Wrexham which would determine which of the two clubs would gain promotion to the Second Division.

Although he was patently and understandably nervous, and his kicking was affected, Peter performed well in the crucial encounter. He could not be faulted for either of Wrexham's goals and made several fine saves in a most praiseworthy individual performance, playing a full part in the 4-2 success that brought about Palace's return to the Second Division.

Oh, and just for the record, Palace won both his other games at the start of 1977/78 too!

CHARLTON, Stan
Full-back 1928-32

Appearances: 135
Goals: 9
Born: 16 November 1900, Little Hutton, Yorkshire
Previous clubs: Oldham Athletic 1920, Rochdale 1922, Exeter City 1923
Subsequent League clubs: Newport County 1932

Stan Charlton was one of the best captains our club has ever had. He was signed for Crystal Palace by his former Exeter manager, Mr Fred Mavin, and made his debut for us in the opening match of 1928/29 alongside another new boy, Tom Crilly, as Palace beat Watford 3-0. Both men received rapturous reports. They played together as Palace's full-back pairing for four seasons and it is no coincidence that in two of them Palace made serious, if unrewarded, attempts to restore Second Division status to Selhurst Park.

Those two terms were certainly Stan's best at the Palace: he missed just one game in 1928/29 and converted four penalties, then in 1930/31 an injury in a London Challenge Cup tie limited him to 33 appearances but his comeback was the 5-1 thrashing we administered to visiting Brentford on Boxing Day.

Stan was the Palace skipper from only his second match in our colours. He retained the post throughout his time at Selhurst Park and was one of the most popular men ever to appear in the claret and blue.

CHATTERTON, Nick
Midfield 1973-78

Appearances: 183
Goals: 36
Born: 18 May 1954, South Norwood
Subsequent League clubs: Millwall 1978, Colchester 1986

Industrious midfielder Nick Chatterton is the fair-haired son of former Palace groundsman Len Chatterton. He made his debut as a teenager on the opening day of 1973/74 when the Eagles were badly beaten by Notts County, but it was a mark of Nick's character and ability that he developed into a valuable, regular member of several successful Palace sides later in that decade.

Thus Nick was fully involved in our run to the FA Cup semi-final in 1975/76 and in the promotion-winning campaign the following term. He appeared to be completely at ease in the old Second Division in 1977/78, his best season with the Palace. Only a cartilage injury prevented him from playing every game and he scored some splendid goals for us too,

finishing as second-top scorer behind Dave Swindlehurst with 9 strikes.

A quiet and thoughtful man, Nick had been ever-present in 1978/79 until he chose to leave Selhurst Park, but he had a successful subsequent career at Millwall, where he became club captain, then at Colchester.

CHERRETT, Percy
Centre forward 1925-27

Appearances: 81
Goals: 65
Born: 12 September 1899, Bournemouth
Previous clubs: Bournemouth, Portsmouth, Plymouth Argyle
Subsequent League clubs: Bristol City 1927

Big, strong centre forward Percy Cherrett joined Crystal Palace in the autumn of 1925 at a troubled time for the club following our relegation earlier that year. But Percy was a proven goalscorer and the Selhurst Park fans warmed immediately to him upon his home debut when he scored twice against Bristol City and inspired Palace to an overdue first victory of the season. The following game he netted a hat-trick of headers and Palace romped to a 4-0 win over Watford.

Percy finished 1925/26 with 26 League goals, then in 1926/27 he did even better with 32, including another hat-trick against Norwich in October.

In cup ties Percy was equally devastating: take the third-round tie of 1925/26 when Palace were three down at Northampton with ten minutes left. Percy burst through to give us a chance, Cec Blakemore got another and then Percy notched an equaliser with two min-

Percy Cherrett.

utes remaining. In the replay our man hit the brace that saw us through to a home tie against Chelsea, when 41,000 fans turned up to create a ground-record attendance that stood for thirty-nine years and witness Palace's 2-1 victory. Any guesses as to who put the Palace on the way to that superb result?

CHESTERS, Arthur
Goalkeeper 1937-40

Appearances: 85
Born: 1912 Salford, Manchester
Previous clubs: Exeter City
Subsequent League clubs: Leicester City
   1941

Arthur Chesters was Palace's goalkeeper for the seasons immediately preceding the Second World War. He would never have challenged for the honour of being Palace's greatest-ever 'keeper, but he played well enough for us to be able to finish in strong positions in our division in both seasons and sufficiently often to deserve inclusion here.

Arthur joined Crystal Palace in the summer of 1937 to play under manager Tom Bromilow and took possession of the goalkeeper's jersey at Selhurst Park after two disappointing results for the club at the start of the season. He appeared regularly for Palace throughout 1937/38 when we finished seventh in the Third Division (South) among a bundle of clubs behind champions Millwall and only went out of the FA Cup in contentious circumstances at Liverpool; and in 1938/39 when we finished as runners-up to Newport County, just pipped for promotion and the title in a thrilling finish. Arthur missed only one game in that entire season.

Safe, strong, tall and assured, the war then blighted Arthur's footballing career. He played occasionally for Palace in 1939/40, but was signed again by Tom Bromilow in February 1941 and joined his old boss at Leicester City.

CHILVERS, Geoff
Wing half 1948-54

Appearances: 123
Goals: 1
Born: 31 January 1925, Sutton, Surrey
Previous clubs: Sutton United

England schoolboy international Geoff Chilvers had been with the Palace as a junior in the early days of the Second World War and had appeared at Selhurst Park in an interesting schoolboy game that was used as an experiment with numbered players. But his extraordinary claim to footballing fame, which will delight fans with a statistical quirk to their nature or an interest in obscure quiz questions, is that he made his debut with a League club as a sixteen-year-old in a match where his side scored double figures! It was actually against Brighton (10-1), here at Selhurst Park on 3 January 1942 in a wartime London League match, but even so, there can be few, if any, other players whose careers have begun so early and so explosively.

Geoff was a sturdy wing half with a refinement and vision of play which were perhaps a little too sophisticated for the Palace teams of his day, when we were forced to perform in the hurly-burly of the old Third Division (South), and in the end his career was finished by a nasty knee injury sustained in mid-1952/53.

CHOULES, Len
Defender 1953-62

Appearances: 280
Goals: 3
Born: 29 January 1932, Orpington

A tall, lean, versatile defender and occasional centre forward, Len Choules played for Crystal Palace for a full decade and fulfilled several roles throughout some really trying seasons. While doing so he accumulated sufficient appearances to remain comfortably within Palace's 'top-twenty' in the all-time lists.

Len was certainly one of the best defenders in the old Third Division (South) in the mid-1950s when he usually featured for us at centre half, a position for which his height and excellent heading ability suited him perfectly, but he also played at wing half and (as on his debut) at full-back and, occasionally as a most effective striker. Thus Len actually played in seven different positions for the Palace, including once as a stand-in goalkeeper!

Among the cherished memories held by Palace fans of the 1950s, which was a pretty grim period for the club as well as for ourselves, are those of goalmouth action at both ends of Selhurst Park in which Len's rangy, angular figure, with its mop of unruly fair hair, was energetically engaged on the club's behalf. Delightfully too, Len remains a Palace man to this day and it has been a pleasure to see him as an occasional guest at Selhurst Park at player reunions and in support of the club to which he gave such unstinting endeavour during some of its most difficult days.

CLARKE, George
Outside left 1925-33

Appearances: 299
Goals: 106
Born: 24 July 1900, Bolsover, Derbyshire
Previous clubs: Aston Villa 1922
Subsequent League clubs: Queens Park
   Rangers 1933

Auburn-haired left-winger George Clarke signed for Crystal Palace in the early summer of 1925 but it is the considered view of most Palace historians that, had he arrived even only a month before the end of the 1924/25 season, then Palace would never have been relegated from the Second Division.

George Clarke.

George immediately became a fixture in the Palace side, and he remained so for seven seasons. He was a magnificent winger – a ball player with craft and artistry – but also fast, clever and with a lethal shot, so his name is etched for all time into the Palace record books. Consider: he remains the third-highest League goalscorer in the history of our club with 99 goals and only two centre forwards, Peter Simpson and Ted Smith, have ever improved on that figure, while no winger has ever approached it. George also holds the record for a single season with a fabulous 22 strikes from the flank in 1927/28.

But George's major contribution to the Palace was actually as a provider of chances from which the club's centre forwards could score their goals. Percy Cherrett fed off him for two seasons, but it was Peter Simpson who benefited most from the work of our talented, flame-haired left-winger, so that it is no coincidence that Peter scored more goals in each of the three seasons in which George was his teammate than in any of the succeeding campaigns.

George Clarke – a prince among Palace wingers!

COLE, Ashley
Full-back 2000

Appearances: 14
Goals: 1
Born: 20 December 1980, Stepney
Previous clubs: Arsenal 1998
International honours: 30 full caps for
   England

Left-back Ashley Cole may today be a household name among England's football fans but, although he had played a single game for Arsenal previously, it was with Crystal Palace that he first came to any degree of prominence.

Ashley joined the Eagles on loan from the Gunners for the final three months and fourteen League matches of 1999/2000, but this was a thoroughly difficult time for the Palace because the club was in administration: morale was at rock-bottom and our prospects were most uncertain.

But although still only a teenager, Ashley's perky, confident, zestful approach added welcome assurance to Palace's performances as we clawed our way slowly towards safety, although his inclusion in this book was ensured by the fact and the manner of his single Eagles' goal. Palace were at home to Blackburn Rovers in our penultimate game and still enmeshed in the relegation struggle. Matt Jansen had put Rovers ahead near the half-hour, but in the sixtieth minute Ashley had us level with a spectacular shot high into the top corner of the Whitehorse Lane netting from the edge of the penalty area and Palace went on to beat the Ewood Park underachievers to ensure our First Division survival.

Of course, Ashley had to go back to Highbury at the end of the season, but Palace fans have always regarded him as 'ours' and followed his flourishing domestic and international career with pride.

COLCLOUGH, Horace
Full-back 1912-15

Appearances: 85
Born: unknown
Previous clubs: Crewe Alexandra

International honours: 1 full cap for England

Horace Colclough was a magnificent left full-back who joined Crystal Palace for 1912/13 and played a few games in his first season, but once he was into our side on any regular basis there was to be no displacing him. Of such quality was he that he took over from Joe Bulcock and shortly afterwards gained Palace's first full international recognition for England, representing his country against Wales at Cardiff (2-0) on 16 March 1914, and he was one of a number of Palace men of that era to earn Southern League honours.

Horace was a member of Palace's best-ever Southern League side of 1913/14. Not only did we retain the London Challenge Cup by beating Tottenham in the final to become the first club to retain that trophy, but it was the League title that we wanted and came within an ace of winning. Everything hinged on the results of the final afternoon's programme but it was eventually clear that we had been denied on goal average alone by Swindon Town.

COLEMAN, Chris
Defender 1991-95

Appearances: 190
Goals: 16
Born: 10 June 1970, Swansea
Previous clubs: Swansea City 1987
Subsequent League clubs: Blackburn Rovers 1995, Fulham 1997
International honours: 32 full caps for Wales
Managerial appointments: Fulham 2003

Chris Coleman.

Although powerful defender Chris Coleman was a Welsh Under-21 international when he joined Crystal Palace, Eagles fans of the early 1990s will recall that it was largely as a stand-in striker that he played for us in his first two seasons at Selhurst Park.

But Chris was finally able to demonstrate the primary reason for his joining our club when new manager Alan Smith deployed him in defence from the start of 1993/94, first at left-back, then as pivot alongside his Welsh international colleague Eric Young. Palace took the First Division title that term with some style and with Chris having played every game it was no surprise when he won the club's Player of the Year award for 1994.

Chris' career progressed both with Wales and in the top flight with Palace throughout 1994/95 but Eagles followers were disappointed when he chose to join Blackburn just before Christmas 1995, although he remains a popular fellow in the hearts and minds of most Palace fans to this day.

COLFAR, Ray
Forward 1958-61

Appearances: 44
Goals: 6
Born: 4 December 1935, Liverpool
Previous clubs: Sutton United
Subsequent League clubs: Cambridge
    United 1961, Oxford United 1962

Ray Colfar was a zippy, exuberant left-winger with the Palace for two and a half seasons in our Fourth Division days. His major contribution was in 1959/60 with 26 League appearances and 5 goals, but once Ron Heckman had arrived from Millwall in July 1960, Ray became a peripheral figure.

Still, his enthusiasm and eager runs down our left flank were a source of pleasure and provided some hope for better things ahead during some depressing times for Palace fans.

COLLINS, Nick
Wing half 1934-39

Appearances: 152
Goals: 7
Born: Chopwell, County Durham
Subsequent clubs: Yeovil Town 1946

It was from the delightfully named Canterbury Waverley club that Palace signed Nick Collins in late August 1934, in the face of opposition from Arsenal.

Palace always had good quality wing halves before and after the arrival of Nick Collins, but he certainly ranked among the best of them. Strong and sturdy – he stood 5ft 8ins and weighed ten and half stone – Nick possessed a venomous tackle and a shrewd, creative footballing brain.

He made his debut a week or two after joining us and soon settled down at left half, making the berth his own, but he was not seen at his supreme best until Palace manager Tom Bromilow signed Les Lievesley from Torquay. These two, with veteran George Walker between them, became one of Palace's most famous middle lines and a potent reason for a serious challenge for the 1938/39 Third Division (South) Championship.

Nick actually captained the Palace on occasions in Walker's absence, and he went on to play regularly for us throughout the first three wartime seasons before his duties in the Royal Navy prevented him continuing his Palace career. However, after the war, Nick joined Yeovil Town and was a member of their side which enjoyed such early post-war success in the FA Cup, including the famous victory over Sunderland in January 1949.

COLLINS, Tony
Forward 1957-59

Appearances: 61
Goals: 16
Born: 19 March 1926, Kensington
Previous clubs: York City 1949, Watford
    1950, Norwich City 1953, Torquay United
    1955, Watford 1957
Subsequent League clubs: Rochdale 1959

Tony Collins was a clever outside left who was well known to patrons of clubs in the old Third Division (South) of the 1950s in that capacity, but he was also a rare black player appearing in the Football League at that time. He was the first such man to play for Crystal Palace.

Tony was signed for Crystal Palace by manager Cyril Spiers in November 1957 as Palace's attempts to avoid founder-membership of the imminent Fourth Division appeared to be lacking sufficient momentum. Tony played 19 games for us in that cause and scored our only hat-trick of the term against Walsall in January, but the Palace could not escape the Fourth Division at the end of the season.

Again, Tony was a prominent member of our 1958/59 side and weighed in with several useful goals, but Palace were never able to contend seriously for promotion, so this intelligent fellow with a penchant for solving crosswords rarely seemed to offer many of the answers that Palace so badly needed at that time.

COLLYER, Harry
Full-back 1906-15

Appearances: 281
Goals: 1
Born: 1885 Bromley

Local boy Harry Collyer joined Crystal Palace for only our second season and was of great assistance in helping to make our club a respected Southern League side while also gaining several personal honours.

Harry was a rugged little full-back with a distinctive 'Pentonville' haircut, so would certainly be in the fashion today! It was at right back that Harry really excelled: he appeared in that position for the Palace until the First World War brought an end to competitive football in 1915. He played in the England international trial in 1909/10, was awarded representative honours when selected for the Southern League in all three inter-League fixtures in 1912/13, the season in

which he became the first Palace player to be awarded a benefit.

Accordingly, it is difficult to think of another player who contributed more towards the early establishment of Crystal Palace than Harry Collyer, and the fact that he was from the Palace neighbourhood makes him even more appealing.

CONNER, John
Centre forward 1919-22

Appearances: 104
Goals: 57
Born: Renfrew
Previous clubs: Belfast Distillery, Sunderland
Subsequent League clubs: Newport County 1922

John Conner was only a little fellow of 5ft 8ins and just 11 stone, but, in spite of his lack of stature, he had gained Scottish junior international honours and was renowned as a powerful header of the ball. Indeed, not only were his 29 League goals (out of a total of 70) the major contribution towards Palace's promotion to Division Two in 1920/21, our first season in the Football League, but many of them had been scored with his head.

John was also extremely fast and nimble, while he possessed a remarkable body-swerve which could prove thoroughly disconcerting to opposing defenders. His shooting was strong, accurate and effective – and much admired within the game.

Formerly with Sunderland, John cracked 18 Southern League goals in his initial season with us, immediately after the First World War, proving the ideal partner for veteran striker Ted Smith. As Ted's star began to wane John became the Palace's leading goalscorer and set them on the way to higher things, and then immediately topped our scoring chart again in our first season in the Second Division, 1921/22.

COOKE, Charlie
Midfield 1972-73

Appearances: 53
Goals: 1
Born: 14 October 1942, St Monace
Previous clubs: Aberdeen 1960, Dundee 1964, Chelsea 1966
Subsequent League clubs: Chelsea 1973
International honours: 16 full caps for Scotland

Refined midfielder Charlie Cooke was an established star of Scottish football who had simply captivated west London soccer fans after he had joined Chelsea. He was recruited for the Palace by Bert Head when our manager sought to add sophistication upon reshaping our side after a dreadful opening to the 1972/73 season. Regrettably though, Charlie contributed little to our fight for survival and just some ten weeks into the following season, as Palace continued to struggle badly in the Second Division, new manager Malcolm Allison offloaded him back to Chelsea.

Thus Charlie was a huge disappointment to Palace fans who had every right to expect more from him than he apparently could or would offer, but nevertheless the Palace club was willing to provide the opposition for his testimonial match at Stamford Bridge in December 1978.

COOPER, George
Forward 1955-59

Appearances: 74
Goals: 28
Born: 1 October 1932, Kingswinford, Worcestershire
Subsequent League clubs: Rochdale 1959

George Cooper was a powerfully muscled, strongly built inside forward and occasional centre forward who came to Crystal Palace in January 1955 as part of manager Cyril Spiers' youth policy. He was quick, eager, and effective in front of goal.

Thus, George netted a debut goal at Walsall (4-1) in early March to help Palace to a marvellous, morale-boosting (if all-too rare) victory and played seven more times that season. He was drafted back into the Third Division (South) side for 1955/56 in September and the following month he continued to demonstrate his goalscoring prowess with a hat-trick to dispose of visiting Coventry City (3-0) going on to make 26 League and Cup appearances for Palace that term.

Season 1957/58 was certainly George's best one at Selhurst Park. He played in 25 of our Third Division (South) games as Palace sought to finish in the top half to avoid forming the new Fourth Division the following term, and his 17 League goals, scored from all three inner positions in our forward line, was far and away our highest tally of that season – and, actually, for four years – though not sufficient, without adequate support, to prevent Palace joining the Fourth Division.

CRAVEN, John
Forward 1971-73

Appearances: 75
Goals: 19
Born: 15 May 1947, St Annes, Lancashire
Previous clubs: Blackpool 1965
Subsequent League clubs: Coventry City
   1973, Plymouth Argyle 1977

John Craven was a talented and versatile forward who was approaching his peak when Palace secured him during manager Bert Head's successful restructuring of our side in the early autumn of 1971. Playing either up front or in a wider role on the right, John proved a considerable asset to our cause. He featured in every remaining match of that season and contributed seven vital goals, enabling Palace to finish in twentieth place with a four-point margin over the two relegated clubs.

Again John was invaluable the following term, even though it ended in disappointment and relegation, but this was through no fault or shortcoming of his. Only Don Rogers scored more goals than John and he retained his place throughout extensive staff alterations, a boardroom upheaval and a change of manager, so that Palace fans were sorry when he moved to Coventry in the close season in order to continue his career at the top level.

CRILLY, Tom
Full-back 1928-33

Appearances: 126
Goals: 1
Born: 20 July 1895, Stockton-on-Tees
Previous clubs: Derby County
Subsequent League clubs: Northampton
   Town 1933

Tom Crilly joined the Palace in the early summer of 1928 as a proven full-back and made his debut for us alongside another new boy named Stan Charlton in the opening match of 1928/29. Palace beat Watford 3-0, with the two men performing really well together and beginning

John Craven.

Tom Crilly.

another of Palace's long-serving full-back partnerships, although ill-health reduced Tom's initial impact in our colours.

Tom's best season with the Palace was certainly 1930/31 when we made our second assault on the Third Division (South) Championship in three years, only to finish in the runners-up position, just as we had in 1928/29. Crilly was a lynchpin of our defence this term – only Bob Greener played more games than Tom, and he netted his single Palace goal this term too, in the infamous Christmas Day rout at Brentford (2-8) equalising The Bees' early opener with a reply from the penalty spot.

Charlie Cross was Palace's regular left-back from 1922-27 and our right-back for 1927/28 after he had joined us in July 1922 in a complex, six-player, exchange deal between Palace and Coventry City, and his partnership with Jack Little for three seasons was a much-admired feature of the Palace defence.

Tough, fit, not in the least prone to injury and highly consistent in his performances, Cross was the epitome of the ideal player, and he was versatile too: at a time when this was not really expected of a footballer, Charlie moved across to right-back after the signing of Scotsman Bobby Orr who much preferred to play at number three.

Perhaps Charlie's best game of all for the Palace was the one on 12 January 1924 when we met and beat mighty Tottenham Hotspur in the (old) first round of the FA Cup at The Nest. Cross' immediate opponent was none other than the great 'Fanny' Walden and the Spurs side was laden with internationals. Charlie completely blotted the great man out of the match and, with this vital piece of their armoury missing, Tottenham were nonplussed and Palace went on to win with two goals scored by Billy Morgan, who had been part of that complex deal which had brought Cross himself to the Palace in 1922!

CROSS, Charlie
Full-back 1922-28

Appearances: 237
Born: Coventry
Previous clubs: Coventry City
Subsequent League clubs:
   Wolverhampton Wanderers 1928

DAVIES, Bill
Outside left 1907-08 and 1910-15

Appearances: 208
Goals: 23
Born: November 1884, Forden, Nr
   Welshpool, Monmouthshire
Previous clubs: Stoke City 1905

Bill Davies.

Subsequent League clubs: West
   Bromwich Albion 1908
International honours: 4 full caps for
   Wales

Bill Davies was a Welsh international winger who played for the Palace in nearly 200 Southern League matches in two spells before the First World War. He will always occupy a unique place in Palace annals because he was the first player from our club to gain international honours. This was against Scotland in March 1908, but later that year Bill joined West Bromwich Albion.

After two seasons at The Hawthorns Bill returned to the Palace and helped us to make a real impact upon the Southern League. Thus, like several of his contemporaries, Bill's best season was 1913/14 when Palace only missed out on the Championship itself on goal average.

Bill was more of a goal-maker than a goalscorer yet he netted some important strikes for the club, several of them in the FA Cup when, for example, he was on target when Palace beat Football League club Bury in 1913, and just before the war when we held Birmingham 2-2 at St Andrews during some trying days for the club. Only three men made more Southern League appearances for Palace than Bill: all of them feature in this book, but none of them gained international honours with our club as Bill did – twice!

DAWES, Albert
Forward 1933-36 and 1937-39

Appearances: 156
Goals: 92
Born: 23 April 1907, Frimley Green, Surrey
Previous clubs: Northampton Town 1929
Subsequent League clubs: Luton Town
   1936, Aldershot 1939

Albert Dawes was a brilliant striker who in two periods at Selhurst Park became Palace's third-highest goalscorer in the Football League at that time behind Peter Simpson and George Clarke. Only Mark Bright and Ian Wright have improved upon Albert's total of 91 League strikes since, but all these other men had longer Palace careers than Albert.

Albert was an outstanding marksman. His powerful shooting, sometimes from long range, was spectacular and effective – and those were the days when the leather ball grew heavier and heavier, soaking up any moisture in or on the pitch and possibly finishing up weighing several pounds! It was some player indeed who could unleash a power drive with a ball that was more akin to a cannonball than a football!

There are several reasons why Albert has a permanent niche in any Palace hall of fame. He hit five goals against Cardiff in September 1934 and only Peter Simpson has bettered that in a single match for us; in 1935/36 he was within a single goal of topping the entire list of Football League marksmen with 38 strikes and that same season Albert was selected for the England squad for the international against Scotland at Wembley, though he was made twelfth man and spent the match idle on the players' bench.

And, for a magnificent finale, Albert became a brilliant utility player during the Second World War seasons: in 1943/44 he played in every outfield position for Palace at least once and he scored glorious goals from all of them!

DAWES, Fred
Full-back 1935-49

Appearances: 237
Goals: 2
Born: 2 May 1911, Frimley Green, Surrey
Previous clubs: Aldershot 1927,
   Northampton Town 1929

Full-back Fred Dawes moved to Crystal Palace from Northampton Town in February 1936, made his debut at Clapton Orient and appeared in all thirteen remaining matches of that season, teaming up again with his brother Albert who had come to Selhurst Park from the Cobblers in 1933.

Fred was appointed as club captain for 1936/37 and played every game for the Palace that season but was badly hampered by injuries the following term. His best season at our club was undoubtedly 1938/39 when he was an ever-present member of the team that was narrowly

beaten in the quest for promotion by Newport County at the end of a thrilling campaign. And Fred notched his brace of senior goals for Palace this season too – one of them, at Exeter, was a forty-yarder!

After the Second World War, Fred put in another 111 League appearances for Palace and thereby became the only player at our club to make a century of appearances on either side of the war. He was awarded a benefit towards the end of the first post-war season, but continued to play for us until October 1949 when his career was abruptly ended by a dreadful head injury incurred at Bournemouth. George Irwin, the former Palace goalkeeper and manager, summed Fred up admirably: 'Fred is a good, honest, clean player, and a credit to the Palace side.' Anyone who saw Fred play will fully agree with those sentiments.

See also Fred Dawes' entry in the Managers section (p.32).

DAWKINS, Trevor
Midfield 1967-71

Appearances: 32
Goals: 3
Born: 7 October 1945, Rochford, Essex
Previous clubs: West Ham United 1962
Subsequent League clubs: Brentford 1971

Trevor Dawkins was a cultured midfield player, moulded in the traditional West Ham style and an England schoolboy and youth international whom Bert Head added to his pool of players in the autumn of 1967 as he sought to guide Palace to top-flight status. Certainly, Trevor added some occasional guile to that quest and a level of refinement which delighted the club's more sophisticated fans, but Palace folk actually saw Trevor at his best after we had reached the First Division as, for example, when his finesse brought him and us two goals to dispose of visiting Wolves in November 1969, then in a more defensive role in January and February 1971.

DEAKIN, Mike
Forward 1954-59

Appearances: 152
Goals: 63
Born: 25 October 1933, Birmingham
Previous clubs: Bromsgrove Rovers
Subsequent League clubs: Northampton Town 1959, Aldershot 1961

Mike Deakin joined the Palace in October 1954 and was among the clutch of bright young men whom manager Cyril Spiers discovered among the smaller, often non-league, clubs, and then drafted into Palace's League side in the mid-1950s. Deakin was one of those who completely justified his boss' faith in him and was in fact Spiers' first signing for the Palace.

Deakin was a striker who found the net regularly and the evidence suggests that, had he been at a bigger club, he would have benefited from a better service and become a prolific scorer. As it turned out he was one of the few successes at Selhurst Park at a particularly difficult time for Crystal Palace.

Mike's style was somewhat ungainly but he always gave 100 per cent and his 23 goals in the Fourth Division (from just 34 appearances!) in 1958/59 established a post-war scoring record at our club that has rarely been improved upon since. Thus, the fans of that period recall Mike

Deakin and his wholehearted displays with pleasure and affection.

DERRY, Shaun
Midfield 2002-

Appearances: 89
Goals: 3
Born: 6 December 1977, Nottingham
Previous clubs: Notts County 1995,
   Sheffield United 1997, Portsmouth 1999

Shaun Derry is a tough-tackling, hard-working, sweet-passing midfielder who joined the Eagles from Portsmouth, where he had been club captain, for £400,000 at the start of 2002/03. His experience has proved most useful to the Palace and his sheer versatility has been invaluable on occasions when he has provided cover in our back four. For example, most recently he filled in at right-back and played down our left flank in the Cardiff play-off final!

Shaun is a focussed, committed footballer who never shirks his responsibilities and produces an occasional goal for his side. The opening matches for 2003/04 saw Shaun wearing Palace's captain's armband and throughout the term he was a valued member of the squad which took the Eagles to the play-offs and to the Millennium Stadium final in which his performance contributed in no small way to the outcome and the club's eventual promotion.

Shaun Derry.

DEVONSHIRE, Les
Forward 1951-55

Appearances: 87
Goals: 12
Born: 15 June 1926, Acton
Previous clubs: Brentford 1948, Chester 1950

Les Devonshire was a useful winger, intelligent and creative, who came to the Palace to play under joint managers Fred Dawes and Charlie Slade in the summer of 1951. He could, and did, operate on both flanks and sometimes at inside left, and weighed in with an occasional useful goal or two, though these were mostly scored on opponents' grounds.

Although within a few weeks of his arrival at Selhurst Park there was a managerial change, it was soon clear that Les' talents appealed to Laurie Scott, but, perversely for Les, it was soon after a match in which he scored his first goal of 1954/55, our 1-7 defeat at Watford in September 1954, that Mr Scott's managerial tenure was ended, and the new incumbent, Cyril Spiers, was much more interested in finding and blooding new talent than utilising the experienced men he had inherited. Les left at the end of the season, not having appeared in Palace's first team since New Year's Day.

However, readers should know that Les made a further, indirect, contribution to Crystal Palace in the early to mid-1950s because it was upon his recommendation that ace sharp-shooter Cam Burgess followed Les to Selhurst Park a month later in the autumn of 1951 – though Palace fans of the 1980s always wished that Les' persuasive powers had been as effective with his son Alan on our behalf!

DOWIE, Iain
Forward 1995

Appearances: 25
Goals: 10
Born: 9 January 1965, Hatfield
Previous clubs: Luton Town 1989, Fulham (loan) 1989, West Ham United 1991, Southampton 1991
Subsequent League clubs: West Ham United 1995
Managerial appointments: Oldham Athletic 2002, Crystal Palace 2003
International honours: 36 full caps for Northern Ireland.

In terms of matches played and goals scored Iain Dowie's Palace career does not appear to have been of much significance, and he was only at the club for eight months, but his is a typical case where statistics fail to reflect the whole truth.

Many modern-day fans know well and everyone reading this should realise that the big, fair-haired Northern Ireland international striker did much to lift morale at Selhurst Park at a testing time. Wholehearted, hard-working Iain added zest, enthusiasm, top-flight experience and, most important, several goals to the tally of a club that was finding goalscoring as difficult as at any time in its history.

Dowie's effectiveness can perhaps best be seen in the way in which, uniquely, Palace reached the semi-finals of both the major cup competitions in the spring of 1995 and came close to a return to Wembley. Ultimately of course we were relegated from the Premiership, but this was in thoroughly controversial and unfortunate circumstances while there was deep regret among all Palace fans when Iain moved to West Ham the following September.

Iain Dowie salutes the Palace crowd after netting his second goal in The Eagles' 4-3 opening-day win over Barnsley in 1995/96.

See also Iain Dowie's entry in the Managers section (p.51).

DOWSETT, 'Dickie'
Forward 1962-65

Appearances: 56
Goals: 22
Born: 3 July 1931, Chelmsford, Essex
Previous clubs: Tottenham Hotspur 1952
  Southend United 1955, Southampton
  1956, Bournemouth 1957

'Dickie' Dowsett was a refined but proven and effective centre forward who had earned a splendidly impressive reputation around the lower divisions of the League with Bournemouth and it was to him that new Palace manager Dick

Graham turned first when he was asked to lead the club away from a perilous situation near the foot of the Third Division as the winter of 1962/63 set in. Palace came from behind to record only their third victory of the season on Dickie's debut and, with the arrival of Cliff Holton soon afterwards, we were soon scoring freely and climbing confidently away from the danger zone.

Dowsett was a craftsman up front. He was clever and experienced, his heading of the ball was sublime even if it lacked great power and he packed a useful shot. He had been brought up at Tottenham under Arthur Rowe, so he passed the ball quickly and accurately to his colleagues, while he was speedy and elusive. He played in every remaining Palace match of 1962/63, when he finished as our second-top scorer with 12 goals from 26 appearances and made a valuable contribution in the first part of our promotion campaign the following term then played a few games as a raiding wide man in the Second Division in 1964/65 before he left us for Weymouth.

DROY, Micky
Central defender 1985-86

Appearances: 58
Goals: 7
Born: 7 May 1951, Highbury
Previous clubs: Chelsea 1970, Luton Town
  (loan) 1984
Subsequent League clubs: Brentford 1986

A towering defensive bulwark, Micky Droy was certainly one of the biggest men ever to appear in the Football League, standing as he did at 6ft 4ins and weighing in at nearly fifteen and a half stone.

Micky Droy.

It is difficult to overstate the worth of Micky Droy to Crystal Palace in the mid-1980s. His presence raised the morale of our players as well as that of our fans and, if he had become somewhat injury-prone by this late stage of his distinguished career, he was part of Palace's best side in the Second Division since our return there in 1981 so that, when he left us, on another free transfer, for Brentford in November 1986, Palace fans were sorry to see him go.

DUNN, Ronnie
Goalkeeper 1931-37

Appearances: 175
Born: 24 November 1908, Southall
Subsequent League clubs: Colchester
United 1937

Micky came to the Palace on a free transfer from Chelsea in Steve Coppell's inaugural season as the Palace boss, as the young manager sought to fend off the looming threat of possible relegation. He provided an immediate stiffening of our rearguard in the vital run-in alongside captain Jim Cannon so that following an important 1-0 success over fellow-strugglers Notts County on Easter Monday, we were ultimately able to record three clean sheets from our last five matches. That additional security was sufficient to see the Eagles through to safety.

But the huge fellow was not content merely to play a stopper's role at the back: he was invaluable at our set pieces, scoring on his debut and then again in a crucial match against promotion candidates Portsmouth in late April, to assist Palace to a priceless three points, while his flick-ons also contributed towards several more important goals.

Ronnie Dunn joined Crystal Palace FC in the spring of 1931 to become the understudy to Billy Callender but had previously starred in a pair of British Army representative fixtures staged at Selhurst Park.

However, events conspired that it was to Ronnie that there fell the unenviable task of taking over from Callender after the latter's tragic suicide, but Ronnie proved emotionally and physically equipped to do so. He missed just one game in 1932/33 and that was because of a dose of flu. He then remained at Selhurst Park for another four seasons and was our regular first-choice 'keeper until the last one. During this period Palace only once finished outside the top six places in our division, but the old Third Division (South) was a hard school, with no margin whatever for mistakes or loss of form, let alone sheer misfortune, because only the top club was promoted – the rest were as good as nowhere.

For this reason, along with several of his contemporaries at the Palace, Ronnie Dunn was only really appreciated by the Palace fans rather than on the bigger stages that his prowess undoubtedly deserved.

DYER, Bruce
Forward 1994-98

Appearances: 153
Goals: 43
Born: 13 April 1975, Ilford, Essex
Previous clubs: Watford 1992
Subsequent League clubs: Barnsley 1998, Watford 2003

Bruce Dyer was a sparkling young winger or striker who caused something of a media sensation when he joined the Eagles as the first teenager in the game to move between clubs for a £1 million-plus fee. He gained 10 England Under-21 caps as a Palace player while his valuable 13 goals in 1995/96 reflected his growing maturity.

Then Bruce produced a rich vein of scoring form when 1996/97 was building to its climax – he began with two goals against his original club in mid-February but his best performance of the term was a fine hat-trick against Birmingham at the end of that month. He followed that up three weeks later with a late brace as a substitute to enable the Eagles to dispose of troublesome, tedious Luton in an evening game at a chilly Selhurst Park.

Possessing great pace and exuberance, Bruce had demonstrated an ability to trouble the best defences so Palace fans looked towards him to produce something similar in 1997/98 with the club back in the Premier League, but Bruce

Bruce Dyer.

rarely showed his best form there after he sustained a nasty ankle injury, although an outstanding FA Cup hat-trick against Leicester was a major highlight to a season which was a disappointing one both for him and the club.

EDWARDS, Ian
Forward 1982-83

Appearances: 25
Goals: 7
Born: 30 January 1955, Wrexham
Previous clubs: West Bromwich Albion 1973, Chester City 1976, Wrexham 1979
International honours: 4 full caps for Wales

Ian Edwards' name will probably mean little to most readers but his reason for inclusion in this book will become apparent if they read on!

Ian was a steady goalscorer and a former Welsh international centre forward who arrived at Selhurst Park in the summer of 1982 as one of Alan Mullery's early signings. Injuries restricted his value to us and he played only 25 games in our colours, but, come the crucial last match of the season, when we met Burnley at Selhurst Park to determine which of the two clubs would be relegated, Ian netted the single goal which ensured our survival!

EDWARDS, Jack
Full-back 1949-59

Appearances: 239
Born: 6 July 1929 Risca, Monmouthshire
Subsequent League clubs: Rochdale 1959
Managerial appointments: Exeter 1963, Torquay 1968 and 1971

Jack Edwards was Palace's stocky, teak-tough full-back throughout the 1950s and became a great favourite at Selhurst Park. His opportunity to break into the limelight came when Fred Dawes' career came to an abrupt end: his debut could scarcely have been more demanding – it was at Millwall! But Jack played a tremendous game and helped to gain Palace a splendid 3-2 victory at The Den, earning himself an accolade from manager Ronnie Rooke.

Fearless and aggressive, Jack became one of Palace's youngest captains up to that time when he took over as skipper in 1956, his determination and enthusiasm admirably suiting him for the role.

His cool, unruffled play was a hallmark of his game along with some immensely powerful clearances.

Jack shared a benefit with goalkeeper Roy Bailey in October 1955, but moved to Rochdale in 1959 (where he once helped to greatly embarrass a visiting Palace side to the tune of 0-4), then subsequently had a successful career in management, the highlight of which was guiding Exeter City to promotion from the Fourth Division in 1964. He still lives in Devon and was a welcome guest at one of Palace's reunions for our former players in 2002.

EDWORTHY, Marc
Defender 1995-98

Appearances: 151
Goals: 1
Born: 24 December 1972 Barnstaple
Previous clubs: Plymouth Argyle 1991
Subsequent League clubs: Coventry City 1998, Wolverhampton Wanderers 2002, Norwich City 2003

Attacking full-back Marc Edworthy was Palace's first close-season signing in the summer of 1995 and he soon impressed at right-back with his flair, style, pace and personality. His consistency was praiseworthy too, for he missed just two Eagles games all season so that discerning Palace folk realised his importance to us as the club came agonisingly close to an immediate return to the top flight, being denied by Leicester only in the last seconds of Palace's first Wembley play-off final.

However, in 1996/97, a late-season injury limited his League and cup appearances to 48 while the Eagles surged to

Marc Edworthy.

ELWISS, Mike
Forward 1978

Appearances: 24
Goals: 7
Born: 2 May 1954, Doncaster
Previous clubs: Doncaster Rovers 1971,
    Preston North End 1974
Subsequent League clubs: Preston North
    End 1979

Palace boss Terry Venables sought out Mike Elwiss on the crowded beaches of southern Spain in the summer of 1978 because he was convinced that the powerful, intelligent Preston North End skipper, with an impressive goalscoring record, could produce sufficient additional striking force to enable the Eagles to challenge seriously for promotion to the top flight in the ensuing season.

Nobody who was privileged enough to see Mike playing in our colours during the first half of that 1978/79 season would dispute Terry's judgement and the new club-record fee of £200,000 appeared to have been money well spent. Mike's second goal for the Palace enabled us to secure a victory that was as late as it was then rare at the home of his former club, Preston, in mid-October and he produced a run where he was on target in five games out of six in November and December, but, just when it looked as if he really could help to take an impressive Palace side on to greatness, he limped from the action at Cambridge just two days before Christmas with a cartilage injury which spelt the end of his career with us and, virtually, in the game.

Mike's inclusion here is justified on the strength of his contribution to us in the first half of 1978/79 when he helped to set us on the way to promotion and the

play-off success in dramatic fashion. By this stage, Marc had developed into a dynamic and forceful wing-back and he also played sometimes as sweeper, so that Palace fans elected him as runner-up in the Player of the Year voting.

In our top-flight season of 1997/98 Marc became Palace's captain. Also sometimes playing in midfield, he was the obvious, clear-cut choice for the Player of the Year honour so that genuine Palace folk were sorry to see him leave Selhurst Park when he joined Coventry early in the following term amid the ferment that had engulfed everything and everyone here at that time.

old Second Division championship: had it not been for the injury he sustained this entry would surely have been an extensive catalogue of his exploits.

EVANS, Gwyn
Defender 1959-62

Appearances: 89
Born: 24 February 1935, Treorchy, Rhondda Valley

Welsh youth international Gwyn Evans was a strapping, fair-haired centre half who hailed from south Wales, where Palace's manager of the mid-1950s, Cyril Spiers, had extensive contacts from his time as manager of Cardiff City in the previous decade. Gwyn signed for the Palace while he was still on National Service and developed into a powerful and effective defender. He was thus approaching his prime when Arthur Rowe became the Palace manager in the summer of 1960 and became a key member of our Fourth Division promotion side of the following season.

Gwyn epitomised the 'stopper' centre half that dominated defences in British football for thirty or forty years. Although rarely moving out of his own half of the field, he presented an imposing, forbidding figure at the heart of our defence and was ideally equipped to cut out crosses from opponents' flanks with either head or foot. Thus, surrounded by experienced, intelligent colleagues, Gwyn helped to form a Palace rearguard that was much more secure than most of its post-war predecessors and was almost always more than able to subdue the opposition. Promotion from the League basement was the outcome and this was

followed for Gwyn by something over a season's consolidation in the old Third Division.

EVANS, Ian
Central defender 1974-79

Appearances: 163
Goals: 16
Born: 30 January 1952. Egham, Surrey
Previous clubs: Queens Park Rangers 1970
Subsequent League clubs: Barnsley 1980
International honours: 13 full caps for Wales
Managerial appointments: Swansea City 1989, Eire Under-21 side 1996

Ian joined the Eagles as a tall, rangy Welsh Under-23 central defender in the early autumn of 1974 and was immediately plunged into Palace's senior side by Malcolm Allison. Ian quickly demonstrated a valuable penchant for scoring goals – indeed, on 30 August 1975 he carved a unique niche in the Palace records by becoming the first defender ever to net a competitive hat-trick when Colchester were our visitors.

Later in that 1975/76 season and under Ian's captaincy, Palace reached the FA Cup semi-final for the first time and as a Third Division outfit, while Ian also gained his first full international cap for Wales.

Ian's best playing season for the Eagles was undoubtedly 1976/77 when he skippered us to promotion to the Second Division, appearing in every match and, alongside Jim Cannon, setting a new defensive record by conceding only 40 League goals in 46 matches. Meanwhile, Ian's international career blossomed: he became the regular centre half for Wales and was part of their most successful side for many years.

However, the precarious nature of a footballer's life was never demonstrated more cruelly than with Ian Evans, for, on 1 October 1977, he was involved in a tackle with George Best, by then of Fulham, and was stretchered from the Selhurst Park pitch with a double fracture of his right leg that kept him out of action for fully two years. In fact it took a revolutionary medical technique to enable Ian to play again – but only for the Palace reserve side. So Ian moved to Barnsley whom he assisted to promotion in 1981.

Ian's link with the Eagles was re-established in June 1984, when he joined Steve Coppell as our assistant manager and he helped to fashion the team that restored top-flight football at the Palace in 1989, although by the time of Palace's promotion, Ian had taken over as manager of Swansea City.

FEEBURY, Albert
Half-back 1914-24

Appearances: 164
Goals: 8
Born: 1891, Hucknall, Nottinghamshire
Previous clubs: Nottingham Forest, Coventry City

Although this big, powerful wing half joined Crystal Palace before the start of the First World War his best seasons with us were those which immediately followed the cessation of hostilities.

Albert played every game for the club in our final season in the Southern League, then missed just one game in our brilliant Third Division Championship-winning team of 1920/21. Indeed, the captaincy of that side fell to Albert in mid-term and he became the first skipper to lead Crystal Palace to a Football League championship.

Albert possessed a crashing shot, so that the 'Feebury Specials' of the early post-war era were guaranteed to generate a great deal of enthusiasm among Palace fans – and no little consternation to opposing goalkeepers.

Albert's later Palace career was plagued by injuries but he was involved in our 6-0 FA Cup rout of Everton at Goodison Park in January 1922, though it ended at another famous northern ground just before Christmas 1923 when Palace lost by the same scoreline at Sheffield Wednesday.

FELL, Les
Forward 1952-54

Appearances: 69
Goals: 8
Born: 16 December 1920, West Ham
Previous clubs: Charlton Athletic

Les Fell had played in the 1946 FA Cup final with Charlton, and Palace boss Laurie Scott was well aware of Les' skill and adaptability as a right-winger of pedigree who could, in addition, find the target on occasions. Mr Scott sought and secured his signature for our club in the autumn of 1952.

And what a start Les made! He scored on his Palace debut at home to Leyton Orient (2-2) in early October, was on target the following week when Walsall were our visitors (4-1) and then again at Shrewsbury (1-1) in the next match! He also helped create the openings from which Cam Burgess, Johnny Rainford and Bob Thomas began to score freely to the point, briefly, of prolifically, then notched another brace of goals himself in a first-round FA Cup replay at Reading (3-1).

However, it is on the flank that Palace fans of the 1950s best remember Les: authoritative, dapper, fleet-footed, calm and visionary – he was an asset unlike any post-war Palace supporters had previously seen in our club's colours, and we recognised his quality as rare the moment we saw it.

FENWICK, Terry
Defender 1977-80

Appearances: 82
Goals: 2
Born: 17 November 1959, Seaham, County Durham
Subsequent League clubs: Queens Park Rangers 1980, Tottenham Hotspur 1988, Leicester City (loan) 1990, Swindon Town 1993.
International honours: 20 full caps for England
Managerial appointments: Portsmouth 1995, Northampton 2003

Although not today to be numbered among the favourites of Palace supporters largely because of his close association with Terry Venables, Terry Fenwick was, once, one of the clutch of superbly talented youngsters who joined Crystal Palace in the early 1970s and matured through the club's junior ranks to the verges of greatness over the next decade. He was a versatile defender or occasional midfield man; eager, shrewd, personable. He had a tackle like a vice, yet, curiously, although he was an England Youth international in a defensive capacity, he first came to the attention of most Palace fans when his long-range goals in the finals earned Palace the 1977 and 1978 FA Youth Cups with Everton and Aston Villa his victims.

Terry matured into a valued member of Palace's 1978/79 Second Division championship side in which he played 24 times for what was, statistically Palace's best-ever defence of all time, then was again a useful part of the Eagles' top-flight side in 1979/80. After Kenny Sansom's move to Arsenal in the summer of 1980 Terry took over at left-back and earned the first of his England Under-21 honours, but, ten days before Christmas and after playing in every one of the matches in the first half of 1980/81, he became one of Terry Venables' first signings for Queens Park Rangers after the manager's defection to Loftus Road.

Thus it has always been with considerable chagrin that Palace fans of the 1970s watched the subsequent career of the former starlet burgeon to distinction with Queens Park Rangers, Tottenham and England. The more discerning always recognised Terry's calibre as a footballer but his close association with our former manager has ensured that he is seldom accorded anything approaching a warm welcome when he returns to Selhurst Park.

FINNIGAN, Tony
Midfield 1984-88

Appearances: 118
Goals: 10
Born: 17 October 1962, Wimbledon
Subsequent League clubs: Blackburn Rovers 1988

Tony Finnigan was a nimble-footed industrious player with the Palace in the mid-1980s and appeared in several widely differing positions.

He began in midfield, where his creative skills were a considerable asset, but, by the end of his first full season with the Eagles, 1985/86, he had settled in at right-back. That was where he began 1986/87, but he had a spell on each wing later that season and donned the left-back and centre forward shirts as well!

The irony of all this is that 'Finn', as he became known to everyone, had been an apprentice here at Selhurst Park in the late 1970s! He had also won 12 England Youth caps and appeared in the World Youth Cup finals in Australia in October 1981, but neither here, or subsequently at Fulham, could he make sufficient impact to be taken on to the professional staff. Eventually, after a spell in Scandinavia, he met Steve Coppell and pleaded with the Palace boss for a trial. Steve agreed, and was rewarded with a versatile and creative player who was a useful asset to Crystal Palace at a rather difficult time.

FLANAGAN, Mike
Forward 1979-80

Appearances: 64
Goals: 13
Born: 9 November 1952, Ilford, Essex
Previous clubs: Charlton Athletic 1971
Subsequent League clubs: Queens Park Rangers 1980, Charlton Athletic 1984
Managerial appointments: Gillingham 1993

Big centre forward Mike Flanagan came to Crystal Palace with an impressive reputation as a goalscoring striker who had gained England 'B' recognition, so that his acquisition for top-flight duty with the Eagles upon our return to the First Division in 1979 appeared to be a first-rate signing by Terry Venables.

Regrettably though, it never worked out that way because, apart from an overdue, though most welcome, hat-trick against Southampton in October 1980, Mike's goals for the Palace were few and far between, and anyway his feat against the Saints was gained from a midfield position to which he had been withdrawn earlier in that season!

Within a couple of months he was on his way to rejoin Terry Venables at Queens Park Rangers, leaving Palace to count the cost of an expensive error of judgement by their former manager, and our fans discomfited by the eagerness our players were showing to leave our ailing club.

FORSSELL Mikael
Forward 2000-01

Appearances: 62
Goals: 18
Born: 15 March 1981, Steinfurt, Germany
Previous clubs: HJK Helsinki 1997, Chelsea 1998
Subsequent clubs: Chelsea 1998, Borussia Mönchengladbach 2003, Birmingham City 2003
International honours: 29 full caps for Finland

Mikael Forssell is the loan player who has contributed most to Crystal Palace and, given his youth and inexperience at the time he was with us, his efforts on our behalf could fairly be described as prodigious.

Mikael Forssell.

Mikael joined the Eagles on loan from Chelsea in February 2000, at a desperate time for the club. Crystal Palace FC was in the legal state of administration and denuded of experienced players to such an extent that our senior side was fielding young men in their teens on a regular basis. Mikael played in thirteen games for us that season alongside Clinton Morrison, and scored three times as Palace struggled to survive, but eventually finished in fifteenth place.

Steve Coppell secured Mikael's on-loan services again for 2000/01 as one of his last signings for Crystal Palace and the young Finn became a valuable First Division goalscorer as the term progressed. His partnership with Clinton Morrison was effective and productive so

that his reputation and popularity burgeoned impressively. Mikael scored 13 First Division goals for Crystal Palace which were absolutely crucial to our eventual survival: he had a wonderful period early in 2001 when he claimed six strikes in five games and he netted the opener in Palace's vital 4-2 victory at Portsmouth in the penultimate game to set us on the way to salvation.

FRANCIS, Gerry
Midfield 1979-81

Appearances: 66
Goals: 9
Born: 6 December 1951, Chiswick
Previous clubs: Queens Park Rangers 1969
Subsequent League clubs: Queens Park Rangers 1981, Coventry City 1982, Exeter City 1983, Cardiff City 1984, Swansea City 1984, Portsmouth 1985, Bristol Rovers 1985
International honours: 12 full caps for England
Managerial appointments: Exeter City 1983, Bristol Rovers 1987, Queens Park Rangers 1991, Tottenham Hotspur 1994

It took a club-record fee of £465,000 to bring Gerry Francis to Selhurst Park but his signing appeared to represent the beginning of a new era for Crystal Palace, newly promoted to the First Division as Champions and, so it was thought, poised to make a lasting impression upon the highest echelons of domestic football. Renowned throughout the game as a supremely skilled and visionary midfield creator, Gerry was a full England international and former captain and approaching what could have been the peak of his career.

Perhaps it was his misfortune (and ours) that he should join the Palace just months before one of the most testing periods in the club's history. In his first season he more or less lived up to his standing, although he was unable to help arrest Palace's decline after Christmas, which saw us fade away to finish thirteenth, but the rigours of 1980/81 were simply too much for him and Palace recouped just one-third of the fee he had originally commanded when he followed the exodus to Loftus Road in February.

FREEDMAN, Dougie
Forward 1995-97, 2000-

Appearances: 247
Goals: 92
Born: 21 January 1974, Glasgow
Previous clubs: Queens Park Rangers 1992, Barnet 1992
Subsequent League clubs:
  Wolverhampton Wanderers 1997,
  Nottingham Forest 1998
International honours: Two full caps for Scotland

Scottish international striker Dougie Freedman was Palace's first-ever signing from Barnet, in September 1995. Genuinely two-footed, nimble, neat and inventive, Dougie's splendid tally of 20 goals from 42 appearances in his first season in Division One was an invaluable contribution to Palace's progress in 1995/96 and included his extraordinary, eleven-minute hat-trick against Grimsby in March 1996 which is, understandably, Palace's fastest of all time.

However, Dougie's most important goals in his first spell at Selhurst Park were the two late strikes he netted as a substitute which ensured the defeat of Wolves in the 1997 play-off semi-final first-leg match at Selhurst Park, and ultimately, our progress to the victorious Wembley final.

Dougie left Palace for Wolves later that year but he received an ecstatic response from our fans when he re-signed for us in October 2000. Dougie quickly repaid our enthusiasm and faith in him by netting four times in his first four games upon his return, while many Palace folk contend that it was his 'double' at Portsmouth in the penultimate game of 2000/01, allied of course to his brilliant late winner at Stockport in the final match, that were his major contribution to the Palace cause.

Another wonderful hat-trick, in the searing heat at Burnley on the opening day of 2003/04, again emphasised Dougie's talent and his value to the Palace, while his total of goals scored for us puts him in the top four post-war strikers at our club (and among the top eight of all time) but his appearances in the latter part of the season became more fleeting and usually from the substitutes bench so that his opportunities to reach a goal tally of three figures for the Eagles became less frequent.

FRY, David
Goalkeeper 1978-83

Appearances: 45
Born: 5 January 1960, Bournemouth
Subsequent League clubs: Gillingham 1983, Torquay United 1985

David Fry was a likeable and accomplished goalkeeper who only emerged

Dougie Freedman celebrates his ninetieth Palace goal with which we defeated West Ham on 12 April 2004, with (from left to right) Andy Johnson, Mark Hudson, Shaun Derry and Tony Popovic.

from the role of understudy to Tony Burns, John Burridge and Paul Barron when injuries prevented those experienced and proven custodians from appearing in the Palace side. But, after the sudden and unexpected departure of Barron to West Bromwich Albion in December 1982, David became Palace's first choice for the remainder of that season.

Number one for Palace in our 1977 and 1978 FA Youth Cup triumphs, David was completely worthy of a permanent place in most football League sides and it is fair to say that on those occasions when he did play for Palace's senior team he was always utterly reliable.

GABBIADINI, Marco
Forward 1991-92

Appearances: 25
Goals: 7
Born: 20 January 1968, Nottingham
Previous Clubs: York City 1985,
   Sunderland 1987
Subsequent League clubs: Derby County
   1992, Birmingham City (loan) 1996,
   Oxford United (loan) 1997, Stoke City
   1997, York City 1998, Darlington 1998,
   Northampton Town 2000, Hartlepool
   United 2003.

Marco Gabbiadini.

Marco Gabbiadini is another player whom many Palace fans would consider to be an impostor in this book, but it is for a single goal of his which made possible a unique and famous victory that it is right to include him.

Marco was an England 'B' international striker whom Palace acquired in far too much haste for a £1.8 million record fee in September 1991 from Sunderland to replace the recently departed Ian Wright. But Palace's direct style of that period was not one that suited him – even though it could upset plenty of top-flight opponents – and it was no doubt a relief to Marco when he moved on to Derby later in the season in which he had joined us.

But Marco was a remarkable goalscorer and he notched several important and memorable strikes for us, with none more so than his riposte to Liverpool's opener at Anfield on 2 November 1991, scything the ball past Bruce Grobbelaar from close range from the overlapping Gareth Southgate's low cross. It was the goal that demonstrated to Palace and their fans that the Reds were fallible and it was the one that made a stunning success possible. For that moment, alone, Marco must appear here.

GAILLARD, Marcel
Forward 1948-51

Appearances: 21
Goals: 3
Born: 15 January 1927, Charleroi, Belgium
Subsequent League clubs: Portsmouth
   1951

Marcel Gaillard made fleeting and occasional contributions to Crystal Palace after joining us in February 1948: he appeared in 21 Third Division (South) games over three years and in four seasons.

He netted on his debut when Palace won 5-0 at Watford, but his reason for inclusion here is that he was the first foreign footballer to play in our colours.

GARRATT, George
Forward 1908-13

Appearances: 185
Goals: 8
Born: 1884, Byker, Tyneside
Previous clubs: Crewe Alexandra 1904,
  Aston Villa 1905, Plymouth Argyle 1906,
  West Bromwich Albion 1907
Subsequent League clubs: Millwall 1913

George Garratt was a sparkling, irrepressible outside right who came to the Palace in the early summer of 1908. His forte was tricky, clever wing play, where he consistently gained sufficient room to put across a steady stream of accurate and testing crosses, from which other forwards regularly benefited. He was tough, strong, disciplined and unselfish – the epitome of the goal-maker whose efforts are recognised by his colleagues and opponents as well as by the discerning fan.

George seldom missed a match for any reason; he was versatile and could play equally effectively on either flank, and it comes as no surprise to find that Palace had two seasons when they finished among the leading Southern League clubs during George's five years in our colours. He also featured in several great FA Cup triumphs, foremost among which was the old first-round success over Cupholders Wolves in January 1908 whom Palace held 2-2 at Molineux then defeated 4-2 after extra time at the Palace – and it was George who netted our second goal to put us ahead and on the way to glory in a mudbath.

GAVIN, Johnny
Forward 1959-61

Appearances: 68
Goals: 17
Born: 20 April 1928, Limerick, Republic of
  Ireland
Previous clubs: Norwich City 1948,
  Tottenham Hotspur 1954, Norwich City
  1955, Watford 1958
International honours: 7 full caps for Eire

Johnny Gavin was a tough, experienced, barrel-chested outside right who joined Crystal Palace in the summer of 1959 as one of manager George Smith's best signings even if it was under the subsequent Palace boss, Arthur Rowe, that we saw Johnny at his pacy, penetrative best on Palace's right wing.

Johnny was almost a veteran when he joined us, and we were his last professional club, but what a swan song he had in our colours! His blend of craft and guile, allied to his knowledge of the game, were perfectly suited to Mr Rowe's 'push and run' tactic, so that he was an invaluable member of Palace's 1960/61 promotion team.

GEORGE, Ron
Full-back 1948-54

Appearances: 126 appearances
Goals: 2
Born: 14 August 1922, Bristol
Subsequent League clubs: Colchester
  United 1954

Ron George was Palace's sturdy full-back for several seasons in the early 1950s. Perhaps Ron did not have the greatest technical ability, but his commitment was never questioned and he could play pretty effectively on either flank so that he was therefore a useful defender.

His appearance record shows that, once Ron had gained a position in the team, he became difficult to displace and probably his best spell with the Palace was as a regular member of the team that finished 1952/53 with such a creditable run of performances.

GILBERT, Billy
Defender 1977-84

Appearances: 273
Goals: 4
Born: 10 November 1959, Lewisham
Subsequent League clubs: Portsmouth
    1984, Colchester United 1989,
    Maidstone 1990

Billy Gilbert was Palace's tough-tackling central defender and occasional full-back from 1977-84 and a vital member of our Second Division championship side of 1979. He was part of our FA Youth Cup-winning teams of 1977 and 1978 but came into Palace's League side in October of the former year as deputy for injured skipper Ian Evans and had taken undisputed possession of our number six shirt by the end of that term.

Thus, Billy became part of the defence which provided the platform for the 1979 title with the best record in our club's history, and he gained the first of his 11 England Under-21 caps that season too.

Billy was a tower of strength for Palace in our two years in the top flight between 1979-81, making his first appearance at that level at rather less than twenty years of age as Palace powered their way to the top of the League with attractive and hugely effective performances that left several of the First Division's most experienced clubs reeling and provided some magnificent victories.

Billy Gilbert continued to serve Palace loyally and dependably after we had returned to the Second Division so that when he opted to leave us for Portsmouth in the 1984 close-season every Eagles fan was sorry to see him go, and a mark of our esteem for him was to be seen in the fact that he had been voted our Player of the Year for his last season at Selhurst Park.

GILES, David
Forward 1982-84

Appearances: 100
Goals: 6
Born: 21 September 1956, Cardiff
Previous clubs: Cardiff City 1974,
    Wrexham 1978, Swansea City 1979,
    Orient (loan) 1981
Subsequent League clubs: Birmingham
    City 1984
International honours: 12 full caps for
    Wales

David was one of those frustrating, enigmatic footballers who perform brilliantly in opposition against you, but who never reproduce such quality of performance when they become a player at your club.

David Giles gained a deserved reputation among Palace fans after playing three superb games for Swansea against us in the FA Cup third round in January 1980, but, having joined us eighteen months later, he lacked the sparkle that had been so evident in those matches.

Still, David was an honest and capable footballer and, even if his Palace career

Billy Gilbert.

was not to reach his previous level, he played some useful games for us and was probably at his best in the autumn of 1983 when he scored some valuable goals for the Palace, including one late winner against his home town club, Cardiff City.

GLAZIER, Bill
Goalkeeper 1961-64

Appearances: 113
Born: 2 August 1943, Nottingham
Previous clubs: Torquay United
Subsequent League clubs: Coventry City 1964, Brentford 1975

Bill Glazier was Palace's aptly named and quite superb goalkeeper throughout most of our sojourn in the Third Division, 1961-64, and he was ever-present during our praiseworthy recovery under Dick Graham in the second half of 1962/63, then in the magnificent promotion season of 1963/64 when the number of goals we conceded was easily the lowest in the division.

When Bill left us in October 1964 for Coventry, with whom we had been promoted just six months previously, it was for the then record fee for a goalkeeper of £35,000 and he repaid that fee to the Sky Blues many times over in a distinguished career with them over the next decade.

GORDON, Dean
Defender 1991-98

Appearances: 241
Goals: 23
Born: 10 February 1973, Thornton Heath

Subsequent League clubs: Middlesbrough 1998, Cardiff City (loan) 2001, Coventry City 2002, Reading (loan) 2004.

Modest, athletic, softly spoken Dean Gordon is a local boy whose pacy contribution on Palace's left flank through six seasons during the mid-1990s really caught the footballing nation's attention when he confounded Palace's First Division opponents as an attacking midfield-cum-winger in the 1993/94 season. Dean also hit some glorious, spectacular goals that term too and was rewarded not

Dean Gordon has just kept Palace in the 1994/95 League Cup with a late equalising header against visiting Lincoln City.

only with a Championship medal but also with an England Under-21 call up, our young star progressing eventually to become the club's most capped player at that level.

Palace were deprived of Dean's talents for the run-in to 1995/96 by an Achilles tendon injury, but this was after he had notched a so-rare defender's hat-trick at West Bromwich Albion just before Christmas. He returned to the Palace side in November 1996 when it was clear that we could, again, challenge seriously for promotion. Dean was a largely unsung hero in that season's eventual triumph but he played in every game after his comeback and discerning fans were well aware of the key role he played in the success.

Disappointing as Palace's Premiership campaign of 1997/98 proved to be, it merely confirmed Dean's quality: he missed just one game and was a pedigree player in a floundering team. As such, few Palace supporters were surprised when he was snapped up by promoted Middlesbrough to continue his career at the highest level.

GRAHAM, Dick
Goalkeeper 1946-50

Appearances: 164
Born: 6 May 1922, Corby,
   Northamptonshire
Previous clubs: Northampton Town,
   Leicester City
Managerial appointments: Crystal Palace
   1962, Orient 1966, Colchester United
   1968

Dick Graham was serving in the RAF when he made his first appearance for Crystal Palace under the guesting

arrangements that pertained during the Second World War and played so well that the club secured his transfer at the earliest opportunity. He was ideally suited for the position of goalkeeper, standing at 6ft 1in and made his official debut in Palace's FA Cup tie with Queens Park Rangers on 5 January 1946, quickly becoming Palace's first-choice between the posts.

Thus, it was in the second League match after the war that Graham made his first claim to a place (albeit an unfortunate one) in Palace's record books. Palace were at Reading and poor Dick had to pick the ball out of our net no less than ten times as Palace slumped to our highest-scoring League defeat.

However, it is interesting and significant to notice how Palace's early post-war fortunes coincided with Graham's appearances. When he was able to play every game, or a large proportion of them, Palace did reasonably well in the Third Division (South) – best was seventh in 1949/50 when Dick missed only four games – but when his back injury prevented him from playing regularly the side suffered badly and we finished bottom of the League twice in three seasons with Graham making only 26 (1948/49) and 11 (1950/51) appearances respectively.

Dick Graham was a brave, stylish goalkeeper who always offered his best for Palace sides and every Palace fan rued the day when it was announced that he would have to give up his playing career. What none of us knew on that bleak day in November 1950 was that something like twelve years later Dick would take over as Palace's manager and perform excellently in that role.

See also Dick Graham's entry in the Managers section (p.36-7).

GRAHAM, George
Midfield 1976-78

Appearances: 51
Goals: 4
Born: 30 November 1944, Bargeddie, Lanarkshire
Previous clubs: Aston Villa 1961, Chelsea 1964, Arsenal 1966, Manchester United 1972, Portsmouth 1974
Managerial appointments: Millwall 1982, Arsenal 1986, Leeds United 1996
International honours: 12 full caps for Scotland

The period that George Graham spent with us at Crystal Palace represents only a modest part of his highly impressive career, but for our club and its prospects it was hugely significant.

George's playing days were on the wane when he arrived at Selhurst Park in November 1976 in the exchange deal which took striker David Kemp to Portsmouth, while Palace themselves were languishing in the middle reaches of the Third Division, desperate to progress. George's vast knowledge and experience of the game provided Palace with the midfield sophistication and direction we required to clamber up the table and clinch the third promotion place in a thrilling, unforgettable finale to the season.

Georges's subtle, refined skills had previously earned him the apt nickname of 'Stroller' and Palace fans certainly enthused over them as they were deployed for the benefit of our club, while in the following season George's maturity was again invaluable as Terry Venables began to mould the young team that would shortly take the Eagles on to even higher things.

So, it is obvious now to everyone and not just to Palace fans of the mid- to late 1970s why George Graham's contemporaries have the highest regard for him, and why he is always such a welcome visitor when he returns to Selhurst Park in any capacity.

GRANVILLE, Danny
Defender 2001-

Appearances: 85
Goals: 6
Born: 19 January 1975, Islington
Previous clubs: Cambridge United 1993, Chelsea 1996, Leeds United 1998, Manchester City 1999, Norwich City (loan) 2000

Danny Granville's Premier League experience has proved invaluable to the Eagles and he again demonstrated his quality after new manager Iain Dowie restored him to our line-up in January 2004 and rejuvenated his career.

Danny reads the game intelligently and enjoys overlapping down Palace's left flank. His first goal of 2003/04 against Wimbledon came from just such a foray, while his headed effort at Nottingham Forest was superbly executed even if, ultimately, it proved to no avail. He is also extremely dangerous when Palace have a free-kick around an opponent's penalty area – ask Millwall about the cracker which decided the south London derby in December 2002!

Predominantly, though, Eagles fans will recall Danny as a key member of our defence throughout the second half of 2003/04 when Palace were transformed into the best side in Division One, gained several important victories over the

Danny Granville shows his pleasure at his headed strike at Nottingham Forest in March 2004.

section's leading clubs to reach the play-offs, won through to the final at Cardiff's Millennium Stadium then beat West Ham to regain our Premiership status... and thus provided Danny Granville with the opportunity to extend his career at the highest domestic level.

GRAY, Andy
Midfield 1984-88, 1989-92

Appearances: 242
Goals: 51
Born: 22 February 1964, Lambeth
Subsequent League clubs: Aston Villa 1987, Queens Park Rangers 1989, Tottenham Hotspur 1992, Bury 1997, Millwall 1998
International honours: 1 full cap for England

Andy Gray is probably the most complex and frustrating Crystal Palace player to describe. At his best he was a huge favourite at Selhurst Park; admired, respected and a potent contributor to our progress. Yet, on both occasions that he left the club he did so as one who had exasperated both management and fans by performances on and off the field that left much to be desired.

Recruited from Dulwich Hamlet in November 1984, Andy netted a goal that contributed to victory at Grimsby the following month in his first full appearance and, deployed as a striker, was our top scorer in 1985/86. But it was in midfield that his career really blossomed, and it was after he returned to the Eagles in August 1989 that Palace fans saw him at his best.

Andy's powerful and creative displays helped Palace to the 1990 FA Cup final, a best-ever placing of third in the top flight in 1990/91 and the Full Members' Cup that April. At his peak Andy fully deserved his international debut for England against Poland in November 1991 and he was unfortunate to be withdrawn at half-time to make way for additional striking potency.

Andy's Palace career record puts him among the foremost participants at our club but, because it was also shrouded by distasteful episodes, the regrettable fact is that he is actually remembered by our fans of the period as something of an enigmatic figure.

GRAY, Julian
Forward 2000-03, 2003-2004

Appearances: 144
Goals: 13

Born: 21 September 1979, Lewisham
Previous clubs: Arsenal 1998
Subsequent clubs: Cardiff City 2003
(loan), Birmingham City 2004

No Palace fan from the early years of the third millennium will ever forget Julian Gray because it was 'Jules' who scored the goals, with a venomous volley and a wicked low cross (though the second one was eventually deemed to have been an opponents' own goal) that sent mighty Liverpool reeling to defeat in front of their own fans at Anfield in an FA Cup fourth-round replay in February 2003!

Julian is a winger of considerable ability. Although he appears rather wraith-like and frail, at his best he terrorises opponents with his speed and control and matured into a really talented player in our colours – as well as a scorer of spectacular, important, morale-boosting goals!

Palace fans welcomed him back to Selhurst Park in midwinter 2003/04 and, usually, he applied himself diligently in our cause, with his performances on our left flank creating havoc in most defences while setting up several important, even decisive strikes. Julian also netted two goals of his own in the splendid away victories at Ipswich and Watford.

GREENER, Bobby
Midfield 1921-32
Appearances: 317
Goals: 6
Born: July 1899, County Durham
Subsequent League clubs: York City 1932

Bobby Greener was a tough, sturdy, driving wing half who joined the Palace in

Julian Gray sees the Gillingham goalkeeper save his headed effort at Selhurst Park on 28 February 2004.

1921. Initially, he was understudy to club skipper Albert Feebury but when the captain was injured just before Christmas 1923, Bobby was ready to grasp the opportunity presented to him. He missed only a couple of the remaining League fixtures and positively starred in Palace's superb 2-0 FA Cup victory over Spurs at The Nest, when some observers considered that he played better than even the legendary Arthur Grimsdell!

Bobby went on from there, season in, season out, to the end of 1931/32. By then he had accumulated 293 League appearances for Crystal Palace – a club record at that time. Even now, over seventy years later, only eight Palace men have exceeded that tally, while Bobby is comfortably inside our 'top-ten' in the all-time charts that include cup-ties.

Bobby's performances were always strong and powerful, yet he almost always seemed to play with a smile on his face and gave every indication that he was delighted to be playing in our colours. The famous Corinthians provided the opposition for his richly deserved benefit in March 1929 and Bobby was a key member of the Palace sides which missed the single promotion place from the Third Division (South) by the closest of margins in 1928/29 and 1930/31.

GREENWOOD, Roy
Full-back 1954-59

Appearances: 116
Born: 22 May 1931, Croydon

Tousle-haired Roy Greenwood played three or four games for the Palace as an amateur in October 1954 but was immediately invited to sign professional forms a month later. Straightaway, he made a niche for himself as our left-back, and his fearless, diving headers made him a tremendous favourite with the Palace fans who dubbed him 'Chopper' in recognition of his decisive interceptions with his unruly mop of fair hair.

After he had had a spell at Southern League Bedford Town, Palace awarded Roy a benefit match on 15 March 1961 in recognition of his services to our club. An eleven of former Palace players turned out to assist Roy's cause – and beat the then current league side 3-2.

GREGORY, Fred
Defender 1937-46

Appearances: 46
Goals: 9
Born: 24 October 1911, Doncaster
Previous clubs: Doncaster Rovers,
   Manchester City, Reading
Subsequent League clubs: Hartlepool
   United 1946, Rotherham United 1947

Palace manager Tom Bromilow secured defender and occasional centre forward Fred Gregory in December 1937 after our right-back Ted Owens had been badly hurt in our FA Cup success at Accrington. Curiously, Owens and Gregory were to become Palace's full-back partners later that season after Ted had made his recovery!

Fred arrived at Selhurst Park with the reputation of being one of the mightiest kickers of a dead ball in the game – and no one who saw him play for or against the Palace would dream of arguing with that! Thus, Fred netted his first goal for Palace from the penalty spot to help secure a home win over Bristol Rovers in January 1938, but it was in September-October 1938, when he was drafted in at centre forward that Fred hit an astonishing five goals in two games! He was also involved in an amazing bout of club goalscoring a little later in the term, when he got the second of three goals we netted against visiting Walsall in the opening three minutes of the game!

Fred played virtually every game for Palace in our wartime season of 1939/40, in which Palace won the League South D Division, but he was away on active service for most of the hostilities, returning late in 1945 to help our club gain another wartime honour and to play in our three FA Cup ties in January 1946.

Fred Gregory.

139

GUNNING, Harry
Forward 1954-57

Appearances: 64
Goals: 4
Born: 8 February 1932, Leigh-on-Sea, Essex
Previous clubs: West Ham United 1952
Subsequent League clubs: Reading 1957

Harry Gunning, nippy, zestful, with a fashionable crew-cut hairstyle, was a little left-winger who was brought to Crystal Palace by manager Laurie Scott in the summer of 1954, but, after Harry's first two games for us – both away, both defeats – Mr Scott was dismissed.

However, Harry was just the sort of player to whom the new Palace manager Cyril Spiers was drawn: he was youthful, eager, possessing talent, enthusiasm and a willingness to learn and work hard. Thus Harry flourished under Mr Spiers' avuncular guidance and was his first-choice outside left for two seasons. It must be admitted though that 1954/55 and 1955/56 were among Palace's worst in the Football League, in terms of finishing positions at least, and after a further twelve months rather in the shadows at Selhurst Park, Harry signed for Reading as soon as 1956/57 was over.

Nevertheless, Harry's energetic running and supply of crosses from the flank provided a measure of excitement for Palace fans of the mid-1950s who were otherwise largely deprived of it – and he helped to fashion the model of a left-winger (if not his haircut!) for at least one aspiring and entirely anonymous supporter!

HAMILTON, Jimmy
Defender 1923-31

Appearances: 196
Goals: 5
Born: 1904, Hetton-le-Hole, County Durham
Subsequent League clubs: Hartlepool 1931, Gateshead 1934
Managerial appointments: Hartlepool 1935-39

Jimmy Hamilton was Palace's regular centre half for six seasons and he appeared in our defence during the eight League terms between 1923 and 1931. It was in February 1924 that he really came to the fore when he was deployed for the third FA Cup replay against Notts County at Villa Park in Palace's longest-ever cup-tie. Palace beat the First Division side 2-1 and Jimmy's claim for a first-team berth had been fully justified.

Another of Jimmy's finest games was the last match of 1924 at Sheffield Wednesday. Played in terrible conditions underfoot and a raging rainstorm, Palace held out under terrific Wednesday pressure and won with a goal scored just before the break. Hamilton was at the heart of our defence and every one of them were heroes, but it was he who subdued Jimmy Trotter (later the manager of Charlton) who was Wednesday's most dangerous forward.

Jimmy incurred a nasty eye injury in February 1925 and was out of the side for the rest of the season as Palace collapsed like a punctured balloon and were relegated. Some players wanted to leave – but not our guardsman centre half. Jimmy stayed for another six years, totted up 180 League appearances and tried all he knew to get Palace back to the

Second Division. He didn't succeed, but it wasn't for lack of trying. But everyone knows, a guardsman never surrenders.

HAMMOND, Paul
Goalkeeper 1972-77

Appearances: 142
Born: 26 July 1953, Nottingham
Subsequent clubs: Tampa Bay Rowdies
  1977

Paul Hammond was the Palace goalkeeper charged by Malcolm Allison to succeed the legendary John Jackson, and it was a measure of Paul's ability that, eventually, he was able to do that successfully in spite of the attitude of some sections of the Palace crowd who made all-too clear their opposition to his selection.

Probably the best measure of Paul's capabilities is that he was an ever-present member of the side which took the Palace to the 1976 FA Cup semi-final and of the promotion team of 1976/77 until he chose to leave us for Tampa Bay in February 1977.

HAND, Bill
Forward 1920-25

Appearances: 110
Goals: 16
Born: 5 July 1898, Codnor, Derbyshire

Bill Hand was a little fellow with a small name – he only stood 5ft 6in in his stockinged feet – but he was tough and sturdy and could play on the wing or at inside forward and did so with considerable effect for the Palace in the early 1920s.

Bill was signed for the Palace by manager Edmund Goodman from Sutton in Ashfield of the Central Alliance in the winter of 1920. He made a useful contribution to Palace's successful run-in to that season when we won some dour, tough games to claim the Third Division Championship in its inaugural season.

Bill was seldom able to put together a consistent run of appearances in our Second Division seasons 1921-25 but, when he did play, his graft and pluck were always appreciated by our fans because Palace continually struggled in the Second Division and the hard-working, tenacious attitude which Bill always adopted was a valuable asset against powerful and more skilled opponents.

Bill also had the happy knack of scoring goals for the Palace when goals were badly wanted. Thus, on his first appearance in the Second Division for us, against Blackpool at The Nest in October 1921, he hit the single goal that gave a weakened Palace side victory, he got another the following week in an excellent 3-1 win at Blackpool, then returned to Selhurst the next Saturday and headed the goal that disposed of rugged Clapton Orient. It was also Bill Hand who rapped the winner to defeat top-flight Notts County in a third replay in an (old) second-round FA Cup tie at Villa Park back in 1924.

Quite a fellow was Bill Hand: a character in the Palace colours indeed!

HANGER, Harry
Defender 1909-15

Appearances: 177
Goals: 7
Born: 1885, Kettering
Previous clubs: Bradford City

Harry Hanger joined the Palace in the summer of 1909 and his stylish performances at wing half were one of the most attractive features of our sides in the years approaching the First World War. Harry's ball control was renowned: 'No player... has shown greater ability to retain possession of the ball and his passes are invariably accurate' eulogised a Palace scribe back in 1913 while a contemporary photograph has captured Harry in graceful airborne action. Thus, Harry was the obvious successor to George Woodger as club captain in autumn 1910.

It was while Harry was skipper that Palace had their best season in the Southern League, coming within a whisker of winning the Championship in 1914.

Neat, precise, clever, controlled – Harry had it all and was a fine and respected club captain. He was also always ready to conjure up the occasional crucial goal. He was honoured by the Southern League and awarded a benefit by the Palace in 1914/15. Sadly, it is highly unlikely that this match ever took place as the designated game against Croydon Common could not be played on its original date and by that time Harry was already away in the services: he was killed in action during the First World War.

HANLON, Wally
Forward 1949-55

Appearances: 130
Goals: 9
Born: 23 September 1919, Glasgow
Previous clubs: Brighton & Hove Albion 1946, Bournemouth 1948

Wally Hanlon was Palace's dapper little outside left throughout the early 1950s and a huge favourite with the fans for his canny wing-play and superb ball control.

With his shorts flapping around his knees and his wispy, thinning hair, he was almost a caricature of a footballer, but Wally could mesmerise his opposing fullback or swerve past him at a deceptive pace, before putting over an accurate, teasing centre.

Wally received a benefit at the end of 1953/54 and almost 4,000 admirers turned out to see the Palace beat a London XI by six goals to five!

HARDING, Ted
Full-back 1946-53

Appearances: 156
Born: 5 April 1925, Croydon
Subsequent clubs: Whitstable Town

Local boy Ted Harding had played for the Palace as early as October 1942 and he became the longest-playing survivor of our 1946/47 Football League side, for he was still appearing for us in April 1953.

Ted was a sturdy, dependable full-back who could be relied upon to play on either flank. He usually turned out for the Palace at right-back and was composed and effective as he succeeded the brilliant Arthur Hudgell, epitomising the honest footballer who would always give of his best for his club whatever the situation. Because of this and his local roots, Ted was always a popular player with the Palace supporters of the period.

HARKOUK, Rachid
Forward 1976-78

Appearances: 63
Goals: 25
Born: 19 May 1956, Chelsea
Subsequent League clubs: Queens Park
   Rangers 1978, Notts County 1980

Born of an Algerian father and a Yorkshire mother, Rachid joined the Palace as one of Terry Venables' earliest signings and quickly demonstrated his ability as a striker of considerable potential by hitting 11 goals to become our top scorer in the Eagles' 1976/77 promotion season. Tall, gaunt and pale, the angular Rachid appeared to be all arms and legs when he was moving at speed so was quickly nicknamed 'Spider' by his teammates, a sobriquet happily adopted by our fans. He carried a shot like a bullet.

For Palace supporters Rachid's valuable contribution to our progress in 1976/77 was epitomised in the dying seconds of our last game of the season, at Wrexham. At 2-2 we were doomed to remain Third Division also-rans behind Wrexham but in an eighty-eighth minute goalmouth mêlée, Rachid hooked the ball above the groping fingers of the Welshmen's goalkeeper and under the crossbar for 3-2, then, moments later, slipped a perfect pass to set up Jeff Bourne for another Palace goal before the final whistle. That result and scoreline were sufficient to put Palace into third place in the table for the first time that season, made promotion a distinct probability and demoralised our opponents before their final (ultimately unsuccessful) game.

HARRISON, Bernard
Forward 1955-59

Appearances: 100
Goals: 12
Born: 28 September 1934, Worcester
Previous clubs: Portsmouth (amateur)
Subsequent League clubs: Southampton
   1959, Exeter City 1960

Bernard Harrison was Palace's last right-winger in the Third Division (South) and a product of manager Cyril Spiers' youth policy of the mid-1950s. He is also one of a select band of Palace players who have appeared in the cricket County Championship, having played for Hampshire fourteen times between 1957 and 1962.

Fair haired, but perhaps somewhat slight of build for the rigours of the lower reaches of the Football League, Bernard was a fast and cagey winger and his talent was recognised when he was selected to play for the Third Division (South) against the Third Division (North) in the fifth and final representative match between the sections at Selhurst Park in October 1957.

HARRY, Albert
Outside right 1921-34

Appearances: 440
Goals: 55
Born: 8 March 1897, Kingston , Surrey
Previous clubs: Kingstonian

This diminutive, bow-legged Palace forward of the 1920s and early 1930s was one of those performers whom fans immediately take to their hearts. A man of character, he always gave 100 per cent effort to his club, and as a winger he was endowed with skills that drew admiration from press, colleagues, supporters and opponents alike, throughout his long career.

Albert signed for the Palace early in the summer of 1921 after manager Edmund Goodman had seen him play for Kingstonian in a local cup final at The Nest. He appeared in eight of the last nine League matches of 1921/22 and scored twice in the last eight minutes of his debut to help Palace beat Bury but all those games saw him feature in his original inside or centre forward positions.

Manager Goodman moved Bert to the wing for the following season during which he played 24 matches. His great merit was that, once he had been given the ball, he was a speedy and direct raider. He had a fierce shot in either foot and excellent ball control. By 1923/24 the outside right position was Harry's own – and he held on to it for another full decade!

The player with whom Albert Harry is often mentioned is Peter Simpson. Those who were lucky enough to see these two together are certainly among the most privileged Palace supporters. The pair blended from Peter's arrival and there can be no doubt that Harry's play on the right flank was one of the key reasons why Simpson was able to crack so many goals.

Bert himself scored 53 League goals for the Palace: how many he laid on for other forwards we can only guess. He put in 410 League appearances for the club and that figure stood as the club record for over thirty years until it was overtaken by Terry Long in the late 1960s. There have been many heroes at Crystal Palace, but only one Albert Harry and articles like this one are a means of ensuring that his name is respected by Palace fans of every generation.

HAVELOCK, Harry
Forward 1927-31

Appearances: 76
Goals: 43
Born: 20 January 1901, Hull
Previous clubs: Portsmouth
Subsequent League clubs: Hull City 1931

Harry Havelock was a strong, well-built centre or inside forward from Yorkshire, who came to Crystal Palace at the beginning of November 1927. He was a most useful goalscorer, but was hugely unlucky with injuries during his time at the Palace, particularly in the early part of his career here. Thus, having scored twice upon his debut to assist Palace to a 5-0 home win over Charlton, it was necessary for Harry to miss the next League game; then, two weeks later, he sustained such a nasty leg injury in our 3-1 win at Dartford in a first-round FA Cup tie that he was unable to play again for ten months.

That said, Harry's career record above, which included 39 League goals from 67 games, does tell of a striker of real ability who made a significant contribution and proved a valuable acquisition.

This was demonstrated most clearly in 1928/29, the season in which Palace came closest to regaining Second Division status. Harry returned from injury in late September and was virtually ever-present thereafter: only goalkeeper Billy Callender, skipper Stan Charlton and Albert Harry played more times than he and he was our top scorer by a distance with 20 League goals, plus four more, including a hat-trick in the snow in a cup replay against Luton, so that it is perfectly legitimate to argue that had Harry been able to start the season, Palace would have taken the title and promotion.

HECKMAN, Ron
Outside left 1960-63

Appearances: 93
Goals: 29
Born: 23 November 1929, Peckham
Previous clubs: Bromley, Leyton Orient 1955, Millwall 1957

Ron Heckman was precisely the sort of goalscoring outside left for whom many clubs today would pay a hefty fee. He already possessed a proven record in the lower divisions and had starred for the England amateur side by the time Arthur Rowe brought him to Crystal Palace, but his debut for us was nevertheless quite remarkable. Ron scored twice and was a constant threat as Palace slaughtered visiting Accrington Stanley 9-2 on the opening day of the 1960/61 season. His second goal, Palace's last, just before the end, was the best of them all and lives in the memory to this day – a flashing, fulminating shot from a narrow angle at the edge of the penalty area which offered the beleaguered Stanley 'keeper no chance whatsoever.

Ron continued to play resourcefully throughout that promotion season and by hitting 14 League goals from the wing established a club post-war record that remains unbroken. Ron himself regarded the best one to be his last one of that glorious season: it was at Millwall on Easter Monday and our 2-0 success made pro-motion almost a certainty. But the fans who saw Ron play for Palace with also insist that he supplied two or three times as many goals as those he scored himself for the main strikers with his clever play and crosses from the flank.

HEDMAN, Rudi
Defender 1988-89

Appearances: 26
Born: 16 November 1964, London
Previous clubs: Colchester United 1983
Subsequent League clubs: Leyton Orient (loan) 1989, Colchester United (loan) 1991

Tall, studious Rudi Hedman was called upon to fill a vital defensive role for Crystal Palace as the 1988/89 season boiled to its climax and we first claimed a place in the play-offs, then secured promotion via those fraught exchanges. Of the regular centre-halves, Gary O'Reilly was injured and Gavin Nebbeling suspended, so Rudi was drafted in after only one full appearance, to perform splendidly and earn an eloquent post-match appreciation from his manager, Steve Coppell, as the Eagles dismissed Swindon over two legs to reach the final against Blackburn.

Even before that sterling show, Rudi had proved a popular fellow with Palace fans, who would chant his name when he was in possession or even when he was warming up as a potential substitute along the touchline.

HEWITSON, Bob
Goalkeeper 1905-07

Appearances: 75*
Born: unknown
Previous clubs: Barnsley
Subsequent League clubs: Oldham
  Athletic 1907, Tottenham Hotspur,
  Croydon Common 1909
*Includes appearances in Southern League
Second Division in 1905/06*

Bob Hewitson was Palace's more-than-capable goalkeeper throughout the first two seasons of the club's existence. His 75 league and cup appearances noted above were made in consecutive matches, with the most memorable and praiseworthy one being the old first-round FA Cup tie at Newcastle in January 1907 in which he kept a clean sheet against the team widely regarded as the best in the country and helped Palace to achieve a sensational victory.

HEWITT, Charlie
Forward 1910-15

Appearances: 162
Goals: 41
Born: unknown
Previous clubs: Middlesbrough, Liverpool,
  Tottenham Hotspur, West Bromwich Albion
Subsequent League clubs: Hartlepool
  United 1919

Charlie was a bustling, enthusiastic bundle of energy who played at inside right for the Palace throughout the five seasons leading up to the end of fully competitive football in 1915.

He came to us in October 1910, scored on his debut, against Plymouth up at the Palace when we romped to a 6-1 win, and went on to play in every remaining match that season. He accumulated a creditable and valuable 39 Southern League goals for Crystal Palace, so that he is our fourth-highest Southern League goalscorer.

Charlie's combination with George Garratt on our right wing was a most pleasing feature of the Palace teams in the pre-war period while Charlie himself was twice selected to play for London against Birmingham in inter-city representative matches.

HILAIRE, Vince
Forward 1976-84

Appearances: 293
Goals: 36
Born: 10 October 1959, Forest Gate
Subsequent League clubs: Luton Town
  1984, Portsmouth 1984, Leeds United
  1988, Stoke City 1990, Exeter City 1991

Vince Hilaire was a supremely talented winger who came to the fore in Palace's FA Youth Cup-winning team of 1977, and then matured in the Second Division in 1977/78 while helping to retain the FA Youth Cup at the same time.

Quicksilver, darting and with wonderful balance and control, Vince was at his best at Selhurst Park in 1978/79 and 1979/80. A teenager throughout the former, it was frequently his magic on our left flank that unlocked the most determined defences provided by our opponents, while in the top flight Vince was subjected to a lot of dubious physical challenges that would not be tolerated today yet was ever-present and scored 5 league goals. He was awarded 9

England Under-21 caps and scored on his debut.

With a style best suited to a bright, attacking side, Vince became something of an enigma when Palace's fortunes began to fade, but he remained loyal to us for three more seasons in the Second Division where he was always a potential match-winner. One perfect illustration of this will never be forgotten by those few Palace fans who were at Selhurst Park on a miserable February afternoon in 1984. Reduced to nine men by wanton refereeing, Palace pushed Vince up front on his own and knocked long balls to him, knowing that the opposing Middlesbrough defence would struggle to contain him on the treacherous surface. Sure enough one of them fouled Vince in the penalty area, Peter Nicholas knocked home the kick and Palace won 1-0!

HINSHELWOOD, Martin
Midfield 1972-78

Appearances: 85
Goals: 5
Born: 16 June 1953, Reading
Managerial appointments: Brighton & Hove Albion 2002.

Martin Hinshelwood was one of the most unfortunate of footballers: he seemed to have a highly promising career ahead of him as a tenacious but creative midfielder – only to have it repeatedly baulked then finally blighted by injuries.

His introduction to the Palace first team in the autumn of 1972 produced his first senior goal in only his second game, but he was absent for most of the next two traumatic seasons, when some pundits believed that his presence

Vince Hilaire.

might have been sufficient to save us from relegation in 1974 or have enabled us to regain some credibility with a prompt return to the Second Division in 1975.

However, Martin was quite superb in the autumn and spring of 1975/76, when Palace were leading the Third Division by a distance and engaging in a club-record-breaking run to the FA Cup semi-finals, but his season ended when he incurred the cartilage injury from which he never fully recovered, when Port Vale visited Selhurst Park on 9 March 1976.

However, his inclusion here is not merely due to sentiment: Martin was at his best for Palace in that marvellous FA Cup run when we competed with, and beat, some of the great clubs in the land, and as a distinguished member of the side that won those famous victories he is fully entitled to be here.

Paul Hinshelwood.

HINSHELWOOD, Paul
Forward/Defender 1972-83

Appearances: 321
Goals: 28
Born: 14 August 1956, Bristol
Subsequent League clubs: Oxford United 1983, Millwall 1985, Colchester United 1986, Southend United 1988

It was on the recommendation of Arthur Rowe that Paul Hinshelwood and his brother Martin were invited to attend Palace trials after playing for Croydon Schools in the 1969 London Schools Cup final, and while Martin's career was dogged by misfortune, Paul went on to wear our colours with distinction.

He began as a striker, but in November 1976 undertook a new role as a full-back

in a remodelled Palace defence. Paul blossomed in this new position and his partnership with Kenny Sansom was a feature of Palace's progress from the Third Division to the First in the late 1970s. The defence of which Paul was a key member, created new records for the club in both promotion seasons and it was in his adopted position that Paul gained 2 England Under-21 caps.

Paul went on to become one of only a handful of Palace players who have appeared for us in ten or more post-war seasons, but perhaps the best measure of his ability and commitment to the Palace was that, although he was never the sort of player who sought publicity or acclaim, he was voted Player of the Year for two consecutive seasons, both of which were spent in the old First Division in 1979/80 and 1980/81.

HOADLEY, Phil
Defender 1968-71

Appearances: 88
Goals: 2
Born: 6 January 1952, Battersea
Subsequent League clubs: Orient 1971, Norwich City 1978

Palace fans of the late 1960s and early 1970s were disappointed when the best parts of Phil Hoadley's career became devoted to the benefit of other clubs, because he had proved to be a dependable and versatile defender and occasional midfield player with our favourites. But there remain two reasons why Phil will be remembered among Eagles supporters for a long, long time to come.

Phil is the youngest player ever to appear in a top-class Palace game – he was just 16 years and 113 days old when he came on as our substitute to make his debut at Bolton in April 1968, but he also went on to become the first man at Crystal Palace FC to wear all the outfield shirts, completing his set of eleven differently numbered jerseys (numbers two to twelve inclusive, in the days of just one substitute) in only his fiftieth game, when he took part, wearing number six, in the League Cup replay at Arsenal in November 1970 which Palace won 2-0.

Phil Hoadley.

HODDINOTT, Tom
Forward 1923-26

Appearances: 89
Goals: 22
Born: 29 November 1894, Brecon
Previous clubs: Watford, Chelsea
International honours: 1 full cap for Wales

A great deal of excitement and interest was generated at Selhurst Park in the summer of 1923 by Palace's signing of Chelsea's centre forward Tom Hoddinott. He was a Welsh international, tall and slim, and possessed pace and elegance. Regrettably however, 1923/24 proved to be the only season in which Tom produced his undoubted abilities for us more than on fleeting occasions – but this term he scored on his debut in Palace's home defeat on the opening day by Port Vale, played 37 League and cup games and was our second-highest goalscorer with 14 goals.

Without question Tom's best game for the Palace occurred this season too, when title challengers Stoke City came to The Nest in late November. Tom hit a first-half hat-trick himself, led the forward line with

149

Tom Hoddinott.

Phil Holder was a rugged little midfield ball-winner and this barrel-chested, chirpy former England Youth international was a useful asset in Palace's 1975/76 run to the FA Cup semi-final and then in the 1976/77 promotion side from the old Third Division.

Strong and sturdy and with big 'presence', Phil was a valuable player to have around in those Third Division days of hustle and bustle where his competitive spirit was constantly driving the Palace forward to success. He later had a spell in charge of Palace's youth side and is still an occasional but welcome visitor to Selhurst Park.

vision and authority in a fog-shrouded game and helped Palace to a splendid, morale-boosting 5-1 win.

Tom made less impression in the relegation season of 1924/25, although he appeared in 36 games in four forward positions, but among his modest tally of 6 goals were two for which Palace fans will always be grateful, because that pair defeated Manchester United at The Nest in mid-February! He left us for north Wales at the end of 1925/26 after a managerial change at Selhurst Park.

HOLDER, Phil
Midfield 1974-78

Appearances: 112
Goals: 6
Born: 19 January 1952, Kilburn
Previous clubs: Tottenham Hotspur 1971
Subsequent League clubs: Bournemouth 1979

HOLTON, Cliff
Forward/Defender 1962-65

Appearances: 112
Goals: 49
Born: 29 April 1929, Oxford
Previous clubs: Arsenal 1947, Watford 1958, Northampton Town 1961
Subsequent League clubs: Watford 1965, Charlton Athletic 1966, Leyton Orient 1966

Following a supremely successful career as a regular goalscorer at his previous clubs, Cliff Holton became Palace manager Dick Graham's solution to the perilous situation the club was in as midwinter 1962/63 approached. Cliff had a magnificent physique, was always commanding in the air and possessed a fearsome shot so his arrival at Selhurst Park was greeted with pleasure as well as anticipation by Palace fans of that time.

Cliff made his debut for us on Boxing Day 1962, teaming up for the first time with another new signing, Dickie

Cliff Holton (centre) has just scored what proved to be his last goal for Crystal Palace at Ipswich (2-3) on 24 April 1965. Picture by Lewis Tassell.

Dowsett, and with Ronnie Allen, and he helped Palace romp home to a thrilling and uplifting 3-0 victory over Millwall on a freezing surface. A few weeks later he scored the first of three hat-tricks he hit for the Palace when we toppled his former club, Watford, 4-1 at Vicarage Road, and Cliff's third strike was an amazing free-kick hit from 'just inside the Watford half'.

Cliff's contribution to the Palace would have been deserving of praise even if it had stopped at the end of 1962/63 with Palace safely in mid-table. But twelve months later, courtesy of 20 goals from the big man himself, Palace were back in the Second Division! Cliff then headed our list of Second Division goalscorers in 1964/65 with 11 more goals – and that was despite spending several matches at centre half!

It will come as no surprise to modern readers to learn that when Cliff was transferred back to Watford early in May 1965, the supporters of that era were greatly displeased, and the move must be regarded as one of the few mistakes that Dick Graham made during his time as our manager. Today, however, Cliff is remembered at Selhurst Park with enormous pleasure by those who were privileged to see him play and he was, without question, one of the most inspiring men ever to appear in the Palace colours.

151

HOPKIN, David
Midfield 1995-97, 2001-02

Appearances: 127
Goals: 33
Born: 21 August 1970, Greenock
Previous clubs: Morton 1989, Chelsea
  1992
Subsequent League clubs: Leeds United
  1997, Bradford City 2000, Morton 2002
International honours: 7 full caps for
  Scotland.

Flame-haired David Hopkin starred on the Eagles' right flank for two seasons in the mid-1990s, making an indelible contribution to Palace's progress as he did so while developing into a powerful and extremely effective performer for the club. Strong-running and possessing a prodigious long throw-in, David was a huge asset to our cause and he had a flair for netting spectacular and important goals.

This was never better demonstrated than in the play-offs at the end of 1996/97. For the second year running Palace only needed a composed performance in the second leg of the semi-final to secure a place in the Wembley showpiece, but, despite a 3-1 first leg victory over Wolves they were now facing a determined rally from the Molineux men, who were backed by their hostile, vocal crowd. They had reduced our overall lead and were now within a single goal of going through by virtue of their away goal, but the night swung Palace's way, thanks to Palace's recently crowned Player of the Year, David Hopkin. Showing the pace, power and eye for goal that had drawn much attention from the Premiership's big clubs, he beat two defenders then shot past the

goalkeeper from the edge of the penalty area to tilt the affair Palace's way again.

But it was at Wembley that David Hopkin produced the moment for which every Palace fan will always remember him. The game was scoreless and into its penultimate minute when Palace gained a corner on the right. Andy Roberts played the ball short for Simon Rodger to put over an in-swinger. It was headed away but fell to David Hopkin some twenty yards out from goal. He controlled the ball on his left foot, transferred it to his favoured right, looked up, adjusted his balance, took aim and then unleashed a stunningly spectacular strike that was fit to settle any final at any level. The ball curled round and over the Blades' rearguard and then dipped into the top right-hand corner, leaving the goalkeeper merely a spectator and bringing delight to every Eagles fan present.

David was at last awarded full international recognition for Scotland, but, to the disappointment of everyone at Selhurst Park, he moved to Leeds for a hefty fee. But, although he never played for Palace in the top flight, he returned to us in March 2001 in a morale-boosting transfer. He quickly completed his century of club appearances and then struck his thirtieth goal for us from the corner of the penalty area to secure a point from our visit to Tranmere, assisting the fight against relegation in the most practical manner.

HOPKINS, Jeff
Defender 1988-90

Appearances: 93
Goals: 4

Born: 14 April 1964, Swansea
Previous clubs: Fulham 1980
Subsequent League clubs: Plymouth
  Argyle (loan) 1991, Bristol Rovers 1991,
  Reading 1992
International honours: 16 full caps for
  Wales

Jeff Hopkins was a softly spoken but tenacious and accomplished Welsh international defender, signed by Steve Coppell to replace Jim Cannon at the heart of the Palace rearguard after the former skipper's retirement in the summer of 1988. Some surprise was expressed at the time at the size of the tribunal fixed fee, and Jeff was Steve's most costly acquisition outside the top flight, but it proved to be an investment at £240,000 for Jeff was a tower of strength for the Eagles in the ensuing season which, eventually and climactically, finished with Palace being promoted to the First Division.

But Jeff was not merely a member of that promotion-winning side – he was the captain of it! It is often overlooked that Palace achieved their success in the absence of skipper Geoff Thomas for more than half the campaign: in fact Jeff Hopkins led the side for the final, vital, twenty matches, including the supremely testing play-offs, during which time the Eagles rose from mid-table mediocrity to become the best team in the division.

Jeff was no mean performer in the top flight either and Palace fans will recall with pleasure his involvement in several splendid First Division matches like the victories at Manchester United and Tottenham. Perhaps most lasting of all would be his equalising goal at Southampton in September 1989, just four days after our 0-9 humiliation at

Liverpool, which restored our prestige and morale at an important time.

HOUGHTON, Ray
Midfield 1995-97

Appearances: 86
Goals: 8
Born: 9 January 1962, Glasgow
Previous clubs: West Ham United 1979,
  Fulham 1982, Oxford United 1985,
  Liverpool 1987, Aston Villa 1992
Subsequent League clubs: Reading 1997
International honours: 73 full caps for
  Eire

Vastly experienced midfielder Ray Houghton was Palace's transfer deadline-day signing in March 1995. At the time he joined us our Premiership prospects were decidedly precarious and, while he immediately provided midfield steel, craft, knowledge and guile, plying passes with creative vision and having an immediate, positive effect upon the play and the players around him, he was unable to prevent the Palace from being relegated.

However, the Eagles came agonisingly close to defeating Manchester United in the FA Cup semi-final, while his contribution as our captain throughout the 1995/96 campaign was nothing short of magnificent. If that season ended in further disappointment for Palace and their fans, Ray was still involved with us in the triumph of 1996/97, even if by the time of the Wembley play-off victory over Sheffield United he had begun to lose his edge.

Ray made a later, equally valuable contribution to Crystal Palace as a member of our coaching staff in 2000/01 when

Eagles fans were pleased to have him with the club again, for his intelligent, industrious style had always held great appeal at Selhurst Park.

HOWE, Bert
Defender 1958-67

Appearances: 212
Goals: 1
Born: 16 November 1938, Charlton
Subsequent League clubs: Orient 1967, Colchester United 1969

Bert Howe was a reliable, consistent and determined full-back, who signed for Crystal Palace just after Christmas 1958 and first appeared for us in the dark days of our Fourth Division existence, but who proceeded to assist the club to an eventual place in the Second Division.

After Bert had completed his national service he became a regular member of the Palace side, making 101 consecutive League appearances between October 1962 and December 1964, including every game of the promotion season of 1963/64.

Once the Palace had regained their place in the Second Division Bert demonstrated his solid ability, coping admirably with some talented wingers from that division and, by the time he left us, he had accumulated well over 200 appearances for the club.

HOY, Roger
Defender 1968-70

Appearances: 62
Goals: 7
Born: 6 December 1946, Poplar

Previous clubs: Tottenham Hotspur 1964
Subsequent League clubs: Luton Town 1970, Cardiff City 1971

Roger Hoy was a fearless but versatile defender or midfielder who stepped out of the shadows of reserve-team football with Spurs, at the invitation of manager Bert Head, and provided Palace with precisely the sort of tenacity, strength and inspiration which a team needs if it is to gain promotion.

Those fans who saw the 1968/69 team that forged its way into the First Division will confirm that Roger was a key member, even if his contribution to our success was never widely acknowledged or publicised outside Selhurst Park, but perhaps his best match of all in the Palace colours was the defeat of his former club, star-studded Tottenham, in a pulsating fourth-round FA Cup replay at Selhurst Park in January 1970. A measure of the fans' appreciation of Roger is that he was given his own song, which was bellowed with enormous gusto from the (then!) Selhurst terraces – though discretion forbids its inclusion here!

HUDGELL, Arthur
Defender 1939-47

Appearances: 29
Goals: 1
Born: 28 December 1920, Hackney
Subsequent League clubs: Sunderland 1947

Arthur's career figures above look to be modest in the extreme, but Arthur played for Crystal Palace as a teenager in the early months of the Second World War and if all his wartime statistics were

Arthur Hudgell.

included his Palace contribution would be seen to have been huge.

Arthur was a defensive left half or full-back. He was exceptional in the Third Division (South) in 1946/47, but his first significant contribution to Crystal Palace was in the League South D Division, of February to June 1940 when he was our only player to appear in every game as Palace took first place in that ten-team competition. Arthur then rarely missed a match for Palace until active service took him away for a couple of years, but upon his return he appeared more times than anyone except skipper Fred Dawes in Palace's Third Division South (South) Championship in the autumn and early winter of 1945.

When League football recommenced after the war, Arthur had appeared in every Palace game, at full-back or in the half-back line, until he was transferred to Sunderland in January 1947 for a record £10,000 fee for a Third Division player after his distinguished performance in Palace's FA Cup tie at Newcastle earlier that month.

HUDSON, Mark
Central defender 2004

Appearances: 14
Born: 30 March 1982, Guildford
Previous clubs: Fulham 1998, Oldham
 Athletic (loan) 2003

Mark Hudson had played for Palace boss Iain Dowie at Oldham but came to Selhurst Park on a three-month loan from Fulham at Iain's instigation in mid-January 2004.

Mark lined up alongside Tony Popovic for most of his 14 matches with us: the pair blended from the beginning, making the previously rather porous heart of our defence much more reliable. In the 14 First Division games prior to Mark's arrival we had conceded 21 League goals and lost 6 times; in his 14 appearances we let in only an average of a goal a game and lost just twice. Thus, by the time his loan expired in mid-April, Mark had helped to take the Palace from the bottom quarter of the First Division to the verge of the play-off places.

Mark's fine physique was a welcome asset and his commanding aerial presence enabled us to repel most of the crosses put in by opposing raiders. So it is that no Palace fan who watched Mark in our colours in the early weeks of 2004 could conceive of this book appearing without proper reference to him.

155

HUGHES, Jimmy
Defender 1909-20

Appearances: 209
Goals: 15
Born: 1886, Bootle, Liverpool
Previous clubs: Liverpool 1904

Big Jimmy Hughes was Palace's creative bulwark at centre half throughout the decade 1910 to 1920, and only the First World War prevented him from amassing a huge total of appearances for the club: even with four seasons lost to the First World War, Jimmy played in 200 Southern league matches for us.

Jimmy began at wing half but was absolutely terrific at the heart of our defence – it is no coincidence that Palace's best Southern League seasons occurred when he was in that position, including the 1913/14 campaign when Palace were denied the Championship itself solely on goal average by Swindon Town; the issue was only settled at the final matches of the programme.

Jimmy was dominating in the air and a tough tackler, but perhaps the best feature of his game was the stream of stylish, sweeping passes he delivered to his wingers after he had won the ball. Consequently, it came as no surprise at all that he was chosen to represent the Southern League.

Jimmy scarcely missed a match for Crystal Palace once he had come into the team at the beginning of October 1909 for a winning debut at Leyton, then he netted with a crashing drive early in the second half of his first senior appearance at the Crystal Palace to ensure a handsome victory (3-0) over visiting Plymouth.

HUGHES, John
Forward 1971-72

Appearances: 23
Goals: 4
Born: 3 April 1943, Coatbridge, Lanarkshire
Previous clubs: Celtic 1960
Subsequent League clubs: Sunderland 1972
International honours: 8 full caps for Scotland

Strapping, fast-running and powerful attacker John Hughes was a great bear of a man who had been nicknamed 'Yogi' after the cartoon character by his fans at Celtic. That epithet followed him to Selhurst Park when he signed for the Palace along with his Scottish international colleague Willie Wallace, as part of Bert Head's first and successful restructuring plan in the autumn of 1971.

Taking advantage of a virtual media blackout caused by a strike in the newspaper industry, Mr Head persuaded Celtic to part with both men for a bargain joint fee of £55,000, and John might have become a prolific scorer for us but he was badly hurt in the game for which he is still remembered by Palace fans, against Sheffield United at Selhurst Park in December 1971. In what proved to be the turning point of the season, John scored two magnificent goals, ran riot among the Blades defence and inspired Palace to a convincing, morale-boosting 5-1 victory.

HUGHES, Michael
Midfield 2003-

Appearances: 41
Goals: 3

Michael Hughes.

Born: 2 August 1971, Larne, Northern
Ireland
Previous clubs: Manchester City 1988,
Strasbourg 1992, West Ham United
1994, Wimbledon 1997, Birmingham City
(loan) 2001
International honours: 69 full caps for
Northern Ireland

Experienced Northern Ireland international midfielder Michael Hughes arrived
at Selhurst Park late in the 2003 close season and immediately impressed with his
hard-working, fierce-tackling, hugely
creative, tenacious and dynamic displays,
so that it was no surprise when he was
made captain in the absence of Neil
Shipperley from Palace's home games
against Reading and West Ham in March
and April 2004.

Michael is a gifted footballer whose
vision and passing ability add an extra
dimension to Palace's midfield and he is
usually at the heart of Palace's most flow-
ing and penetrative moves. He is the
architect at many Eagles free-kicks, while
his exquisite control enabled him to
score a delightful goal against Stoke to
assist Palace's surge up the First Division
table – he dribbled the ball quite forty
yards before looping it over the 'keeper.

That said, few would argue that
Michael's most important strike for the
Palace was not one that features in any
statistics – the winning penalty which
defeated Sunderland in the 2004 play-off
semi-final and took Palace to the
Millennium Stadium, Cardiff for the first
time. He was selected as the Man of the
Match in that dramatic, victorious finale.

HUGHTON, Henry
Midfield 1982-86

Appearances: 137
Goals: 1
Born: 18 November 1959, Stratford, London
Previous clubs: Orient 1978
Subsequent League clubs: Brentford 1986

Henry Hughton was snapped up on a free transfer for Palace from Orient and was arguably one of manager Alan Mullery's best signings for the club because Henry's amazing versatility became extremely useful in several difficult seasons at Selhurst Park. Henry actually played in nine differently numbered shirts, including the goalkeeper's jersey on one occasion, when George Wood was injured during a game against Shrewsbury in November 1984, and although Henry never wore a number five for the Palace, he played alongside Jim Cannon in central defence at Fulham in March the following year.

Henry's wholehearted displays in such a variety of roles, allied to his self-effacing modesty combined to endear him to all Palace fans of the mid-1980s.

HUMPHREY, John
Full-back 1990-95

Appearances: 203
Goals: 2
Born: 31 January 1961, Paddington, London
Previous clubs: Wolverhampton Wanderers 1979, Charlton Athletic 1985
Subsequent League clubs: Charlton Athletic 1995, Gillingham 1996, Brighton & Hove Albion 1997

John Humphrey.

John Humphrey was a tall, stylish right full-back who joined Crystal Palace from Charlton early in the close season of 1990, during the period when the Valiants were tenants at Selhurst Park.

John was a fine acquisition. He played in each of Palace's 52 games in his first season with the Eagles and his top division experience, previously gained at Wolves, was invaluable. His completely unflappable temperament was a considerable asset as well, and it is no coincidence that upon his arrival Palace immediately had the best single season of their entire existence, finishing third in the old First Division and beating Everton at Wembley to win the Full Members' cup. John's reserve in the Palace dressing room was also extremely beneficial – his quiet, dry humour and studious capacity to solve the most testing crossword puzzles helped to ease any pre-match tension and prepare his teammates for the serious business ahead.

Understandably, John rarely featured among the Palace goal scorers, but no one who saw his crashing, thirty-yard drive into the Holmesdale Road goal to level matters against Wolves in a televised match in October 1993 will ever forget it.

HYND, Roger
Central defender 1969-70

Appearances: 38
Born: 2 February 1942, Falkirk
Previous clubs: Rangers 1964
Subsequent League clubs: Birmingham City 1970, Oxford United 1975, Walsall 1975

Related to both Bill Shankly and Sir Matt Busby, Roger Hynd was a towering central defender, who was recruited by manager Bert Head to bolster our rearguard for top-flight duty after our promotion to the First Division in 1969.

Roger was in the mould of the traditional 'stopper' centre half – he was tough and strong, possessed a fearsome tackle, never shirked a challenge, always gave 100 per cent every time he played, and was certainly influential in helping Palace to maintain their hard-won senior status in 1969/70 which was the single season he spent with us. But, so important was that to the club itself and to its fans, that Roger is deserving of record here.

IMLACH, Stewart
Forward 1962-64 and 1965-66

Appearances: 54
Goals: 3
Born: 6 January 1932, Lossiemouth, Morayshire
Previous clubs: Bury 1952, Derby County 1954, Nottingham Forest 1955, Luton Town 1960, Coventry City 1960
International honours: 4 full caps for Scotland.

Stewart Imlach was a winger of acknowledged refinement who originally joined the Palace under Arthur Rowe, but who played for us mainly under the management of Dick Graham, providing culture and elegance on the Palace left flank to bring considerable pleasure to our fans of the mid-1960s.

Although most statistical records of Stewart's career fail to show it, the fact was that he had two spells with the Palace. He left us in mid-season after helping us to gain promotion in 1964, returning a little more than a year later as something of a veteran, but nevertheless he added his unique touch of guile to our side before moving into a successful coaching career with Notts County and Everton.

INNERD, Wilfred
Wing half 1905-09

Appearances: 133*
Goals: 7
Born: unknown
Previous clubs: Newcastle United 1900
Includes appearances in Southern League, Second Division 1905/06

Wilfred Innerd was a Geordie who joined Crystal Palace at the club's inception in 1905 and played a major part in its establishment. He usually featured at wing or centre half, although he was able to provide cover for several forward positions. Consequently, until he was badly hurt during Palace's tremendous FA Cup victory over Wolves in January 1909, he was seldom absent from the team and he holds the unique record of having appeared in every one of the club's first twenty-two FA Cup ties.

Wilf took over as Palace's captain in 1906 after Ted Birnie had left the club. Palace were now embarking upon their initial season in the First Division of the Southern League – a very much tougher assignment than the Second Division in which the team had played in 1905/06. Yet, under Wilf's captaincy, and well motivated by his experience, inspiration and talent, the club immediately produced a magnificent FA Cup run to the quarter-finals in 1906/07, and then its best overall performance and final League position of fourth the following term, that was to remain our best until 1913/14. Readers can now appreciate that the sheer perversity and contrariness of the club we follow today is absolutely nothing new!

IRVINE, Alan
Forward 1984-87

Appearances: 127
Goals: 14
Born: 12 July 1958, Glasgow
Previous clubs: Everton 1981
Subsequent League clubs: Dundee United 1987, Blackburn Rovers 1989

Alan was Palace's pacy winger who brought a welcome touch of sophistication to our attack with his talented displays over three seasons in the mid-1980s.

Alan was able to beat defenders both by scorching speed or by sorcery and guile before delivering a telling cross or a powerful shot, and he was involved in many of the goals we scored during his period with us. But Alan was also capable of netting brilliant goals himself and his tally of fourteen in our colours have included some really spectacular efforts, with none more so than the one which beat visiting Nottingham Forest in a third-round FA Cup tie on a snow-covered surface in January 1987.

JACKSON, Cliff
Forward 1966-70

Appearances: 120
Goals: 30
Born: 3 September 1941, Swindon
Previous clubs: Swindon Town 1958, Plymouth Argyle 1963
Subsequent League clubs: Torquay United 1970

Cliff Jackson was one of new manager Bert Head's first signings for Crystal Palace and, initially as a winger, then as a striker, Cliff played an immensely valuable role in the Palace sides of the later years of that supremely successful decade for the club, culminating in promotion to the top flight with a team in which Cliff was the top scorer with 14 goals.

Cliff's first goal for the club, a searing twenty-yard drive from the left wing that put Palace on the way to probably our best victory of 1966/67, but it is his srtikes in the promotion season of 1968/69 for which he is best remembered. He was on target twice in the first game – a 4-0 win at Cardiff – and again in both the two final ones. Many readers will recall his winner for Palace against Fulham in the match which confirmed our first-ever promotion to the top flight, but a few Palace folk were at Blackburn for the last, tempestuous game of the season, where Cliff took advantage of a defensive blunder to put us ahead with a lob.

Inevitably, goals were much harder to come by in the First Division, but Cliff's effort in the second match of 1969/70, against Sunderland, ensured the establishment of a club record of eighteen league matches without defeat, while his last Selhurst Park goal was important too – a close-range finish completed a Palace success over Southampton in mid-March and the points gained from it were utterly crucial in the final analysis.

JACKSON, John
Goalkeeper 1964-73

Appearances: 388
Born: 5 September 1942, Hammersmith
Subsequent League clubs: Orient 1973,
   Millwall 1979, Ipswich Town 1981,
   Hereford United 1982.

Even among the illustrious company that is made up of Crystal Palace goalkeepers there is one name that will always stand out: John Jackson, who made a prodigious 346 League and 42 various senior cup appearances. Jackson signed for Palace in early March 1962 and made his debut in Palace's second match of our first Second Division season for thirty-nine years, at Swindon in August 1964.

Palace lost 0-2 but within a couple of months first-choice 'keeper Bill Glazier had signed for Coventry, and, although manager Dick Graham signed Welsh international Tony Millington to play in his stead, by the end of the year it was Jackson who was earning praise in the Palace goal and by the end of the season 'Jacko' was our undisputed first choice between the posts.

Over Palace's next four seasons John Jackson was a model of consistency and became one of only three ever-present players in the team that took Palace into the First Division for the first time in 1968/69.

In the top flight 'Jacko' really came into his own. He played 138 consecutive top-flight matches before missing the game at Wolves, through illness. No other Palace player ever attained one season's maximum appearances in the club's first three terms in the First Division – 'Jacko' did play so often because, time and again, as any Palace fan of that period will confirm, it was his superb displays that salvaged precious points for Palace against the odds; points that at the end of the season, made all the difference between survival and relegation.

Ultimately of course not even Jackson could keep Palace in the top flight. He had played in all but four of the First Division fixtures that Palace had contested and many fans around the country acknowledged that he had had the misfortune to be a great goalkeeper in an age of great goalkeepers. In a different generation, or, perhaps, at a more fashionable club, John Jackson would surely have gained many more honours than his single appearance for the Football League.

It has been marvellous for Palace fans of the 1960s and 1970s to have seen

'Jacko' back at the Palace occasionally in recent years at the reunions of former players and it is quite evident that his popularity remains totally undimmed at Selhurst Park.

JANSEN, Matthew
Forward 1998

Appearances: 33
Goals: 10
Born: 20 October 1977, Carlisle
Previous clubs: Carlisle United 1996
Subsequent League clubs: Blackburn Rovers 1998, Coventry City (loan) 2003

Matthew Jansen was a bright, eager young forward who oozed quality and chose to join Crystal Palace in preference to several of the leading clubs in the land in February 1998, although by that time Palace's Premiership future was beginning to look extremely doubtful.

Despite a series of defeats in his earliest Palace games, in which he usually featured as a substitute, no one could doubt Matt's talent and he was rewarded with a fabulous goal at Aston Villa, then further strikes in the victories at Newcastle and over Derby County. Matt was included in an England 'B' call-up too, then netted some more useful goals for Palace in the early part of 1998/99, but with financial problems looming large over the club it came as small surprise when Matt was transferred to Blackburn Rovers for some £4 million, though every Palace fan was desperately sorry to see him go.

JEFFRIES, Derek
Midfield/Defender 1973-76

Appearances: 122
Goals: 1
Born: 22 March 1951, Manchester
Previous clubs: Manchester City 1968
Subsequent League clubs: Peterborough United (loan) 1976, Millwall 1977, Chester City 1977

Derek Jeffries was bought for £100,000 for Crystal Palace in September 1973 by manager Malcolm Allison, who had previously been Derek's boss at Manchester City, to help to boost Palace's struggling midfield as we sought desperately to come to terms with life after relegation to the Second Division.

However, Derek was actually seen at his best with the Palace when playing in the 'sweeper' role, which grew to some prominence while he was at Selhurst Park and was much favoured by Mr Allison, or when lining up alongside Ian Evans in the centre of defence: he appeared in both roles in Palace's fabulous run to the FA Cup semi-final in 1976.

Always a footballing footballer, even when under pressure in defence, Derek's quality was evident for everyone to see, and the appreciation of the Palace fans of the period was shown when Derek was elected as our Player of the Year in 1975.

JOHNSON, Andy
Forward 2002-

Appearances: 83
Goals: 46
Born: 10 February 1981, Bedford
Previous club: Birmingham City 1997

*Andy Johnson
celebrates a goal in
his trademark style!*

Andy Johnson was a neat, inventive, hugely industrious attacking player who joined the Eagles in the summer of 2002 as a component in the deal which took Clinton Morrison to Birmingham City, in which Andy was valued at £750,000. Many Palace folk would say that ours was the better part of that transfer!

Andy sported a fashionable, completely shaven-headed hairstyle, but his Palace colleagues and fans would have had no difficulty whatever in picking him out because he quickly demonstrated his qualities for us to admire, while he will long be remembered at Selhurst Park for sequences of goalscoring that were quite outstanding!

The first one of these established a unique record at our club! By the time Andy notched a brace of goals in our 3-0 League Cup defeat of Coventry in early November 2002 he had scored 10 times in just 5 games, including hat-tricks in consecutive League matches!

Then, during 2003/04, Andy produced another devastating spell of intense goalscoring when, within 10 League games from mid-December, he hit 14 strikes including another hat-trick in the Eagles' stunning 6-3 rout of visiting Stoke City.

With the benefit of yet another hat-trick, at Crewe in late April, Andy ultimately finished 2003/04 as the Football League's leading goalscorer with 28 First Division strikes and thus created a new Eagles record by exceeding Ian Wright's tally of 27 in the also extended term of 1988/89. Thus, no one could possibly deny that Andy thoroughly deserved not just Palace's Player of the Year award but also that of the entire Nationwide League as well.

JOHNSON, Jeff
Midfield 1973-76

Appearances: 98
Goals: 5
Born: 26 November 1953, Cardiff
Previous clubs: Manchester City 1970, Swansea City 1972
Subsequent League clubs: Sheffield Wednesday 1976, Newport County 1981, Gillingham 1982, Port Vale 1985

Jeffrey Johnson was a strong and clever former Welsh schoolboy international who had been at Manchester City with Malcolm Allison early in the 1970s then joined his former mentor at Selhurst Park to augment Palace's midfield.

The move proved beneficial both to the player and his new club. Jeff quickly came to the attention of the Welsh selectors and gained Under-23 recognition, then was called into several of Wales' full

international squads. He played in every remaining Palace match in 1973/74 after his move to us and was a first-team regular throughout 1974/75 and most of 1975/76 when his industry was much appreciated by Palace fans.

JOHNSON, Joe
Goalkeeper 1907-15

Appearances: 295
Born: 1884, Tibshelf, Derbyshire
Previous clubs: Aston Villa, Plymouth Argyle 1906
Subsequent League clubs: Nottingham Forest 1919

Joshua Johnson (nicknamed 'Joe' by the Palace fans) was the club's goalkeeper from early December 1907 until the First World War. Following his unforgettable debut at Bristol Rovers on a waterlogged pitch he played in every remaining Southern League match of 1907/08 and

'Joe' Johnson.

in the three FA Cup ties – and was only absent from the Palace defence through injury during the next seven seasons!

By the time the war ended Joe's Palace career he had played 276 Southern League games for the club, the highest in our history. But when these are seen in context they assume even greater value, for not only were the maximum possible appearances lower than today (only one of Johnson's seasons with the Palace included even a forty-two-match programme) but goalkeepers were subject to much more physical attention than is permitted now. The shoulder charge was commonplace and the buffeting he received required him to be strong and brave. At 6ft tall and 13 stone, Joe was ideally equipped, yet off the field he was a quiet and serious fellow, a Sunday School teacher who frequently declined to play on Good Friday or Christmas Day.

Joe's prowess was quickly recognised and when the first representative match was staged between the Southern and Football Leagues in April 1910 (2-2) our man was between the posts for the Southern League.

The days of Palace as a Southern League outfit may appear remote today. But even at this distance in time we can clearly recognise in Joe Johnson a sterling player of immense character and value to our club.

JONES, J.T. ('Tom')
Defender 1920-22

Appearances: 66
Goals: 6
Born: Rhosymedre, Near Wrexham
Previous clubs: Stoke City

J.T. (Tom) Jones.

Subsequent League clubs: Coventry City 1922
International honours: 15 full caps for Wales

Tall, dependable defender and current Welsh international centre half J.T. 'Tom' Jones, joined the Palace in the summer of 1920, though such was the calibre of Palace's defence at that time in the first season for the club in the Football League, that Tom only found a niche in the line-up after the unfortunate injury to wing half Roy McCracken in early December. But Tom took over most ably from the Irishman and playing at right half was certainly a key member of Palace's successful side throughout the second half of that season.

Tom also netted four valuable goals to assist our Third Division side to the championship, but the strike for which he will always be remembered at the Palace came in the club's inaugural match in the Second Division at the start of the following season when he netted Palace's opener and first at the higher level to put us ahead and on the way to a quite wonderful 4-1 victory over promotion favourites Nottingham Forest at The Nest. It was a towering header from a corner and left Forest's former England custodian Sam Hardy rooted to the spot and grasping nothing but air!

That was Tom's greatest Palace moment – and the club's best match at that Second Division level between 1921 and 1925 – and at the end of the season he moved back to the Midlands to join Coventry City.

JUMP, Stewart
Defender 1973-77

Appearances: 91
Goals: 2
Born: 27 January 1952, Crumpsall, Manchester
Previous clubs: Stoke City 1969
Subsequent League clubs: Fulham (loan) 1976

Stewart Jump was an intelligent, mobile defender who was recruited for Crystal Palace by manager Malcolm Allison and certainly his arrival caused our rearguard to quickly tighten up, enabling us to make a brave if eventually unavailing attempt to avoid a second successive relegation.

However, it was in the early spring two seasons later that Palace fans saw Stewart Jump at his very best for us, because he was quite outstanding as our sweeper in the Eagles' team which forged its way to the FA Cup semi-final as a Third Division side, and starred in the victories at Leeds and Chelsea. Although Palace then won at Sunderland without him, some thinking Palace fans have always wondered if his injury-induced absence from the semi-final cost us dearly as we faltered to defeat at Stamford Bridge without him.

KELLARD, Bobby
Midfield 1963-65, 1971-73

Appearances: 137
Goals: 10
Born: 1 March 1943, Edmonton, London
Previous clubs: Southend United 1959
Subsequent League clubs: Ipswich Town 1965, Portsmouth 1966, Bristol City 1968, Leicester City 1970, Portsmouth 1972, Hereford United 1975, Torquay United 1975

Tough little Bobby Kellard (he stood just 5ft 6ins tall) made two impressive contributions to the Palace cause for which he is remembered at our club with pride, pleasure and affection.

He first joined us early in 1963/64 to become an important feature of our promotion drive that season in a role that was several years ahead of its time. He usually played at number seven or number eleven, but combined the traditional attacking duties of a winger with those of midfield grafter, and he continued in that position as a valued member of our Second Division squad until November 1965 when he moved to Ipswich.

But in late September 1971 Bobby was recalled to Selhurst Park to make an even more significant contribution. His task was to replace popular skipper Steve Kember, who had just left us for Chelsea for a hefty fee: no easy role! But Bobby was always a man for a difficult task and he was no mean footballer. His industry and skill, now mainly deployed in midfield, were amply demonstrated again and he led Palace slowly but surely out of trouble, not only succeeding the gifted Kember in midfield but also as skipper of the team.

Bobby not only missed just one game in the remainder of that tense season, he also scored three invaluable goals, two of which were absolutely crucial. One helped Palace claim a vital point from Arsenal; the other ensured that we beat Stoke City to stay in the top flight.

No wonder this cheery little fellow is made so welcome when he returns to us for the reunions of the former Palace players.

KELLY, Noel
Forward 1950-51

Appearances: 43
Goals: 6
Born: 28 December 1921, Dublin
Previous clubs: Glentoran, Arsenal 1947
Subsequent League clubs: Nottingham
    Forest 1951, Tranmere Rovers 1955
International honours: 1 full cap for Eire

Inside forward Noel Kelly was the single player of quality at Crystal Palace during our quite dreadful 1950/51 season. He was one of several experienced players whom manager Ronnie Rooke recruited during the spring/summer of 1950, but none of them contributed as much to the ailing, fading Palace side as Noel did.

Noel scored his first goal for the club in a wind-affected Easter Monday 2-1 victory at Reading, but his four strikes in 1950/51 made him our joint-second top League goalscorer! That said, his consolation strike for Palace against Millwall in the FA Cup, in Ronnie Rooke's last game in charge, was sufficient to put him on

terms with the former Arsenal sharpshooter at the end of our overall season's scoring list!

Noel's guile and craft offered lustre where there was little else to be found, so that it was no surprise to anyone at Selhurst Park in the summer of 1951 that he joined promoted Nottingham Forest, and he remains the only Palace player from that awful time to be spoken of with any admiration at all.

KEMBER, Steve
Midfield 1965-71, 1978-80

Appearances: 295
Goals: 38
Born: 8 December 1948, Croydon
Subsequent League clubs: Chelsea 1971,
    Leicester City 1975
Managerial appointments: Crystal Palace
    1981, 2001, 2003

Steve Kember is a local lad and as such has always been a great favourite at Crystal Palace. He signed for us as an apprentice in 1963 and as a full professional on his seventeenth birthday.

In Steve's first spell with us, he matured under Dick Graham and quickly became an important part of the teams in the late 1960s when his talented midfield displays were one of the hallmarks of Palace's performances. He was an ever-present member of the promotion side of 1968/69 that gained the club a place in the top flight for the first time, netting several vital goals in the process. When playing at the highest level Steve shone as brightly as any of the illustrious players who opposed him and he gained his first England Under-23 cap in October 1970.

Steve Kember early in his playing days for the Palace.

Steve succeeded John Sewell as Palace's captain after the latter's retirement, but in September 1971 he moved to Chelsea for a fee quoted as £170,000 as Bert Head sought funds in order to drastically re-shape his Palace squad for First Division survival. An impressive four years were followed by a move to Leicester, where he played 117 League games in a little over three seasons.

In the autumn of 1978, after an initial spell with Vancouver Whitecaps, Steve returned to Selhurst Park when Terry Venables paid £40,000 to add his experience to the precocious skills of a young team that was seeking to put Palace back into the top flight. Steve missed just one of our remaining games and his mature influence was an important feature of Palace's glorious Second Division Championship.

Steve remained with Palace in the First Division until the following March, when he re-crossed the Atlantic to play for Vancouver for a couple of seasons, but as the entry under his name in the previous chapter concerning Palace's managers has already shown, Steve has been

involved with us in productive fashion at that level too.

Discussion sometimes focuses upon which of Steve's manifold achievements with and for our club has been the most significant and, certainly, there have been few men who have made a greater contribution to Crystal Palace than he.

See also Steve Kember's entry in the Managers section (p.42-3).

KEMP, David
Forward 1975-76

Appearances: 44
Goals: 16
Born: 20 February 1953, Harrow, Middlesex
Subsequent League clubs: Portsmouth 1976, Carlisle United 1978, Plymouth Argyle 1979, Gillingham 1981, Brentford 1981
Managerial appointments: Plymouth Argyle 1990

David's initiation into League football was with Malcolm Allison's Eagles in a meaningless fixture at Tranmere Rovers in May 1975 after he had joined us from Slough Town the previous month. Particularly in the early months of 1975/76 David was a highly effective striker and Palace supporters of the period remember him as a lively, tousle-haired goal-poacher whose efforts produced an important ingredient towards our run that season to the FA Cup semi-finals as a Third Division club.

But David was to make a later and more distinguished contribution to Crystal Palace because he rejoined us – again, ironically, from Slough Town! – to become a member of the coaching staff at Selhurst

Park under new manager Alan Smith in the summer of 1993, and helped to lead the Eagles to a prestigious Division One Championship the following season.

KETTERIDGE, Steve
Midfield 1985-87

Appearances: 71
Goals: 6
Born: 7 November 1959, Stevenage, Hertfordshire
Previous clubs: Wimbledon 1978
Subsequent League clubs: Leyton Orient 1987, Cardiff City (loan) 1988

Steve Ketteridge, tall, angular, experienced and competitive, was secured by Steve Coppell as season 1985/86 approached, to add new and much-needed steel to Palace's midfield, and if the hard-working, eternally running 'Ketts' was not the most refined of footballers, he certainly became part of our most effective team since our return to the Second Division in 1981.

As such, Steve was one of the men who helped to restore dignity and credibility to Crystal Palace: fans of the mid-1980s were grateful to him for that, and will confirm the rightness of his inclusion here.

KOLINKO, Aleksandrs
Goalkeeper 2000-03

Appearances: 99
Born: 18 June 1975, Latvia
Previous clubs: Interskonto 1994, Skonto Metals 1995, Skonto Riga 1996
International honours: 51 full caps for Latvia.

'Alex' Kolinko was a goalkeeping enigma! At his best he was spectacular and a quite brilliant shot-stopper, demonstrating precisely why he is Latvia's first choice in his position – but let's just say that Alex wasn't always quite able to reproduce such form in every match!

Nevertheless, Alex quickly became a considerable favourite with the Palace fans, and in his first season with us he revealed a remarkable talent for saving penalties. He also possessed a long, powerful, and accurate throw-out which perhaps Palace could have used to greater advantage.

KURZ, Freddie
Forward 1946-51

Appearances: 154
Goals: 49
Born: 3 September 1918, Grimsby
Previous clubs: Grimsby Town
Subsequent League clubs: Boston United.

Having seen Freddie Kurz 'guest' successfully for the Palace during the wartime competitions of 1944 and 1945, including the scoring of a hat-trick upon his debut against Queens Park Rangers in August 1944, Palace supporters of the period petitioned the board of directors to secure the free-scoring centre forward on a permanent basis. When the Palace were then drawn to face Rangers again in the third round of the first post-war FA Cup competition in January 1946, in which no 'guests' were eligible to play, the club hurried the petitioned move through at what was then a club-record fee of £5,000.

Freddie did not manage to keep us in the cup against the powerful Rangers out-

Alex Kolinko.

fit but, usually playing at centre forward, he steadily repaid his fee several times over during the first five post-war seasons, for not only has his tally of 48 League goals rarely been exceeded by subsequent Palace strikers, but his goals were all scored for struggling Palace teams, which only once finished in the upper half of the League table. Freddie was our leading goalscorer in 1947/48 and 1948/49 with 18 and 12 goals respectively.

LAZARUS, Mark
Outside right 1967-69

Appearances: 70
Goals: 17
Born: 5 December 1938, Whitechapel
Previous clubs: Leyton Orient 1957, Queens Park Rangers 1960, 1962 and 1965, Wolverhampton Wanderers 1961, Brentford 1964
Subsequent League clubs: Orient 1969

Mark Lazarus was renowned as a widely travelled, occasionally volatile but powerful and vastly experienced raiding winger before he was secured for the Palace by our club's astute manager Bert Head, who believed, correctly, that Mark's goals from the right flank for which he was justly famous among London's footballing fraternity, allied to his tenacious, creative service to his colleagues, could help to turn Palace from a good Second Division side into serious promotion contenders.

Strong, fast and with a low centre of gravity, Mark was extremely difficult to stop once he was in possession and on the move. He was also a tremendous character, and Palace fans immediately responded to his zest, enthusiasm and robust attacking forays – and dramatic celebratory tours after he had scored a goal, from which no one was safe! He would run to embrace several other players, the occasional supporter, a policeman or two and even John Jackson at the other end of the ground!

Mark netted 11 vital goals in Palace's promotion season of 1968/69 and was thereby Palace's joint-second-highest scorer along with Bobby Woodruff, but his sheer energy, strength and exuberance also helped to create many of the other goals scored by his teammates, so that there are fans of that period who will argue that it was Mark's charisma which was the crucial factor in Palace's eventual success that season in gaining the long-coveted place in the top flight for the first time.

LEIGERTWOOD, Mikele
Central defender 2004-

Appearances: 15
Born: 12 November 1982, Enfield

Previous clubs: Wimbledon 2001, Leyton Orient (Loan) 2001

Mikele only started ten Palace games towards the climactic finish to 2003/04, and to begin with was often only used as a substitute, but, after Mark Hudson returned to Fulham, Mikele became a first-choice centre half and played with real and increasing confidence at the heart of our defence to help lift us into the play-off places, then to emerge victorious from them.

LEWIS, Glyn
Forward 1942-48

Appearances: 66
Goals: 4 goals
Born: 3 July 1921, Abertillery, Gwent
Subsequent League clubs: Bristol City 1948

Glyn Lewis was a tough, industrious and versatile little Welshman with Crystal Palace who played occasionally for us during the war years and then throughout the first two post-war seasons.

Usually Glyn appeared at inside forward, with a preference for inside right, but he could also play on both flanks, so that in both the post-war terms he lined up in four different forward positions.

Probably Glyn's best match for the Palace was the second-round FA Cup tie at Bristol City in December 1947 when his constant probing provided the inspiration that gave Bert Robson the extra-time opening from which he netted the only goal of the contest. Certainly the Robins didn't forget his contribution – they signed him at the end of that season!

LEWIS, Jack
Wing half 1938-50

Appearances: 130
Goals: 5
Born: 26 August 1919, Bloxwich,
  Staffordshire
Previous clubs: West Bromwich Albion
Subsequent League clubs: Bournemouth
  1949, Reading 1951

Jack Lewis was a brilliant attacking wing half whom Palace obtained for nothing more than a signing-on fee from West Bromwich Albion in the summer of 1938. He made his teenage debut in Palace's penultimate League game of 1938/39 at Selhurst Park in a goal-less draw against Bristol Rovers.

Like so many players of that era, Jack's footballing career was blighted by the Second World War, but he was available to help Palace to the regional championship of the Third Division (South) in the first half of 1945/46, then upon the resumption of League football in 1946/47 he shone as a half-back of real quality in a none-too-great Palace team. Inevitably his performances quickly drew the attentions of several First Division sides but Jack played on for the Palace, appearing in every match that season, the only player besides skipper Fred Dawes to do so.

Jack was tall and strong, a ball-winner, always constructive and eager to set his forwards in motion with an accurate, perhaps penetrative pass. He gained representative honours when he was selected for a London XI to play in Brussels in 1948 but in the end, as had become obvious, Palace could not hold on to him. Discerning fans of the period thought that Jack could well have played at a much higher grade, but his subsequent career was spent with stronger teams in the old Third Division (South).

LIEVESLEY, Les
Defender 1937-39

Appearances: 82
Goals: 3
Born: July 1911, Staveley, Derbyshire
Previous clubs: Manchester United,
  Torquay United

Les Lievesley was signed for Crystal Palace by manager Tom Bromilow right at the end of season 1936/37 and made his debut in the final match of that term when Palace gained a deserved if rare victory at Queens Park Rangers.

Les was one of the best wing halves ever to play for the Palace. He was a powerful, dynamic fellow at all but 6ft and over 12 stone and his acquisition was unquestionably a key reason for a much-enhanced Palace showing in 1937/38, and the best performance for a full decade the following term.

Les put in 53 consecutive appearances after joining us and, with George Walker and Nick Collins, helped to form an outstanding half-back line that is still spoken of with awe at Selhurst Park today. But sadly, Les' life was to end in tragedy: after training paratroopers and commandos during the Second World War, Les joined Turin of Italy, only to be killed with twenty-nine other members of that club when the plane carrying them from a match against Benfica in Lisbon hit the cathedral at the top of Superga Hill on the edge of the city, before plunging into a courtyard in flames.

Andy Linighan in action against Wolves.

LINIGHAN, Andy
Central defender 1997-2000

Appearances: 128
Goals: 4
Born: 18 June 1962, Hartlepool
Previous clubs: Hartlepool 1980, Leeds
United 1984, Oldham Athletic 1986,
Norwich City 1988, Arsenal 1990
Subsequent League clubs: Oxford United
2000

Andy Linighan was already a vastly experienced and distinguished central defender when he joined the Eagles from Arsenal as manager Dave Bassett's last signing in January 1997, but his impact upon our vulnerable defence was such that he immediately assisted us towards the play-offs and was a key member of the Palace backline which kept Sheffield United at bay throughout the Wembley final before David Hopkin's wonder goal in the last minute took Palace back to the Premiership.

As an economy measure at a dire time for the Eagles, Andy spent the final weeks of 1998/99 on loan at Queens Park Rangers where, on the last day of the season and after helping the Hoops to a convincing victory over us, he trotted over to the phalanx of Palace fans after the final whistle to applaud their efforts with a gesture that was warmly appreciated by the travelling members of the red and blue army.

Then came Andy's best season for the Palace and his greatest contribution here. In 1999/2000 he played in every League game while many of the club's best players were transferred for financial reasons, and deservedly won the supporters' Player of the Year award for his resolute displays which were a key reason for Palace's First Division survival.

LITTLE, Jack
Full-back 1919-26

Appearances: 261
Born: c.1884, Ryton-on-Tyne
Previous clubs: Barnsley 1908, Croydon
   Common 1912

Jack Little was Palace's first-choice right-back for some seven seasons after the end of the First World War, but he was already well known to local football fans when he joined us because he had played regularly for Croydon Common and had helped them to gain a prestigious promotion in 1913/14.

Jack's usual full-back partner was 'Dusty' Rhodes and the duo are usually mentioned in the same breath with goal-keeper Jack Alderson – these three Palace heroes played an amazing 100 consecutive matches together (including cup ties and friendlies), helping the club into the Football League and then into the Second Division as the first Champions of the newly formed Third Division in 1920/21.

It is worth noting that over half of Jack's 242 League appearances for Crystal Palace were made in the Second Division of the Football League – at the time only Roy McCracken played more times than Jack between 1921 and our relegation in 1925 so that it was not until the late 1960s that any other Palace man was able to improve upon Jack's efforts at that level. A man who helped to 'make' Crystal Palace indeed!

LOCKE, Gary
Defender 1983-86

Appearances: 101
Goals: 1
Born: 12 July 1954, Kingsbury
Previous clubs: Chelsea 1971

Gary was a steady, reliable and unspectacular right-back and former England Youth international who joined the Palace at manager Alan Mullery's instigation in January 1983 and he certainly helped to bolster our somewhat suspect defence in the trying days at the Palace in the early to mid-1980s.

Gary also managed a goal for us, which brought him, as well as Palace fans, great delight, for it was netted against his former club, Chelsea, and helped us to secure a 2-2 draw upon his return to Stamford Bridge with the Eagles in November 1983; then as his career with us drew towards its close he also revealed a perhaps unexpected talent by performing competently at the centre of our defence.

LOMBARDO, Attilio
Forward 1997-99

Appearances: 47
Goals: 10
Born: 6 January 1966, Zelo Buon Persico,
   Italy
Previous clubs: Pergocrema 1983,
   Cremonese 1985, Sampdoria 1989,
   Juventus 1995
Subsequent League clubs: Lazio 1999,
   Sampdoria 2001
International honours: Italy – full international
Managerial appointments: Crystal Palace
   1998

It was a terrific morale-booster for the Eagles and their supporters when the audacious signing of thirty-one-year-old

Italian international winger Attilio Lombardo was announced in August 1997. He was a household name among home-based football fans through Channel Four's live Sunday afternoon coverage of Italy's Serie A, and he made an immediate impact for Palace, newly promoted to the Premiership, helping to inspire the club to victories in the opening two away games at Everton (2-1) and at Leeds (2-0).

Yet, if ever a man looked a parody of a footballer, it was Attilio. He was prematurely bald, bandy-legged, with an awkward gait and an almost gnome-like stance. But in terms of sophistication and vision it seems unlikely that Palace have ever possessed so much in a single player. Perhaps, inevitably, he found the sheer pace and intensity of the Nationwide First Division too much at times, but, during what developed into a thoroughly difficult time for the club and its players, it was always apparent that he gave of his best to our cause.

Palace fans certainly took Attilio to their hearts. We loved to sing 'Just one Lombardo' to *'O Sole Mio'* which was the tune to an Italian ice-cream advertisement at the time in his honour and there were unquestionably times when he demonstrated levels of skill in our colours that no contemporary British player could approach.

See also Attilio Lombardo's entry in the Managers section (p.48).

LONG, Terry
Forward/Wing half 1955-69

Appearances: 480
Goals: 18

Born: 17 November 1934, Tylers Green, Buckinghamshire
Previous clubs: Wycombe Wanderers

Terry Long joined Crystal Palace in May 1955 and did not leave until the autumn of 1973, so that Bobby Greener, Johnny McNichol and Steve Kember are the only players who have served the club for longer than him. Terry was originally a wing half who had captured the eye of manager Cyril Spiers and after making his debut and settling to the demands of League football in 1955/56 he put together a run of 214 consecutive League appearances (234 with major Cup ties), a club record at the time and only once surpassed – and that by the superb John Jackson.

Terry's sequence ended just a month before the end of 1960/61, Palace's first promotion season for forty years, and his splendid, regular performances were a key feature of that success. He remained a cornerstone of the defence as the side was remodelled in the Third Division, so that only Terry himself and George Petchey from the 1961 team were members of the 1963/64 squad which took the club back into the Second Division after an absence of thirty-nine years.

Terry was a marvellous club man. His faithful service to Crystal Palace was rewarded with a testimonial in October 1966 and a crowd of over 17,000 came to support and thank him.

Although Terry was a steady and capable defender, he could and did play upfield as an inside forward. He did not often score goals but no one who saw it will ever forget the one he hit from twenty-five yards in the floodlit friendly against Real Madrid. Another memorable one was the last one he netted for the club on 30 September 1967 when, in front of a then record crowd for a League fixture at Selhurst Park of 38,006 Terry struck the only goal of the game against Queens Park Rangers to put Palace top of the Second Division for the first time in the club's history.

Terry was still making League appearances for us in 1968/69 when Palace gained promotion to the First Division but, to his disappointment and that of all Palace followers, he was never to turn out for us in the top flight. Nevertheless, Terry was appointed as assistant manager to Bert Head in 1972. He remains a most welcome visitor to Selhurst Park to this day, but all Palace fans were delighted when he agreed to make a public return here in October 1984 to give recognition to Jim Cannon, the only player to have appeared in more games for Crystal Palace than Terry himself.

LOUGHLAN, John
Defender 1968-71

Appearances: 77
Born: 12 June 1943, Coatbridge,
    Lanarkshire
Previous clubs: Morton 1965
Subsequent League clubs: Wrexham 1971

John Loughlan was a splendid left-back secured by Bert Head along with Tony Taylor from Morton in the autumn of 1968 to complete the squad which would take the Palace to promotion to the First Division for the first time some seven months later. In fact, only a chipped anklebone prevented John from playing in all the remaining fixtures of that triumph, although he did appear in the last four games with fractured ribs!

Obviously then, John was a tough and courageous fellow, while his fierce tackling and excellent control after he had won possession made him a valuable asset in our rise to senior status, and in our early fight to stay there.

McCORMICK, John
Central defender 1966-73

Appearances: 229
Goals: 7
Born: 18 July 1936, Glasgow
Previous clubs: Third Lanark 1959,
    Aberdeen 1964

Centre forward Tom White had been Palace manager Bert Head's principal target from Aberdeen early in the close season of 1966, but he brought a big central defender, craggy John McCormick back with him as well as a makeweight – all for a mere £1,500! John became a staunch and resolute pillar of Palace defences later in the 1960s, helped to guide the club to promotion to the top flight and then to relative, short-term, security there.

Not only did John play every game in the Palace promotion side of 1968/69, but he absolutely relished the challenge of the First Division, and, unless you saw him playing for Palace at that level, you will never know just what he did for our team there. With Mel Blyth alongside and John Jackson in goal, John was part of the triumvirate who did most to keep the club in that section for four years. John made international strikers appear anonymous; he constantly inspired his colleagues; his headed clearances saved Palace in scores of tight situations and his red hair stood out like a beacon. It was only after John

John McCormick.

had given up playing that Palace fell out of the First Division – and it was entirely proper that in September 1974 the club awarded him a richly deserved testimonial for his magnificent service.

Speaking about John McCormick many years later, Bert Head said that he regarded this signing as the best one he had made for Crystal Palace, and even after a great deal of thought, it is impossible to argue with Bert's judgement. Some makeweight!

McCRACKEN, Roy
Wing half 1920-26

Appearances: 190
Goals: 2
Born: 25 June 1895, Dromore, County Down
Previous clubs: Belfast Distillery
Subsequent clubs: Portadown 1926
International honours: 4 full caps for Northern Ireland

Roy McCracken was a stylish wing half who joined the Palace in the summer of 1920 and, until he had the misfortune to break a leg in December, was our first-choice right half in the promotion-winning team of 1920/21. However, Roy made a successful comeback when Palace made their Second Division debut and he played more games for us at that level than anyone else during our four-year tenure between 1921-25. Such consistency was of enormous value to Palace as they sought to become established in that division and it should be understood that our ultimate relegation in 1925 was certainly not the fault of the side's overworked defenders.

Roy's intelligent, mature, skilful performances earned him a deserved reputation as a neat and clever footballer. He won 4 full international caps for Northern Ireland and was the first Third Division player to be so selected.

Roy was the younger brother of the Newcastle and Northern Ireland defender Billy McCracken, who so manipulated the offside law of that period that it was ultimately altered in 1925. Roy is less well known than his famous brother except at Crystal Palace where he graced the best teams in the first sixty years of the club's existence and is still recognised as having been among the most cultured players ever to have appeared in our colours.

McDONALD, Harry
Full-back 1950-55

Appearances: 146
Goals: 1
Born: 11 September 1926, Salford
Previous clubs: Ashton United
Subsequent clubs: Kettering Town 1955

Harry McDonald was a strong, sturdy left-back but he possessed a turn of speed that was unexpected in a defender and which frequently surprised his opposing wingers, so that he was our first choice at number three for over three seasons.

Interestingly Harry had come into the game unusually late because he was already twenty-four-years-old when chief scout Charlie Slade spotted him playing in a local league game in Lancashire and urged Ronnie Rooke to sign him. Certainly, Palace fans of the early 1950s will agree, there was no doubting the quality of Mr Slade's judgement on this occasion.

Harry always looked immaculate and unruffled, and he was one of those players on whom the manager, team colleagues and supporters can always rely for a composed and controlled performance, so he was held in considerable esteem at Selhurst Park.

McGOLDRICK, Eddie
Midfielder/Defender 1989-93

Appearances: 189
Goals: 17
Born: 30 April 1965, Corby,
    Northamptonshire
Previous clubs: Northampton Town 1986
Subsequent League clubs: Arsenal 1993,
    Manchester City 1996, Stockport County
    (loan) 2003
International honours: 15 full caps for
    Eire.

Eddie McGoldrick teases the Southampton defence at The Dell in October 1992.

Dapper Eddie McGoldrick was a twinkling little winger who joined the Eagles in January 1989 as the final component for our promotion-winning squad of that season. He became a huge favourite with Palace fans and won the Player of the Year award for 1991/92.

Eddie's teasing runs to the byline and supply of crosses were an integral and attractive feature of Steve Coppell's Palace teams. While Eddie was at Selhurst Park they were a major reason for the club's success via the 1989 play-offs, then our growing top-flight maturity in the early 1990s. Eddie's skill however, was not limited to wing play, although that was primarily why Steve Coppell bought him, for he could also perform as an immaculate sweeper behind the back four and Palace deployed him there most effectively in the latter part of his career at the club, though many supporters would have preferred to see him used in a more adventurous role.

Partly, no doubt, because of his adaptability, Eddie was called up for international duty with Eire, but he chose to leave the Eagles in the summer of 1993 after our relegation from the Premier League.

McKENZIE, Leon
Forward 1995-2000

Appearances: 98
Goals: 8
Born: 17 May 1978, Croydon
Subsequent League clubs: Fulham (loan) 1997, Peterborough United (loan) 1998, Peterborough United 2000, Norwich City 2003

Leon McKenzie was a vibrant young striker who made his Palace debut as a seventeen-year-old, and by scoring against visiting Southend in a second round second leg League Cup tie in October 1995 became Palace's first teenager to achieve that feat since Jim Cannon had done so over twenty years before.

Leon's goals had been a major reason for several junior successes in the earlier 1990s, but as the Palace club regained momentum and forced its way back into the Premier League so Leon's role here became more that of a substitute, and then upon our return to Division One it became apparent that the greater striking talents of Clinton Morrison, Mikael Forssell and Dougie Freedman would seriously limit his opportunities here so that he moved on to Peterborough early in 2000/01.

McNICHOL, Johnny
Midfielder/Defender 1958-63

Appearances: 205
Goals: 15
Born: 20 August 1925, Kilmarnock

Previous clubs: Newcastle United 1946, Brighton & Hove Albion 1948, Chelsea 1952

Johnny McNichol came to Selhurst Park in March 1958 as manager Cyril Spiers' last desperate attempt to prevent the Palace from becoming founder members of the new national Fourth Division to be formed at the end of that season. Johnny was immediately made captain, a position he held for nearly five years, and he scored the only goal of the game upon his debut to defeat visiting Port Vale, but even his 7 goals from the 12 remaining fixtures could not keep Palace out of the new basement division.

Johnny was an old-fashioned inside forward, but he gradually moved, via wing half, to full-back and it was from there that he skippered Palace's first promotion side for forty years in 1960/61. He had another couple of seasons as a Palace player extending his club record (still

Johnny McNichol (right) and Real Madrid skipper Francisco Gento exchange pennants before the floodlit friendly at Selhurst Park on 18 April 1962.

unbeaten) of consecutive League appearances from a debut to 153 but had to retire after a particularly nasty fractured cheekbone and broken jaw early in 1962/63. His subsequent career, mentioned in a previous chapter in this book, in the commercial side of the game was equally valuable to Crystal Palace so that his contributions to our club, both on and off the field, will long be remembered with gratitude.

MABBUTT, Kevin
Forward 1981-84

Appearances: 88
Goals: 24
Born: 5 December 1958, Bristol
Previous clubs: Bristol City 1976

Kevin Mabbutt's career was blighted at Crystal Palace by an awful injury, but before that occurred he had lifted the hopes of all Palace folk at a dreadfully depressing time for both the club and its fans.

The fact was that Kevin was one of the most unlucky footballers of all time – and at Crystal Palace FC we seem to have had our share of these. He was an exciting acquisition at the time of his arrival at Selhurst Park as Dario Gradi's last signing for Palace in October 1981: he was intelligent, articulate, a former schoolboy and youth international and a gifted footballer with a fine career in prospect as a mobile, elusive and effective striker.

Kevin played in every remaining match of 1981/82 for us when his 8 goals were invaluable to our somewhat troubled cause and made him our leading scorer. He lost four months of 1982/83 to a pelvic injury yet still led our scoring charts by a distance, so that his and Palace's prospects at the dawning of 1983/84 still appeared bright enough. However, two weeks before opening day, Kevin sustained the injury that ultimately wrecked his career: within minutes of the start of the friendly against Southampton at Selhurst Park, he overstretched while chasing a ball near the touchline and ruptured all the ligaments in his left knee.

Bravely, Kevin tried to resurrect his career several times, after lengthy absences and repeated knee surgery, but it was to no avail and Palace and their fans were left to rue the mischance that deprived them of this skilful and likeable young man.

MADDEN, Dave
Midfield 1988-90

Appearances: 33
Goals: 6
Born: 6 January 1963, Stepney
Previous clubs: Southampton 1980, Bournemouth (loan) 1982, Arsenal 1983, Charlton Athletic 1984, Reading 1987
Subsequent League clubs: Birmingham City (loan) 1989, Maidstone United 1990

Creative, brooding, skilful Dave Madden arrived at the Palace virtually unnoticed on a free transfer in the summer of 1988 – but he was a household name among Eagles fans by the following spring, having made an important contribution to Palace's exciting run to the Second Division play-offs at the end of the season and to our eventual promotion.

At the crucial time, with several senior men having proved worryingly fallible from the penalty spot, Dave assumed responsibility in these matters and converted all the five spot kicks we were awarded in the last fifteen matches, including the vital one in the play-off final second leg at Selhurst Park against Blackburn Rovers, which levelled the aggregate scores, provided the Palace with the advantage, plus new impetus from which ultimately and after extra-time we achieved success.

It was an acknowledgement of Dave's value to us at that important stage that Palace were pleased to send a full, top-flight squad to play a testimonial for him in April 1992 at his subsequent club, Maidstone United, after his career had been terminated through injury.

MANDERS, Frank
Forward 1931-35

Appearances: 102
Goals: 34
Born: 13 June 1914, Camberley, Surrey
Previous clubs: Aldershot
Subsequent League clubs: Norwich City
1935

Frank Manders was a tall, clean-cut, good-looking lad who signed for the Palace on his seventeenth birthday in June 1931, having caught the eye of the manager Jack Tresadern. Frank quickly became a prolific scorer for our reserve team but it was as the foil to the great Peter Simpson that he graduated to our League side, having initially deputised for the master when Peter was out due to injury.

Frank developed into a useful striker in his own right: stylish, poised and unselfish. Inevitably, he came under scrutiny of the bigger clubs and Tottenham and Brentford made offers for

him, but he eventually moved rather suddenly in October 1935 to Norwich when the Canaries paid their record fee to obtain his services, and he played for the Carrow Road club until the outbreak of the war.

MARTYN, Nigel
Goalkeeper 1989-96

Appearances: 349
Born: 11 August 1966, Bethel, near
St Austell, Cornwall
Previous clubs: St Blazey, Bristol Rovers
1987
Subsequent League clubs: Leeds United
1996, Everton 2003
International honours: 23 full caps for
England

Nigel Martyn became the country's first £1 million goalkeeper when he joined the Eagles in November 1989 as manager Steve Coppell sought to improve the Palace defence after some early top-flight embarrassments. Strong and powerful at 6ft 2in, but possessing an ideal temperament, plus essential 'presence' Nigel soon impressed with his performances at the highest domestic level, and in our run to the 1990 FA Cup final.

His top-division experience continued and he became part of the Palace's best ever defence at that level in 1990/91 and it became apparent that he was on the verge of international recognition. After earning a series of 'B' caps, Nigel gained his first full England honour as a substitute in Moscow in April 1992 against the newly formed Confederation of Independent States. Everyone at the Palace was delighted for him as he had been in tremendous form and had clearly

Nigel Martyn.

deserved his selection. That 1991/92 season also saw Nigel move smoothly into the top ten in the list of appearances of Palace goalkeepers. By then he had already kept more top-flight clean sheets than anybody else in our club apart from the magnificent John Jackson.

Nigel was an ever-present member of the Division One Championship side of 1993/94 and completed an unbroken sequence of 100 consecutive League appearances for Palace back in the Premier League, at Leicester in October 1994, when he kept a third clean sheet in eight days to ensure a narrow Palace victory over the Foxes.

Despite the absences necessitated by an injury to his hand in the 1995 FA Cup semi-final, by the early weeks of 1996 Nigel passed his 250 League appearances for the Eagles, then entered the top five places in the club's all-time chart in February 1996, going on to complete another season of full appearances. But Palace's unfortunate defeat by Leicester in the 1996 Wembley play-off final was to cost the club its brilliant goalkeeper. Having played 349 senior games for Palace, he moved to Leeds for £2.5 million as the country's costliest goalkeeper for the second time. Palace fans rued his departure, but fully realised that such a quality goalkeeper both wanted and needed to be playing in the top flight and we wished him well for his future.

MENLOVE, Bert
Forward 1919-22

Appearances: 65
Goals: 21
Born: Croydon, Surrey
Subsequent League clubs: Sheffield
  United 1922

Centre forward Bert Menlove was a local boy who joined Crystal Palace in the spring of 1920. He made an immediate impact, scored 6 goals in his 12 Southern League outings that season, including a hat-trick at Gillingham (4-2) at the end of March, and contributed five more towards Palace's Third Division Championship of 1920/21 plus an additional seven in the Second Division in 1921/22.

Bert was also a useful striker in major cup ties. He netted Palace's second and decisive goal in our dazzling 2-0 win over top-flight Manchester City at The Nest in January 1921 and was twice on target in the 6-0 rout of Everton at Goodison Park twelve months later, to re-emphasise Palace's ability to topple the biggest outfits which – to the delight of modern-day supporters – continues to the present time.

MORGAN, Billy
Forward 1922-25

Appearances: 84
Goals: 16
Born: 3 November 1900, Old Hill, Birmingham
Previous clubs: Birmingham City, Coventry City

Billy Morgan was a dark, swarthy-featured young man who joined the Palace in the summer of 1922 in an extraordinarily complex transfer deal with Coventry City which involved no fewer than six players! He became a useful goalscorer for us and fully justified his £500 fee in one match alone.

Billy became the captain at Crystal Palace from Christmas Day 1923, so he was our skipper when illustrious Tottenham visited The Nest for a first-round FA Cup tie the following January. The heavy pitch soon cut up and a typical cup game ensued with the breakthrough coming just after half an hour. Albert Harry delivered a cross from the right that was never more than a couple of feet off the ground. Several players went for it, but it was Billy Morgan, diving low among boots and studs, who got to it and glided a perfect header past the Spurs goalkeeper for an inspirational goal.

Ten minutes after the break it was all over, Billy finally netting from close range after shots from Tom Hoddinott and Bill Hand were blocked. In all conscience, Billy was to do little more for the Palace in his career with us, but he had done enough in the match against Tottenham to earn a niche in any Palace chronicle. It also earned him possibly the most curious nickname ever accorded to a Palace footballer – 'The Spurs Undertaker'. You don't need to be a parson to appreciate that one!

MORRISON, Clinton
Forward 1998-2002

Appearances: 189
Goals: 72
Born: 14 May 1979, Tooting
Subsequent League clubs: Birmingham City 2002
International honours: 21 full caps for Eire

Clinton Morrison was Palace's lively striker who marked his debut by scoring the only goal of our Premiership match against Sheffield Wednesday in May 1998 after joining the action as a late substitute. Brimming with confidence in his own ability, Clinton proved a regular goalscorer for Palace in Division One. While still a teenager he notched 12 League goals in the demanding 1998/99 season and established himself as an immediate choice, playing more games in the League and in total than anyone else except his friend Hayden Mullins.

In 1999/2000 Clinton was again the club's top scorer – despite a protracted lay-off necessitated by a dislocated shoulder. In 2000/01 he once more headed our list of strikers, though curiously he didn't score at Selhurst Park after mid-January. However, many Eagles fans will recall with delight several of his League Cup goals against Premier League opposition. He was on target in the 3-0 demolition of Leicester at Filbert Street, then struck a glorious winner to beat Sunderland at Selhurst Park just before Christmas. His rising drive into the top corner of the Holmesdale Road goal put the first leg of the semi-final beyond the reach of even mighty Liverpool and crowned Palace's best performance of the entire season.

It was exploits like these which brought about Clinton's call-up for Eire six months later and no Palace fan was surprised when he marked his international debut with a goal in August 2001.

Clinton Morrison.

He passed his 50th Palace strike quicker than Ian Wright was able to do, netted a tally of 24 goals in 2001/02 but then moved to promoted Birmingham in the summer of 2002.

MULLIGAN, Paddy
Defender 1972-75

Appearances: 66
Goals: 2
Born: 17 March 1945, Dublin
Previous clubs: Chelsea 1969
Subsequent League clubs: West Bromwich Albion 1975
International honours: 51 full caps for Eire

Paddy Mulligan was a proven full-back who joined the Palace with Charlie Cooke from Chelsea and Ian Philip from Dundee in September 1972 as Bert Head attempted another escape from the clutches of relegation, and it was perhaps crucial to the outcome that injuries prevented Paddy from playing a full part.

Paddy was certainly a quality defender, but Palace fans of the early 1970s will always remember him best for the two goals he scored – both splendidly executed efforts, in the same game – for his victims were no less than Manchester United whom Palace routed 5-0!

However, and to the surprise of many Palace fans, after Malcolm Allison had taken over at Selhurst Park, Paddy was seldom a first choice, so that we had the bizarre experience of seeing him called up regularly to play for Eire while spending long periods in the Palace reserve side!

MULLINS, Hayden
Midfield/Defender 1998-2003

Appearances: 257
Goals: 20
Born: 27 March 1979, Reading
Subsequent League clubs: West Ham
United 2003

Although Hayden Mullins was only nine-teen years old when he made his senior Palace debut in August 1998, he immedi-ately established himself as a permanent fixture in Palace sides and remained so until he moved to West Ham in the autumn of 2003. Nevertheless, few would argue that Hayden's best season with the Eagles was actually his first one. After all, so well did he perform in 1998/99 that he was the club's Player of the Year and earned England Under-21 recognition.

Hayden Mullins.

Hayden is extremely versatile – he can perform admirably, stylishly and effec-tively anywhere in the defence (including as a sweeper) and midfield. He exudes class of the highest order, though his nickname 'Cas' (for Casual) belies his one potential flaw.

Equally Hayden can score wonderful goals, with perhaps his best for Palace a scorching volley at Walsall in mid-April 2000. He captained the Eagles for most of his career with us, joined the ranks of the elite men who have gained the Player of the Year award more than once when he won it again in 2003, and, on his day, was certainly one of the most complete footballers ever to have starred for Crystal Palace.

MURPHY, Jerry
Midfield 1976-85

Appearances: 269
Goals: 25
Born: 23 September 1959, Stepney
Subsequent League clubs: Chelsea 1985
International honours: 3 full caps for Eire

Jerry Murphy was an outstandingly tal-ented young footballer who was part of the acclaimed Palace junior side which won the FA Youth Cup in 1977 and 1978 then, demonstrating a silken left foot, he became a vital member of our team which won the Second Division Championship in 1979 and went on, ini-tially at least, to take the top flight by storm.

Jerry had vision, culture and refine-ment. He possessed a temperament which sometimes made him appear aloof from the proceedings around him, but some of his goals were absolute gems.

Jerry earned 3 full international caps for Eire (qualifying on his father's nationality) but once Palace began to lose their way, his laconic, if delicate and sometimes moody style became, occasionally at least, something of a luxury which our struggling side could scarcely afford. That said, Jerry's final season with the Eagles was the first of Steve Coppell's management career and no one doubted Jerry's commitment to the cause then, so that Palace fans everywhere were disappointed when, having become a free agent in the summer of 1985, he chose to move across town to play for Chelsea.

MUSCAT, Kevin
Defender 1996-97

Appearances: 61
Goals: 3
Born: 7 August 1973, Crawley, Surrey
Previous clubs: Sunshine 1989, Heidelberg 1991, South Melbourne 1992
Subsequent League clubs: Wolverhampton Wanderers 1997, Millwall 2003
International honours: 40 full caps for Australia

Kevin was a fierce-tackling Australian international full-back who loved nothing better than to push forward and overlap his winger to add weight to an attack. He could play on either side of the defence and proved a most shrewd late-summer 1996 signing for the Palace by manager Dave Bassett.

Kevin was a feature of our side which finished his first (indeed, only) full season at Selhurst Park in sixth place, and appeared in the play-offs at Wolves and at Wembley when Palace beat Sheffield United to gain promotion. But Wolves were sufficiently impressed with Kevin's assertive style that they paid Palace £200,000 for him early in 1997/98.

NASH, Carlo
Goalkeeper 1996-97

Appearances: 25
Born: 13 September 1973, Bolton
Previous clubs: Clitheroe Town
Subsequent League clubs: Stockport County 1998, Manchester City 2001, Middlesbrough 2003

Carlo was the tall, blond adonis in the Palace goal for the climax of our promotion season of 1996/97, although he had made his Eagles' debut in September in Palace's storming 6-1 win at Reading upon our final visit to Elm Park.

Although Carlo lacked Football League experience, he was hugely impressive in the upper reaches of Division One for the Eagles. His initial, three-match tenure saw Palace undefeated with a goal aggregate of 14-4 while the last third of the term saw Palace power to the play-off places with some towering performances among which our 3-0 victory at Wolves in mid-February (with Carlo's League experience now stretching to all of six games!) was perhaps the most glorious. In the play-offs themselves, Carlo was assured, safe and thoroughly reliable even when Palace were under intense pressure at Wolves in the semi-final second leg.

Carlo spent 1997/98 in Palace's reserve side, then moved back to his native North-West but he did so with the warmest good wishes of all Palace fans.

NDAH, George
Forward/Midfield 1992-97

Appearances: 100
Goals: 10
Born: 23 December 1974, Camberwell
Subsequent League clubs: Bournemouth
  (loan) 1995, Gillingham (loan) 1997,
  Swindon Town 1997, Wolverhampton
  Wanderers 1999

Gorge Ndah looked to be something of a prodigy out on the left wing of the Palace juniors side which reached the final of the 1991/92 FA Youth Cup and his earliest senior appearances confirmed that he had sufficient potential to make a major contribution.

Tall, lithe and pacy, possessing a fantastic body-swerve, George was quiet to the point of diffidence off the field, but he showed tremendous confidence and maturity in Palace's League Cup side in the midwinter of 1992/93, scoring an opportunist first goal to help the Eagles dismiss Chelsea on a rain-soaked evening at Selhurst Park to reach the last four in the competition for the first time. Regrettably, George's progress was then arrested by a couple of debilitating injuries but, following a successful loan spell at Bournemouth, he returned and approached his best form again.

George's value to the Palace in 1995/96 was typified by two important goals scored in consecutive games in mid-March, to set us on our way to 'doubles' over visiting Tranmere, and at Grimsby, which asserted our credibility for the top places and then by his late brace, which emphasised Palace's first victory at Millwall's New Den as our run-in gathered momentum, then George played in all three play-off fixtures in which the

A youthful George Ndah receives the 1993 Palace Young Player of the Year award.

Eagles were engaged. However, 1996/97 saw George rather more of a peripheral figure and he featured increasingly as a substitute for us as his Selhurst Park career wound towards a disappointing end.

NEBBELING, Gavin
Defender 1981-89

Appearances: 173
Goals: 8
Born: 13 May 1963, Johannesburg, South
  Africa
Subsequent League clubs: Fulham 1989

Gavin Nebbeling was a tall, upright South African central defender who played for the Palace throughout the 1980s, but his career was continually dogged by injury and this inevitably rather limited his value to the club, although his League appearances exceeded 150 by the time he moved on to Fulham in the summer of 1989.

Quiet, steady and composed, Gavin was an ideal partner for Jim Cannon at the heart of the Palace defence and if the early 1980s were a time when our back four was often under a lot of pressure, Gavin played his part in Palace's revival at the end of the decade, although in spite of skippering our successful 1988/89 promotion side for a few matches in mid-season, he incurred yet another injury and was prevented from playing in all but the final three games.

NEEDHAM, Archie
Midfielder/Defender 1905-09

Appearances: 122*
Goals: 26*
Born: unknown
Previous clubs: Sheffield United
Subsequent League clubs: Glossop 1909
This includes appearances and goals in the Southern League Second Division 1905/06

Archie Needham was a talented and extremely versatile footballer who came to the Palace from Sheffield United when our club was formed in 1905.

To begin with, Archie featured at inside forward and was easily the leading scorer in our first season with 20 goals in the Southern League Second Division, and as such he was a primary reason for Palace's elevation to the First Division for 1906/07. Midway through that term Archie was deployed at right-back in the Palace line-ups, although he had a few

outings on the right wing and he played throughout our fabulous progress to the FA Cup quarter-finals. Then, in the spring of 1908, Archie became our regular, goalscoring left-winger, while in 1908/09 he divided his appearances between outside left and left-back!

The moment for which Archie will always be remembered by Palace fans was when he scored our fourth and conclusive goal after a marvellous solo run from the centre circle to defeat the FA Cup holders, Wolves, in a thrilling replay up at the old Crystal Palace in January 1909.

NEWMAN, Ricky
Midfield 1993-95

Appearances: 62
Goals: 3
Born: 5 August 1970, Guildford, Surrey
Previous clubs: Maidstone United (loan) 1992
Subsequent League clubs: Millwall 1995, Reading 2000

Ricky had been on the fringes of Palace's first team for some eighteen months but made huge progress when he was drafted into the Eagles' Premier League side in the autumn of 1994, providing dramatic evidence of this when he scored the best goal of the night, his first for our club and arguably our most spectacular of the entire season, with a crashing drive of stunning accuracy and prodigious power to complete Palace's fine victory at Coventry (4-1) in early November. He followed this with a similar effort to set us on the way to another success over Ipswich the following Saturday, and in both matches was clearly the most influential midfielder on the park, thoroughly deserving his Man of the Match awards.

Ricky was a sublime passer of the ball, even if his rather angular style masked that fact from less-discerning observers, and a feature of his game became the long, raking ball from deep in the Palace half, out to John Salako on the left flank, which would instantaneously turn the play to Palace's advantage.

NICHOLAS, Peter
Midfield 1977-81, 1983-85

Appearances: 199
Goals: 16
Born: 10 November 1959, Newport, Gwent
Subsequent League clubs: Arsenal 1981, Luton Town 1985, Aberdeen 1987, Chelsea 1988, Watford 1991
International honours: 73 full caps for Wales.

Peter Nicholas was a magnificent, driving, defensive midfield player, whose whole-hearted commitment to the club endeared him to every Palace fan. He was in the Palace junior side which won and then retained the FA Youth Cup in 1977 and 1978 and he became a regular member of our Second Division Championship side of 1978/79, as well as of the team which did so well in the early part of the 1979/80 campaign in the top flight.

Arsenal were pleased to pay a bargain fee for Peter in March 1981 but he came back to Selhurst Park in October 1983 when his tenacious and skilful experience was a key reason for Palace's Second Division survival in a most difficult season. Palace secured Peter's full registration for

1984/85 but, to the regret of all Palace folk, he signed for First Division Luton in mid-winter.

Peter was seldom a goalscorer for the Palace, although he never had a blank season. He netted three times – still as a teenager, remember – during the 1978/79 promotion campaign, usefully augmenting a modest aggregate tally, and it was Peter who most memorably beat Manchester United at Selhurst Park in November 1980. After his return to the Palace he took responsibility for our penalties. Best remembered of these was the first one he converted for us in February 1984 to defeat Middlesbrough here at Selhurst Park when we were playing with just nine men on a gluepot of a pitch.

Peter won 14 full caps for Wales while registered with Crystal Palace and has always been held in great affection by our fans as well, of course, as huge respect.

NOAKES, Alf
Full-back 1955-62

Appearances: 209
Goals: 14
Born: 14 August 1933, Stratford
Previous clubs: West Ham United 1950, Sittingbourne
Subsequent League clubs: Portsmouth 1962

Alf Noakes was a tough little full-back who served the Palace loyally and well for more than six seasons in the mid- to late 1950s and then in the promotion side of 1960/61. He could play on either flank of our defence, and indeed, on occasions early in his career in positions further forward, but it was at left-back

Peter Nicholas.

that he settled in to give of his best to our club.

Thus, it was at number three that Alf made forty appearances in Palace's first promotion side for forty years to help us climb out of the Fourth Division, and with his cup tie appearances he is part of the group of only fifty or so men to have played over 200 games for the Palace.

O'DOHERTY, Ken
Defender 1985-88

Appearances: 51
Goals: 1
Born: 30 March 1963, Dublin
Previous clubs: University College, Dublin
Subsequent League clubs: Huddersfield Town 1988, Exeter City (loan) 1991

Tall academic central defender or full-back Ken O'Doherty was signed by Steve Coppell during the first season of the latter's managerial tenure at the Palace, as part of a policy which proved highly successful at that stage, of securing talent from clubs in the lower divisions or outside the Football League altogether.

During the period that Ken was with the Eagles he had several useful spells in our defence, although he was never really able to make any position his own. Our fans respected him because he was so obviously committed to our cause and our best memory of him is his single goal for Palace, which could not have been scored in more distinguished surroundings. Palace were at Old Trafford in a League Cup third-round tie in October 1987, but were not performing at all well. We were two goals adrift as the interval approached and it appeared possible at least that we would go down to an embarrassing defeat. But Ken rifled home a spectacular strike from a Neil Redfearn corner and, in the second half, a revitalised Palace most certainly extended United and could even have embarrassed them.

O'REILLY, Gary
Defender 1987-90

Appearances: 85
Goals: 4
Born: 21 March 1961, Isleworth, Middlesex
Previous clubs: Tottenham Hotspur 1979, Brighton & Hove Albion 1984
Subsequent League clubs: Birmingham City (loan) 1991, Brighton & Hove Albion 1991

Gary O'Reilly was a dark-haired, eloquent but injury-prone central defender who joined the Palace midway through the 1986/87 season, although it was two years before he made more than a transient contribution.

However, Gary then became a key figure in Palace's assault on the promotion race from the old Second Division: he helped to form a determined and resolute partnership with Jeff Hopkins at the heart of our defence in the second half of the season, as Palace inexorably climbed the table to become the best team in the division. But then an injury deprived us of his services for the last four matches of the normal programme and he also missed the first three play-off games.

He was recalled by Steve Coppell for the vital, climactic showdown against Blackburn Rovers at Selhurst Park in the second leg of the play-off final, when it was absolutely essential that Palace prevented Rovers from adding to the lead they had gained at Ewood Park. Steve's judgement proved flawless; Gary played impeccably in probably his best-ever game for the Eagles and Palace triumphed 3-0 to win promotion back to the top flight.

Gary made another indelible, unforgettable, contribution to the Palace cause as a member of the squad that took us to the FA Cup final at Wembley in 1990 for the first time. He lined up against Liverpool in the semi-final at Villa Park, where his close-range drive put us ahead 2-1, rocked Liverpool and set us on the way to victory, and then he netted the opening goal of the final after little more than a quarter of an hour, his header from a Phil Barber free-kick looping off a Manchester United defender, over the goalkeeper and into the net for Palace's first-ever goal in an FA Cup final and our first at the national stadium.

ORR, Bobby
Full-back 1926-28

Appearances: 71
Goals: 2
Born: Hardgate, Dumbartonshire
Previous clubs: Third Lanark, Morton

Intelligent and experienced full-back Bobby Orr was probably manager Alec Maley's best signing for Crystal Palace upon taking charge of the club in 1925 and beginning a policy of introducing Scotsmen at Selhurst Park.

Tall (for those days), strong and possessing a powerful dead-ball shot, Bobby was installed at left-back after his summer 1926 signing and played 38 Third Division (South) matches for us that season to help Palace finish sixth – one of

them was at centre forward, when his goal defeated Norwich at their Nest! In 1927/28 he began at right-back but switched to number three in mid-January after a change of manager and completed 32 League appearances as Palace finished fifth in the table, but he was not retained at the end of the term and retired from the game.

OSBORN, Simon
Midfield 1991-94

Appearances: 72
Goals: 5
Born: 19 January 1972, Croydon
Subsequent League clubs: Reading 1994, Queens Park Rangers 1995, Wolverhampton Wanderers 1995, Tranmere Rovers 2001, Port Vale 2001, Gillingham 2001, Walsall 2003

Simon was a tenacious and attractive midfielder with a prodigious work rate, who came to the fore at Selhurst Park during Palace's top-flight tenure under

Simon Osborn.

Steve Coppell – indeed his League debut was during Palace's splendid 1-0 victory over Tottenham here in April 1991. A product of the club's youth scheme, he was dubbed one of 'The Bisto Kids' after some fine midfield displays with Simon Rodger.

Popular among Eagles supporters because of his high level of commitment, Simon also won our sympathy because his career with us was dogged by one unfortunate injury after another, and no one who was present on the opening day of the 1993/94 season will ever forget the sickening dismay and disappointment we all experienced when Simon was once more forced to leave the fray with another bad injury to his shoulder, early in those proceedings against Tranmere Rovers.

Ted Owens.

OWENS, Ted
Full-back 1934-39

Appearances: 172
Goals: 1
Born: 1913, Trimdon Grange, County Durham
Previous clubs: Stockport County, Preston North End

Ted Owens was one of the stalwarts of Crystal Palace FC during the inter-war period, when his resolute performances at right-back during the latter half of the 1930s made him a firm favourite at Selhurst Park.

Ted signed for the Palace in the summer of 1934, had a magnificent first season and was only prevented from playing every game by an injury sustained at Torquay on Christmas Day. He continued as Palace's first choice at number two

until the Second World War brought a halt to fully competitive soccer – and, the record books show, well beyond it. Ted will always be remembered at the Palace for his full-back partnership with Fred Dawes for three and a half years before the war when the pair played 106 matches together in League and cup games including most of those of the Third Division (South) in 1938/39 when Palace made their best attempt to lift themselves into the higher sections of the League between 1931 and 1964, and, in a thoroughly exciting season, were only denied by Newport County.

PARDEW, Alan
Midfield 1987-91

Appearances: 168
Goals: 12

Born: 18 July 1961, Wimbledon
Previous clubs: Yeovil Town
Subsequent League clubs: Charlton
   Athletic 1991, Barnet 1995, Tottenham
   Hotspur 1995
Managerial appointments: Reading 1998,
   West Ham United 2003

Versatile midfielder Alan Pardew was another of manager Steve Coppell's terrific signings from the ranks of non-league soccer. He made such tremendous progress with the Palace that he missed only one match of the extended 1988/89 promotion season, for which his drive, energy and cultured right foot proved invaluable components, then just two games the following season upon the Eagles' return to the top division.

During that 1989/90 season, Alan was Palace's joint-third-top scorer with 6 priceless goals, while it was he who notched Palace's extra-time winner against Liverpool in the FA Cup semi-final to secure the club's first-ever appearance in an FA Cup final while earning himself everlasting fame and glory among Palace supporters, along with the nickname 'Super Al' by which he will always be remembered at Selhurst Park.

Another supremely important and morale-raising strike by Alan Pardew was the one which secured victory at big-spending Tottenham in March of the same year, some five weeks before the semi-final. This one demonstrated both vision and technical skill when he spotted Spurs 'keeper Erik Thorstvedt off his line as Tottenham sought to defend a long Andy Thorn free-kick, and, from just inside the penalty area, Alan headed a poor clearance back over him and into the untenanted net to secure three price-less top-flight points to help ensure Palace's ultimate survival.

PARKIN, Brian
Goalkeeper 1988-89

Appearances: 25
Born: 12 October 1965, Birkenhead
Previous clubs: Oldham Athletic 1983,
   Crewe Alexandra 1984
Subsequent League clubs: Bristol Rovers
   1989

Brian was a tall, lean, quietly spoken goalkeeper who played a useful deputy's role to Perry Suckling in the 1988/89 promotion season, making nineteen consecutive appearances for us after Perry was injured in only the second game of the term.

Brian Parkin.

Reliable and spurning the spectacular, Brian was the ideal foil to the glamorous Suckling, and he played a single top-flight game for us before travelling in the reverse direction when Palace secured Nigel Martyn from Bristol Rovers.

PARRY, Oswald
Full-back 1931-36

Appearances: 150
Born: 16 August 1908, Dowlais, Nr Merthyr Tydfil
Previous clubs: Wimbledon
Subsequent League clubs: Ipswich Town 1936

Oswald Parry was a strong, tall, fair Welshman who seemed to have a lock of hair perpetually curling across his broad forehead and joined the Palace in the summer of 1931. He came with something of a reputation as a centre half but his five-year Palace career was spent largely at full-back.

Parry made his Palace debut in our fourth match of 1931/32 when he helped us to secure a superb 3-0 victory at Brighton and he became a regular member of the side for that season. He began at left-back, got switched to centre half but by the end of the campaign was firmly established at number two.

Oswald's best season with the Palace was probably 1933/34 when he topped our list of appearances with 39 games, although perhaps his finest display for the club was in that season's second-round FA Cup tie at Stockport when the Palace came from being in arrears to win 2-1. After this he was a little unlucky with injuries and left us at the end of 1935/36 having served us honourably and well.

He joined Ipswich Town, for whom he made over 150 appearances, helped them to gain League status and reappeared at Selhurst Park with them in 1938/39, then again after the war.

PAYNE, David
Midfield 1965-73

Appearances: 326
Goals: 12
Born: 25 April 1947, Croydon
Subsequent League clubs: Orient 1973, Millwall 1978

David Payne was a Dick Graham protégé. He made his senior, then Football League debuts as a seventeen-year-old in quick succession in 1964 and he became a regular member of Palace's Second Division side during 1965/66. Over three seasons he rarely missed a match, although a mid-term injury at Millwall restricted his appearances in the club's 1968/69 promotion team to a mere 30. However, David was fit for the final, crucial, eight games of that season, and was immediately restored to the side which clawed its way remorselessly to the runners-up position in which David's tireless, ceaseless energetic displays along with his tough tackling and midfield vision in tandem with Steve Kember were all vital components.

David was not a big man but, like several Palace midfielders and defenders of that time, he excelled under intense and almost continuous pressure in the top flight. As circumstances demanded, David would play almost anywhere – he actually wore eight different numbered shirts for Palace in our four First Division seasons 1969-73 – and rarely, if ever, even in such illustrious company, was he out-shone.

Thus, with his unflagging work rate, intelligent and selfless running and accurate distribution proving him to be a high-calibre footballer, it was no surprise to Palace fans when Sir Alf Ramsey included David as a substitute for the England Under-23 side against Wales at Swansea in November 1967 – but we were always disappointed that no further or higher honours were accorded to him.

David eventually left Selhurst Park for Orient in August 1973, joining several other former Palace stalwarts at Brisbane Road, but his departure was greatly regretted by Palace fans of the period who had always held this likeable young man in immense respect and affection. Delightfully though, in recent years David has reappeared in public at the Palace where his efforts in forming a former Palace players' association have been greatly appreciated by his contemporary colleagues and Eagles fans of all generations.

PEMBERTON, John
Full-back 1987-90

Appearances: 105
Goals: 2
Born: 18 November 1964, Oldham
Previous clubs: Rochdale 1984, Crewe
    Alexandra 1985
Subsequent League clubs: Sheffield
    United 1990, Leeds United 1993, Crewe
    Alexandra 1997

John Pemberton was Palace's genial and gutsy full-back throughout the Club's promotion drive to the First Division in 1988/89 and then in the Eagles' progress

John Pemberton.

to the FA Cup final and subsequent replay of 1990. Indeed, John's surging, sixty-yard run immediately after half-time in the semi-final against Liverpool at Villa Park, which took him past several bemused defenders before he delivered the cross from which Mark Bright put Palace on terms and on the way to a stunning victory, will always remain in the memories of those who saw it.

'Pembo' also impressed enormously in the two FA Cup final matches against Manchester United's sophisticated and costly imports. Inevitably therefore, the club and our supporters were disappointed when John chose to leave Selhurst Park in July 1990 to join Sheffield United.

John was capable of filling several defensive roles where his versatility and sheer athleticism proved invaluable to our club on many occasions, although it was as a right or left-back that he usually featured – although always wearing the number two shirt – and he was without question among manager Steve Coppell's most astute and most effective signings.

PENNYFATHER, Glenn
Midfield 1987-89

Appearances: 41
Goals: 1
Born: 11 February 1963, Billericay, Essex
Previous clubs: Southend United 1980
Subsequent League clubs: Ipswich Town 1989, Bristol City 1993

Glenn was a diminutive but forceful midfielder, recruited by Palace to replace Andy Gray when the latter left us for Aston Villa in November 1987. Dapper and intelligent, Glenn was an ideal replacement for Gray because he possessed considerable experience and was eager to prove himself with a club that had real prospects of reaching the First Division. However, injuries prevented him from making quite the impact he (and we) would have wished at Selhurst Park, so that he rather remained on the fringe of matters when Palace were challenging towards the climax of 1988/89, although he did appear as substitute in the two away legs of the play-offs.

PERRIN, Steve
Forward 1976-78

Appearances: 58
Goals: 14
Born: 13 February 1952, Paddington
Previous clubs: Wycombe Wanderers

Subsequent League clubs: Plymouth Argyle 1978, Portsmouth 1979, Northampton Town 1981

Steve Perrin was a qualified schoolmaster who took the eye of Malcolm Allison while playing for Wycombe Wanderers in their pre-League days, and then proved Big Mal's judgement to be sound by netting on his debut to help beat previously undefeated Mansfield Town in Palace's promotion season of 1976/77.

Tall, strong and intelligent, either with the ball or off it, Steve made an invaluable input to the Eagles' success that term. He provided useful physical presence in a division where defenders were usually pretty combative, and contributed effective goalscoring support to Dave Swindlehurst and Rachid Harkouk, netting 9 times in the League campaign, including the only strike of the game at Oxford and Palace's second in the victory at Wrexham in our final, crucial game of the season.

PETCHEY, George
Wing half 1960-65

Appearances: 153
Goals: 12
Born: 24 June 1931, Whitechapel
Previous clubs: West Ham United 1948, Queens Park Rangers 1953
Managerial appointments: Leyton Orient 1971, Millwall 1978

George Petchey was a driving, inspirational wing half who joined Fourth Division Crystal Palace in the summer of 1960 to play under manager Arthur Rowe.

He proved a terrific signing, for he helped the Palace to gain promotion from the league basement in his first season at Selhurst Park, during which he was ever-present, then continued as a first-team regular to become one of only two men who starred in both the 1961 and 1964 promotion sides. In fact, George's strong, assertive displays were a feature of Palace's progress back to the Second Division but his playing career was brought to a premature end by a troublesome eye complaint and his final match for the club was the delayed sixth-round FA Cup tie against mighty Leeds in March 1965.

After manager Dick Graham left Palace in January the following year, George assisted Arthur Rowe and then Bert Head in the role of team coach, helping to mould the side that earned top-flight status in 1969. In acknowledgement of his efforts for our club, both as a player and in support of the managers, Palace awarded George a testimonial in November 1967 when an International XI came to provide the opposition and Palace won 6-3 to the delight of over 10,000 fans who had come along to show their appreciation of this greatly admired player.

PIERCE, Barry
Forward 1955-59

Appearances: 93
Goals: 27
Born: 13 August 1934, Liverpool
Subsequent League clubs: Millwall 1959, York City 1961, Exeter City 1962

Barry was a bright, sharp, energetic and intuitive goal-getting forward who joined Crystal Palace at the instigation of manager Cyril Spiers, and was ultimately deployed in an intriguing dual-centre forward role with Mike Deakin that was many years ahead of its time.

It was certainly seen at its most effective in what was probably Barry's best game in the Palace colours, against Brentford in a second-round FA Cup replay at Selhurst Park in December 1956, which had a big crowd in ferment as Palace won 3-2 after extra time. Barry netted a hat-trick to see us safely through – it was his only one for the club and Palace's first in the FA Cup for more than a quarter of a century!

It consisted of two headers (the first and last goals) and a hook shot that The Bees' goalkeeper did well to get a hand to but could only watch as Barry followed up and tapped the ball over the line.

Barry fell out of favour after his mentor left the Palace and twelve months later Barry moved on too but Palace fans of the mid-1950s have never forgotten his eager, enthusiastic style which served our club well.

PITCHER, Darren
Midfield 1994-96

Appearances: 83
Goals: 3
Born: 12 October 1969, London
Previous clubs: Charlton Athletic 1990

This fiercely competitive, uncompromising midfielder was recruited for the Palace by Alan Smith in the summer of 1994 for Premiership duty. In the second half of that season Darren was able to establish himself in our side and he became a regular member of the team that played its way to two cup semi-finals, even if the season was to end in the disappointment of relegation.

Darren Pitcher.

Darren is not renowned as a goalscorer, but his superb, spectacular, dipping half volley from some thirty yards at Wolves in March 1995 was as fine a goal as any scored anywhere that season and helped to bring about Palace's comprehensive Molineux victory and our third appearance in an FA Cup semi-final.

Darren's playing career came to an abrupt end when his cruciate ligaments were damaged in an away game at Huddersfield in August 1996 following which he was never able to play for our senior side again.

POPOVIC, Tony
Central defender 2001-

Appearances: 106
Goals: 7

Born: 7 April 1973, Australia
Previous clubs: Sydney United 1989, 1996, Wolverhampton Wanderers 1995, Sanfrecce 1997, Hiroshima 1999
International honours: 43 full caps for Australia

Tony Popovic is a tall, powerful, experienced central defender who has proved an invaluable presence at the heart of our backline, though injuries have sometimes prevented his availability and therefore reduced his value to the club. But Palace fans invariably respond to his commitment and professionalism and were delighted for him when he scored a glorious goal for his country to help Australia to defeat England at Upton Park in February 2003.

Tony captained the Eagles against Nottingham Forest (1-0) in December 2003 and nets an occasional goal for us too, but in mid-September 2001 he hit a brace in Palace's 5-0 demolition of visiting Grimsby Town in only his fourth game with the Palace.

POSSEE, Derek
Forward 1973-74

Appearances: 61
Goals: 16
Born: 14 February 1946, Southwark
Previous clubs: Tottenham Hotspur 1963, Millwall 1967
Subsequent League clubs: Orient 1974

Diminutive Derek Possee was manager Bert Head's last signing in the latter's unsuccessful quest to retain our hard-won (and even harder-retained!) top-flight status in 1972/73. He joined us for £115,000 from Millwall in January.

Tony Popovic.

A nimble, speedy winger, Derek responded positively to the challenge, even if the First Division of those days was rather beyond his capabilities, and no one laid any of the blame for our eventual relegation at his feet.

The following term, after another dreadful start to the season, was better for Derek. Either on the flank or some-times up the middle, he was one of new manager Malcolm Allison's first choices in our line-ups and finished as second-top scorer only to Don Rogers.

POWELL, Darren
Central defender 2002-

Appearances: 61
Goals: 3
Born: 10 March 1976, Hammersmith
Previous clubs: Brentford 1998

Former Brentford skipper and towering centre half Darren Powell joined the Eagles in a £400,000 deal in the summer of 2002 and played so well for us in his first season in Division One that his raw, uncompromising style put him among the front-runners for the club's Player of the Year award.

Darren perhaps surprised even himself when he poked home Palace's first goal of the season as we came from behind to win at Preston back in August 2002, though he scored in more traditional manner for a centre half when he headed the opening goal in Palace's 2-1 extra-time victory over Plymouth in an early-term League Cup encounter. But the goal for which every Palace fan will forever remember him was Darren's crashing, close-range header at Sunderland in the 2004 play-off semi-final which took that titanic contest into extra time and enabled Palace to power on to the final, to victory, promotion and glory!

QUEEN, Gerry
Forward 1969-72

Appearances: 131
Goals: 30
Born: 15 January 1945, Glasgow
Previous clubs: St Mirren 1961, Kilmarnock 1966
Subsequent league clubs: Orient 1972

Gerry Queen was a brave, exciting, intelligent goalscorer who came to the Palace in July 1969 as manager Bert Head sought additional and experienced striking power for the First Division battles which lay ahead. Gerry was probably Mr Head's most effective signing for Palace over the four top-flight years 1969-73.

Gerry made an immediate impact at the Palace by scoring on his debut for the club in the 2-2 draw with Manchester United on the opening day of 1969/70; he went on to become our top scorer that season. On his day, Gerry was as good a centre forward as any in the land and he would almost certainly have won a string of Scottish international caps had he been with a more fashionable club. He had skill, grace and power and was strong in the air, yet he was also willing to battle against the odds for his club.

The value of Gerry Queen to Crystal Palace can perhaps be measured by the fact that he was easily Palace's top scorer in the First Division between 1969-73 with 24 top-flight goals while his 18 strikes in the first two seasons represented a quarter of the club's total tally in that period. And some of Gerry's goals were crucial, point-saving or point-winning ones, so that they were real morale-boosters for his manager, his colleagues and, of course, the fans.

RAINFORD, Johnny
Forward 1949-53

Appearances: 67
Goals: 10
Born: 11 December 1930, Camden Town
Subsequent League clubs: Cardiff City 1953, Brentford 1953

Johnny Rainford was an inside forward, tall, strongly built and fashionably glossy-haired, who made his debut for the Palace as an eighteen-year-old in Palace's last game of 1948/49, under Jack Butler's management. He next appeared in the penultimate fixture of 1950/51, but then at last began to blossom, briefly, for us under Laurie Scott from the autumn of 1951.

Johnny was a rare product of the early post-war juniors to make an impact in our senior side and he was certainly highly thought of around the game at that time. Thus after a couple of seasons' involvement with us, mainly as an industrious foil to Cam Burgess and Bob Thomas, Johnny signed for First Division Cardiff City in a major transfer deal.

Johnny's best contribution to Crystal Palace was on 1 November 1952 when both he and Cam Burgess netted hat-tricks to secure a stunning, unforgettable 6-3 win for us at Swindon Town.

REDFEARN, Neil
Midfield 1987-88

Appearances: 65
Goals: 10
Born: 20 June 1965, Dewsbury, West
    Yorkshire
Previous clubs: Bolton Wanderers 1982,
    Lincoln City 1984, Doncaster Rovers 1986
Subsequent League clubs: Watford 1988,
    Oldham Athletic 1989, Barnsley 1991,
    Charlton Athletic 1998, Bradford City
    1999, Wigan Athletic 2000, Halifax Town
    2001, Boston United 2002, Rochdale
    2004

Neil was a highly regarded midfield player whom Steve Coppell secured for the Eagles in the face of stiff opposition from other possibly more distinguished clubs than Second Division Palace, but Steve's persistence was amply rewarded because Neil played more games than anyone else in 1987/88 and scored eight goals for us as Palace came agonisingly close to a play-off place.

Accordingly, Palace fans were sorry when Neil requested a transfer early in 1988/89 after he had been substituted on a number of occasions, and he moved to Watford in mid-November for a fee of £150,000.

REECE, Tommy
Wing Half 1938-48

Appearances: 81
Goals: 5
Born: 17 May 1919, Wolverhampton
Previous clubs: Wolverhampton Wanderers

Hardworking Tommy Reece was a tenacious, constructive wing half or occasional inside forward who joined Palace in September 1938 and made his debut for us as a teenager at Watford (1-4) on the last day of that year in place of injured Nick Collins, but his later appearances that season were much more happy and positive ones as Palace sought to catch Newport County at the top of the Third Division (South). The quest was ultimately unsuccessful but ended in a thrilling finish.

Inevitably, the war years spoiled Tommy's football career, although he played a few games for us during the hostilities, but he became a regular member of the Palace's post-war League side for two seasons and accrued 66 League appearances during this period.

RHODES, Ernie
Full-back 1913-23

Appearances: 142
Goals: 1
Born: South Bank, Teesside
Previous clubs: Gravesend

Although Ernie Rhodes was with Crystal Palace before the First World War it was after that dreadful event that he made his major contribution to our cause.

Ernie appeared in all but the initial match of 1919/20, making the left-back position his own, and played in every game of the 1920/21 promotion season. His six FA Cup appearances included the fabulous 6-0 rout of Everton at Goodison Park and another triumph over a top-flight outfit, Manchester City, at The Nest in January 1921, which reignited Palace's tradition of upsetting the big outfits in cup ties which continues to this day.

An impressive feature of the early post-war Palace side was the triumvirate of Alderson in goal with Little and Ernie at full-back, and those who watched them play together for the Palace will tell you of an understanding between them that bordered on the uncanny.

Soon after the start of Palace's Second Division career in 1921/22, it was calculated that Ernie and his colleagues had played precisely 100 consecutive matches together (including cup-ties and friendlies.) A presentation was made by the club to each one of them to mark a record that is without parallel at Crystal Palace to this day and which is certainly unusual in football's annals overall.

RIIHILAHTI, Aki
Midfield 2001-

Appearances: 126
Goals: 8
Born: 9 September 1976, Helsinki
Previous clubs: Valerenga (Norway) 1999
International honours: 51 full caps for Finland

Aki Riihilahti signed for Palace just a day or two before he scored for Finland against England in a World Cup qualifier at Anfield in March 2001, so Eagles' fans knew that we were obtaining a most useful performer.

Aki quickly established a bond between himself and Palace followers with his wholehearted, energetic, long-striding style in our midfield and he netted an invaluable goal for Palace in our crucial penultimate game of 2000/01 at Portsmouth, while of his strikes for the Eagles, probably his spectacular twenty-five yard drive against Wimbledon in October 2001 is the most memorable.

Unfortunately, Aki was troubled by injuries in 2002/03 when Palace certainly missed the experience and ability of this flamboyant personality, but he was a dominant, invaluable member of Iain Dowie's resurgent squad which gained promotion back to the Premiership by winning the final at the Millennium Stadium in Cardiff, where Aki was regarded by a significant number of fans and pundits to have been Palace's most influential player.

ROBERTS, Andy
Midfield 1995-98

Appearances: 130
Goals: 3

Aki Riihilahti heads for goal at Bradford City on 24 January 2004.

Born: 20 March 1974, Dartford, Kent
Previous clubs: Millwall 1992
Subsequent League clubs: Wimbledon
   1998, Norwich City (loan) 2002, Millwall
   2002

Palace paid a club record fee of some £2 million when Andy Roberts joined the Eagles from Millwall in the summer of 1995. Blessed with a fine physique and immensely powerful, Andy took a little while to settle into his defensive duties with us but it was when we deployed a sweeper system with him at the heart of the backline that Palace fans saw him

blossom to his best form. Andy's role was further refined by new boss Dave Bassett to a position further upfield in an attempt to exert more sustained pressure upon our opponents. The ploy proved so highly effective that Palace claimed third place in the table and reached the Wembley play-off final. Andy himself received the Player of the Year award and scored his first goal for the club at Wembley, though the Eagles lost 1-2 to Leicester in extra time.

But 1996/97 saw Palace gain promotion via the play-offs with increasingly authoritative performances. Andy was in excellent form throughout; he continually impressed, missed just one match in the entire campaign and was considered by some pundits to be heading towards full international honours having already captained the England Under-21 side.

However the following term was bizarre. Andy was a Premier League regular for the Eagles but, as hints mounted of an imminent and perhaps not very satisfactory boardroom takeover and our FA Cup prospects were dashed by Arsenal in a fifth-round replay at Selhurst Park, so Andy decided to join Wimbledon in another major transfer deal in order to ensure himself of continuing his top-flight career.

ROBERTS, 'Dickie'
Forward 1905-08

Appearances: 99*
Goals: 25*
Previous clubs: West Bromwich Albion, Newcastle United, Middlesbrough
Including appearances and goals in Southern League Second Division 1905/06

'Dickie' Roberts was an experienced campaigner who had over 100 Football League appearances to his name before he joined Crystal Palace for our inaugural season. He was a powerful, raiding, goalscoring left-winger who was also something of a character. So, too was his wife, who was Dickie's greatest fan and was to be heard whenever her husband was bearing down on an opponent's goal to shout 'shoot, Dickie, shoot' to the delight and amusement of all our other supporters!

Dickie was Palace's first-choice outside left for two-and-a-half seasons, but

his career was brought to an end by injuries incurred in an FA Cup tie down at Plymouth; then, finally, in a fierce London Challenge Cup tie against our local rivals Croydon Common in September 1908.

ROBSON, Albert
Forward 1936-48

Appearances: 88
Goals: 23
Born: 14 November 1916, Crook, County Durham

Albert Robson was a versatile footballer, well able to play in a variety of forward positions but at his most successful as a striker. His close control was impeccable and his delicate skills could bemuse the very best of centre halves.

Albert joined the Palace groundstaff in 1935 and signed professional forms the following year. His best League season was 1938/39: he came into the Palace side on 17 December when we played host to Mansfield Town and he hammered a second-half hat trick in just fifteen minutes to help demolish the Stags 6-2. In the second half of that 1938/39 season Robson was our best goalscorer as Palace chased along at the heels of Newport County in the quest for the single promotion place in the Third Division (South), and he finished the season's scoring charts here as second only to Albert Dawes with 11 goals from his 20 games.

Albert came to the peak of his career in the early wartime seasons and there can be little doubt that, had the normal peacetime arrangements still pertained, he would have been greatly sought after at this time by the topmost clubs.

Bert Robson.

Robson continued his excellent scoring form in the first three wartime seasons. He hit the target regularly, including three occasions where he scored four goals in a match, including what was unquestionably his best single performance, against no less a centre half than the redoubtable Stan Cullis at Fulham in March 1941 in the London War Cup.

That Palace's success in 1940/41 was largely due to Albert's goalscoring is demonstrated in that he scored a phenomenal 36 goals from his 40 competitive appearances and it is worthy of mention that these goals came from matches which included opponents of the highest calibre.

Regrettably, though, for Crystal Palace and our supporters, Albert was past his best by the time Football League soccer recommenced after the war. He was a member of our forward line in the first two seasons, playing in four positions over 48 Third Division (South) matches but, by his own later admission, his lightning pace had gone and his cutting edge had been blunted by the passage of time, so that it remains the fact that only those relatively few Palace fans who could follow the club in the early 1940s ever really saw Albert Robson at his majestic best.

RODGER, Simon
Midfield 1991-2002

Appearances: 326
Goals: 12
Born: 3 October 1971, Shoreham, Sussex
Previous clubs: Bognor Regis Town
Subsequent League Clubs: Brighton & Hove Albion 2002

Simon Rodger was a fair-haired, industrious and tenacious midfielder whose career was hit by recurring injury but who was always a great favourite with the fans who quickly nicknamed him 'Jolly'.

Quiet and reserved off the pitch, Simon's eager, pacy and hard-working contribution to the Palace cause was initially linked with that of his fellow 'Bisto-Kid' Simon Osborn, but while 1993/94 provided nothing but frustration for his colleague, for Simon Rodger it developed into probably the best one of his career. He played a major role in Palace's Division One Championship, missing just four matches in that splendid campaign.

After a year's lay-off due to a cruel back injury Simon played a full part in guaranteeing his and Palace's presence in two consecutive Wembley play-off finals in 1996 and 1997. Indeed, some of the fans would contend that his 39 Premiership games in the Eagles' traumatic 1997/98 season actually represent the best indicator of his loyalty and commitment to the club.

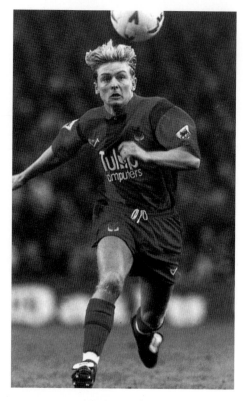

Simon Rodger.

Former Palace manager Steve Coppell was a huge admirer of Simon. Steve not only oversaw Simon's early development with the Eagles but later appointed him as skipper. It was largely with Simon as the Palace captain that the side put on such performances of dogged resistance throughout the dreadful, worsening adversity of 1999/2000, for the entirety of which the club was in the legal state of administration, but which we finished comfortably in mid-table despite losing player after player to rival clubs at cut-price fees just to enable our club to stay afloat.

By the time Simon left Selhurst Park, rejoining Steve Coppell at Brighton, he had moved up our all-time appearances chart to sixth place and is certain to retain a position in the affections of all Palace fans for many years to come.

ROGERS, Don
Forward 1972-74

Appearances: 83
Goals: 30
Born: 25 October 1945, Paulton, Wiltshire
Previous clubs: Swindon Town 1962
Subsequent League clubs: Queens Park
    Rangers 1974, Swindon Town 1975

At his peak Don Rogers was unquestionably a goalscoring winger of supreme ability and had he been at a more fashionable outfit than Swindon Town he would surely have won a string of England international caps. His former Robins' boss, Bert Head, paid a Palace club-record fee of some £150,000 to bring Don to Selhurst Park in the late autumn of 1972, when Palace badly needed a goalscorer to remedy an awful start to the season, so Rogers immediately obliged with the only goal of his debut match to defeat visiting Everton and produced the marvellous return of 13 strikes from 26 First Division outings in the remainder of the term.

Don's talent was a cultivated and lethal left foot, phenomenal acceleration even on a slippery pitch, and top-class control. His shooting was accurate and sometimes explosive. He revitalised Palace for a while in that 1972/73 season, terrorising several distinguished defenders (none more so than those of Manchester United whom Palace routed 5-0 in December with Don twice on target), but without another established goalscorer in the side and Rogers' reputation quickly making him a heavily

marked man, Palace failed to survive and were relegated.

Regrettably, though, Don was just past his best by the time he joined us and new manager Malcolm Allison tended to play him in far less assertive roles, so that at times he became almost anonymous in the Second Division of 1973/74. But, that said, Palace fans of the early 1970s remember Don Rogers as a wonderfully gifted forward who provided them with some marvellous memories, especially at Selhurst Park.

ROOKE, Ronnie
Forward 1933-36, 1949-50

Appearances: 64
Goals: 32
Born: 7 December 1911, Guildford, Surrey
Subsequent League clubs: Fulham 1936,
    Arsenal 1946

Ronnie Rooke has already received an appraisal in the earlier chapter about Crystal Palace managers, but, because of his post-war goalscoring efforts, he demands further inclusion in this section too.

Appointed as Palace's player-manager in the summer of 1949, Ronnie netted 21 League goals to set up a post-war scoring record that stood for ten years and was an improvement upon all but one of Albert Dawes' efforts and those of all others back to the early 1930s in the days of Peter Simpson. It was prodigious by Palace standards and remains among our club's best post-war tallies by an individual marksman to this day.

Ronnie's goals were sufficient to lift Palace from re-election applicants to seventh place in the Third Division (South), but with little support, that was to be the limit of his and our achievements and of course what followed was nothing short of ruinous both on and off the field.

See also Ronnie Rooke's entry in the Managers section (p.32).

ROUSE, Vic
Goalkeeper 1956-1962

Appearances: 257
Born: 16 March 1936, Swansea
Previous clubs: Millwall 1953
Subsequent League clubs: Northampton Town 1963, Oxford United 1963, Leyton Orient 1965
International honours: 1 full cap for Wales

It is a clear indication of the quality of Vic Rouse's goalkeeping that he succeeded the great Roy Bailey between the Palace posts, and then went on to set a club record of 238 Football League goalkeeping appearances, a tally which has only been exceeded by the invincible John Jackson and England international Nigel Martyn. He also gained full international recognition on himself – he was actually the first international player to be chosen from the ranks of the old Fourth Division, but Palace fans should be aware that his selection for Wales against Northern Ireland in Belfast in April 1959 was no freak choice because Vic had impressed many with his splendid performances and was in a run of 143 consecutive League games with just a single absence.

A major feature of Vic's game was the accurate and powerful throw he developed which could reach the halfway line, by which means he frequently set up a fast counter-attack via one of his wingers.

Understandably Vic was a great favourite with the Palace fans of his day and it has been a great pleasure to many that he has returned to Selhurst Park several times recently to attend the reunions for former players.

ROUTLEDGE, Wayne
Forward 2001-

Appearances: 83
Goals: 10
Born: 7 January 1985, Eltham

At just 5ft 6ins, Wayne Routledge is tiny for a footballer, but he made his senior Palace debut as a sixteen-year-old and his frame is packed with a winger's talent. His career is still in its infancy at the time this book is being compiled, but Palace fans already know that Wayne is a major star in the making.

Wayne's pace, balance and control frequently bemuse experienced First Division defenders and as well as making openings for others, Wayne has also demonstrated an ability to score explosive, spectacular goals himself. His first for the club – netted inside the first minute of his first appearance in a League starting line-up in mid-September 2002 – was a powerful fifteen-yard drive across the face of the Whitehorse Lane goal and into the far top corner of the netting. It rocked Wolves, put Palace on route for an impressive 4-2 win and revealed a dimension to his talent which Palace fans hope will continue to delight them for many years to come.

But, perhaps Wayne's most spectacular strike, which included a delightful pirouette at pace, was Palace's last in the

Wayne Routledge.

6-3 rout of visiting Stoke on St Valentine's Day in 2004 and brought connoisseurs and hardened ex-professionals to their feet in admiration and delight.

SALAKO, John
Forward 1986-95

Appearances: 273
Goals: 34
Born: 11 February 1969, Ibadan, Nigeria
Subsequent League clubs: Coventry City 1995, Bolton Wanderers 1998, Fulham 1998, Charlton Athletic 1999, Reading 2001

International honours: 5 full caps for England

John Salako came up through Palace's junior sides as a pacy winger who could also score goals. However, after the Eagles' return to the top flight in 1989 he also revealed himself as capable of fulfilling other roles and performed splendidly as a mobile left wing-back in the latter stages of the 1989/90 season, notably in the FA Cup semi-final against Liverpool and in the Wembley finals – and as Palace's stand-in goalkeeper against Wimbledon on a torrid night in August 1991.

John Salako, though in an unfamiliar role!

both cruciate ligaments behind his left knee.

The rebuilding technique was a new one and John was only able to play properly again after an absence of nearly two years, but his first full appearance against Stoke City on a waterlogged pitch at Selhurst became a personal triumph for him and his hat-trick brought the Palace crowd to a fever pitch of delight and excitement.

SANSOM, Kenny
Full-back 1975-80

Appearances: 197
Goals: 4
Born: 26 September 1958, Camberwell
Subsequent League clubs: Arsenal 1980, Newcastle United 1988, Queens Park Rangers 1989, Coventry City 1991, Everton 1993, Brentford 1993, Watford 1994
International honours: 86 full caps for England

Curiously, of John's first 100 senior appearances almost half were as a substitute and although he demonstrated great potential he never really established himself as a regular member of the Palace side until the autumn of 1990. But the exciting promise he now revealed was rewarded with a place on the England tour of Australasia in June 1991 where he again showed his capacity to excite the crowd and bemuse the opposition.

John's progress was then cruelly cut short in October 1991 when he fell badly after putting in a header in a night game against Leeds and was stretchered to the Selhurst Park dressing room, subsequently to learn that he had severed

Kenny Sansom was probably the most polished and certainly the best full-back to have played for Crystal Palace – his 86 full England caps simply put that point beyond the realms of any debate.

He made his Palace debut as a sixteen-year-old: within two years he had become the skipper of the England Youth team, led the Palace juniors to an FA Youth Cup triumph in 1977 and been an ever-present member of the senior Palace side that won promotion from the Third Division. Kenny missed just one match in three seasons from 1976-79.

Kenny simply excelled in the higher divisions. He helped the Palace gain the Championship of the old Second

Kenny Sansom.

Division with the club's best-ever defensive record and to reach the top of the entire League in September 1979. He was also the only player to make full appearances in both Palace's promotion seasons of the late 1970s. But by now Kenny was a prized Palace asset and was eagerly sought by the biggest clubs in the land. Fresh-faced and perky, Kenny was ideally built for a full-back: he was strong and sturdy and with a low centre of gravity and possessed remarkable stamina and resilience. His tackling was precise and he was seldom beaten in any tussle for the ball, his positional sense was mature, and although the game of the 1970s and 1980s required less overlapping from defenders than it does today, Kenny had blistering pace.

Ultimately Kenny won 9 full England caps while at the Palace. He was our Player of the Year for two seasons, 1977 and 1979, and is the youngest Palace player ever to have won that award. It took a record fee to take him to Arsenal in an exchange deal in the close season of 1980 when both he and Clive Allen were valued at £1 million. Palace fans

213

were desperately sorry to see Kenny leave, recognising that such ability as his was irreplaceable at any price.

SAUNDERS, Jack
Defender 1954-56

Appearances: 62
Born: 24 August 1924, Middlesbrough
Previous clubs: Darlington 1946, Chelsea 1948
Subsequent League clubs: Chester City 1957

Jack Saunders was an experienced wing half who originally came to Crystal Palace in the summer of 1954 when the club was managed by Laurie Scott, but, following one of the most disastrous debuts in Palace's entire history when he came into our team for a 1-7 defeat at Watford in early September, which ultimately led to Mr Scott's dismissal, Jack became a dependable defender and club captain under the newly appointed Cyril Spiers.

Playing now invariably at centre half, Jack was a rarity in Mr Spiers' Palace sides which were largely composed of much younger and less experienced men, and inevitably perhaps, the sides of which he was skipper, struggled badly, finishing twentieth, then twenty-third in the Third Division (South). But Jack was a dignified footballer: the situation he found himself in was one that could bring him no glory, but he acquitted himself honourably, giving what he could to the club and the team, and discerning Palace fans recognised his ability and quality during those difficult times.

SCOTT, Jimmy
Forward 1970-71

Appearances: 53
Goals: 6
Born: 21 August 1940, Falkirk
Previous clubs: Hibernian 1958, Newcastle United 1967
Subsequent League clubs: Falkirk 1971
International honours: 1 full cap for Scotland

Jimmy Scott was a tall, clever, ball-playing Scottish international winger secured by manager Bert Head in an attempt to increase the supply of crosses and other opportunities for our strikers, in order to revive a flagging Palace goal tally early in 1970, as the last critical quarter of our first, and decidedly arduous, season in the top flight approached.

Neat, composed, intelligent in his passing and running, Jimmy was a typical thoroughbred footballer from north of the border, but his talents were perhaps too subtle for a Palace side that spent most of the time he was with us struggling in or near the relegation zone. However, for those fans who enjoy the sight of sophisticated performers in the Palace colours, Jimmy Scott's spell at Selhurst Park certainly offered refinement and artistry.

SEWELL, John
Full-back 1963-71

Appearances: 258
Goals: 9
Born: 7 July 1938, Brockley
Previous clubs: Charlton Athletic 1955
Subsequent League clubs: Orient 1971

John Sewell has a unique place in any Palace gallery because he was the popular and talented skipper of the team which took the club to the top flight for the first time in its history, back in 1969.

He joined the Palace in October 1963, scored his first goal for the club the following month, made eighteen consecutive League appearances, some of them as captain, but then was injured at Millwall in February 1964 leaving Palace to claw their way into the Second Division without his assistance. The climax of his entire playing career was undoubtedly 1968/69, but he maintained his high level of performance by helping to keep the Palace in the top flight for the two seasons in which he remained at the club.

John's efforts in assisting Palace to retain their hard-won place in the First Division were magnificent. Often playing with or against men who were ten years his junior, this immaculate full-back always looked fresh and resilient and his presence was a boost to the confidence of every Palace side. He made 70 top-flight appearances for the club, and, at a time when the defence was usually under considerable pressure, most of the matches were tense affairs and the demands upon the skipper were, consequently, much greater. His 70 games were only bettered over that period by the evergreen John McCormick, goalkeeper John Jackson and the much-younger Mel Blyth, which speaks volumes for the fitness, charisma and sheer determination of the man.

After Palace's 1970/71 season had ended, the club marked his retirement with a testimonial match against FC Bruges from the Belgian League. John had played 258 senior games for the club overall and nearly 9,000 Palace fans came

along to show their appreciation – some of them were also at Selhurst Park in March 2000 to see John Sewell and his colleagues from the 1969 promotion team when they returned to the Palace as guests for the club reunion.

SHAW, Richard
Defender 1987-96

Appearances: 268
Goals: 3
Born: 11 September 1968, Park Royal
Subsequent League clubs: Coventry City
 1995.

Richard Shaw was a thoroughly versatile player who was one of the first products of the resourceful youth development programme at Crystal Palace during the 1980s. He was Palace's Young Player of the Year for 1986 and became a useful back-up member of the Eagles' promotion squad of 1988/89. He continued to progress during Palace's first season back in the top flight and played a full part in the tremendous FA Cup semi-final victory over Liverpool and the two Wembley FA Cup finals against Manchester United.

Perhaps 1990/91 was Richard's best season. He missed only two matches in the entire campaign and became one of the youngest players at Palace to complete their first century of appearances when he had an outstanding game in the 4-1 Wembley success over Everton that brought the Zenith Data Systems Cup to Selhurst Park.

Richard could fill a central defensive role with distinction yet was equally effective at full-back but it was in the former position that he earned Palace's Player of the Year award for 1994/95.

SHIPPERLEY, Neil
Centre forward 1996-98, 2003-

Appearances: 119
Goals: 32
Born: 30 October 1974, Chatham Kent
Previous clubs: Chelsea 1992, Watford
   (loan) 1994, Southampton 1995
Subsequent League clubs: Nottingham
   Forest 1998, Barnsley 1999, Wimbledon
   2001

Neil Shipperley came to Crystal Palace in the autumn of 1996 at a time when the Eagles were needing extra focus and goalscoring craft as we attempted to put a play-off final defeat behind us and re-apply ourselves for another assault on the top places in Division One.

Neil certainly delivered! He netted twice in only his second outing for Palace, at Bradford City at the end of October to help Palace to another impressive away win, and finished his season with a firm, downward header in our home leg of the play-off against Wolves which set up an astonishing finale at Selhurst Park and the gripping Molineux return. Neil's 1996/97 tally was 13 Division One goals from 35 outings and was crucial to our cause.

Inevitably, Neil was not so prolific in the Premiership in 1997/98, but he had a wonderful run of five goals in five games in late October, November and early December, with probably his most important, as well as the most memorable, the audacious, side-footed, near-post flick that beat Spurs at White Hart Lane on Sky TV.

Former Palace boss Dave Bassett took Neil to Nottingham Forest early in 1998/99 to continue his top-flight career, and whenever Palace fans watched Neil in

Neil Shipperley.

opposition line-ups they recognised that this was a player whose services we should have retained at all costs, so that there was universal approval when Palace re-signed him in the close season of 2003. He became Palace captain after the departure of Hayden Mullins, led our attack with verve plus intelligence laced with the craft that only experience can provide, was an ideal foil for the prolific Andy Johnson and netted several useful strikes himself including three in four games in late January/early February to enhance our upwards surge under Iain Dowie. But, for all Neil's goals in our colours, the one for which he will always be remembered is the four-yard tap-in which won the 2004 play-off final at Cardiff's Millennium Stadium. Knowledgeable fans reckon that this was a fitting reward for a loyal, hardworking player.

SILKMAN, Barry
Forward 1976-78

Appearances: 54
Goals: 7
Born: 29 June 1952, Stepney
Previous clubs: Hereford United 1974
Subsequent League clubs: Plymouth
   Argyle 1978, Luton Town 1979,
   Manchester City 1979, Brentford 1980,
   Queens Park Rangers 1980, Orient 1981,
   Southend United 1985, Crewe Alexandra
   1986

Barry Silkman was a versatile front man who could play on the flank or as a striker, by whom Malcolm Allison was completely enthralled. Big Mal subsequently signed Barry for at least two other clubs while his opinion and influence ensured that Terry Venables brought Barry to the Palace shortly after Malcolm had left us.

Fashionably hirsute, with a mop of cultivated curly hair, Barry's potential was indeed tremendous. In only his fourth game for the Eagles he brought the crowd to its feet with a stunning, match-winning strike, scored from way out on the wing. It flew into the net just under the crossbar to provide Palace with a 2-1 victory over Bury. It was one of those goals that if you saw, you've never forgotten!

Thus, Barry was a useful member of our 1976/77 promotion side and he helped us to settle in the Second Division

the following term, but it appeared to many Palace folk that this level was rather beyond his regular capabilities, even if he did later play in the top flight with Manchester City under the management of his great mentor Malcolm Allison.

SIMPSON, Peter
Centre forward 1929-35

Appearances: 195
Goals: 165
Born: 13 November 1905, Leith
Previous clubs: St Bernards 1925,
   Kettering Town 1927
Subsequent League clubs: West Ham
   United 1935, Reading 1937

Peter Simpson must rank among the best strikers in the history of Crystal Palace. He signed for the Palace in the summer of 1929 having played and impressed against us in a first-round FA Cup tie for Kettering the previous season. He made his Palace debut in mid-September and notched a hat-trick to despatch visiting Norwich.

Peter became famed as a goalscorer for Palace. He was that – but much more too. His distributive skills were prodigious: he fed Albert Harry and George Clarke on Palace's flanks with rare ability and they returned the compliment with a stream of centres and crosses. Simpson read and paced the game brilliantly, his high-scoring feats telling of a man who could always find the split second of time, the extra half-yard of space or ounce of energy to beat an opponent. Thus, he set a new goalscoring record of 36 League goals in his first season, topped the Third Division (South) chart and was only bettered by two men in the entire Football

Peter Simpson.

League. In 1930/31 he was absolutely magnificent. He rattled up 46 League goals (an all-time record for the club which would seem to be invincible) including six in succession in the 7-2 defeat against Exeter in October. He went on from there to top Palace's list of scorers for each of his first five seasons, netting a total of 153 League goals from 180 appearances and establishing a tally which no one at our club has ever approached, either before or since.

The Peter Simpson era began to fade after a knee injury in 1934/35 caused him to lose some of his sparkle. He was transferred to West Ham the following summer, then moved to Reading for whom he played against the Palace in January 1938, scoring twice in the second half to send us home defeated by a margin of 2-3.

Palace staged a Benefit for Peter on Wednesday 31 October 1934, against the popular local amateurs The Corinthians, but the weather was so awful that only a few more than 1,000 fans turned up to see Peter well-policed by Bernard Joy. Palace won 3-2.

After his retirement, Peter took over a newsagent and tobacconist's shop in West Croydon. He died in March 1974 at the age of sixty-nine, but here at Crystal Palace FC at least, the memory of Peter Simpson remains immortal.

SMILLIE, Andy
Forward 1961-63

Appearances: 59
Goals: 26
Born: 15 March 1941, Ilford, Essex
Previous clubs: West Ham United 1958
Subsequent League clubs: Scunthorpe
United 1963, Southend United 1964,
Gillingham 1968

Andy Smillie was a neat, compact, nimble and cultured footballer who had been brought up at West Ham. He was therefore precisely the sort of inside forward or midfielder to whom manager Arthur Rowe would be attracted and the great man brought Andy to Selhurst Park to augment and refine our Fourth Division promotion side as it aimed to further improve Palace's status in 1961.

Andy – and Mr Rowe's Palace – were initially hugely successful. Andy was our top scorer in 1961/62, blended perfectly with Johnny Byrne, Ronnie Allen and company and helped to form one of Palace's most effective and attractive sides. In October 1962, Andy had an astonishing run of six goals in just four games, but by this time Palace were beginning to lose their way as the manager's health gave out, and new boss Dick Graham had no place for this refined and clever player, so that our fans were sorry to learn that he had left us at the end of the 1962/63 season.

SMILLIE, Neil
Forward 1976-82

Appearances: 97
Goals: 8
Born: 19 July 1958, Barnsley

Subsequent League clubs: Brentford
(loan) 1977, Brighton & Hove Albion
1982, Watford 1985, Reading 1986,
Brentford 1988, Gillingham 1993

Neil Smillie, intelligent, flaxen and curly-haired, and wide-midfielder or winger, was an early product of Palace's youth scheme which was so successful under John Cartwright in the mid- to late 1970s.

After being on the fringe of Palace's Second Division Championship side of 1978/79, Neil came to maturity just as the Eagles were beginning to find the First Division rather too rigorous, both for management and our teams, but he missed only one match in the demanding 1981/82 season when Palace had a tough time indeed in fending off the threat of further relegation.

Neil Smillie.

Neil was a wholehearted player and Palace fans were pleased for him when he appeared in the 1983 FA Cup final with Brighton, then helped Reading to win the 1988 Full Members' Cup.

SMITH, Jamie
Full-back 1997-2004

Appearances: 176
Goals: 2
Born: 17 September 1974, Birmingham
Previous clubs: Wolverhampton Wanderers 1993, Fulham (loan) 1999
Previous clubs: Bristol City 2004

Jamie Smith.

Jamie Smith is a popular, steadfast full-back who plays with commitment, flair and evident relish. He has been extremely unfortunate with injuries in more recent seasons, but those many fans who have witnessed his full Palace career recognise just what a splendid signing he has proved for the Eagles.

Actually though, Jamie revealed two wonderful (if unexpected) and hugely appealing additional talents during 2000/01 when he was called upon to support our attack rather more emphatically. Now he played more as a wing-back, and in doing so he showed a dribbling skill on the flank which would be the envy of any aspiring winger, along with the ability to cross the ball as accurately as anyone.

SMITH, Keith
Forward 1964-66

Appearances: 56
Goals: 15
Born: 15 September 1940, Woodville, Derbyshire

Previous clubs: West Bromwich Albion 1958, Peterborough United 1963
Subsequent League clubs: Darlington 1966, Orient 1967, Notts County 1967

Keith Smith has an honoured place in virtually every football statistician's charts because of his astonishing six-second goal for the Palace at Derby County on 12 December 1964 which ended in a 3-3 draw, but Palace fans will be eager to know how it came about. Peter Burridge kicked off, Cliff Holton slipped the ball to Brian Whitehouse and his long ball skidded through all the Rams' defenders to Keith, who stabbed it past the exposed Reg Matthews in Derby's goal.

Keith had only joined the Palace the previous month, having been signed by Dick Graham with whom he had served at West Bromwich Albion. He was a tough, mean goalscorer, spare at only 5ft

10ins, who was emphatically at his best for us in the four to five months immediately after coming to Selhurst Park, for he was a key member and second-top scorer of the team which took promoted Palace to a most praiseworthy seventh place in the Second Division in our first season in the higher divisions for forty years and to a place in the FA Cup quarter-finals.

SMITH, Ted
Centre forward 1911-21

Appearances: 192
Goals: 124 goals
Born: 1884, Birmingham
Previous clubs: Hull City 1910

Ted Smith was a marvellous goalscorer for Crystal Palace on both sides of the First World War. He joined the Palace from Hull City in December 1911 and immediately scored a hat-trick on his debut at West Ham at the end of the month, then repeated the feat when Bristol Rovers came to the Palace a week later. Ted simply went on from there: he topped the club's list of scorers for the remaining four pre-war seasons, and again in 1919/20 so that during that period his record was the equal of any in the game.

Ted was burly and strong, weighing in at 12 stone and standing 5ft 9ins tall. As a header of the ball he was phenomenal and it is amazing how many of his goals came from his head, while he also possessed an extremely powerful shot – and of course it should be remembered that in those days the leather ball collected any moisture on the pitch and could end up weighing several pounds!

Ted's efforts for the club were recognised by everyone at Crystal Palace and he was awarded a Benefit in 1920/21. It was the Third Division match against Gillingham in March: some 12,000 Palace fans were at the game, the band played 'For he's a Jolly Good Fellow' and Ted kicked off, even though a persistent injury had prevented him from playing since New Year's Day.

After the First World War Ted became the captain of the Palace side: only an exceptional centre forward could do that. He skippered the Palace through the first half of the Third Division championship season of 1920/21, then again in the opening matches of 1921/22 in the Second Division. A 'jolly good fellow' indeed!

SOUTHGATE, Gareth
Midfield/Defender 1990-95

Appearances: 191
Goals: 22
Born: 3 September 1970, Watford
Subsequent League clubs: Aston Villa 1995, Middlesbrough 2001
International honours: 57 full caps for England

Gareth Southgate matured to stardom under the guidance of his mentor, Alan Smith, when the latter was in charge of Palace's youth, then reserve teams, and it was obvious from an early stage to judicious Palace fans that Gareth was a future skipper in the making. Sure enough, just after he had completed 100 senior appearances for the club, he captained our Division One side to victory for the first time at Barnsley in November 1993.

Gareth Southgate, seen here in typically imperious action (at Luton (1-0) in April 1994), was Palace's skipper in our last Championship season.

Versatile, and admired as well as respected by Palace fans, Gareth played at full-back, in central defence and in the middle or on the right of midfield, but wherever he performed he exuded confidence, authority and class, and in 1993/94 he began to score some valuable, often spectacular goals, to usefully augment Palace's charge to the top of Division One. His 9 league strikes actually made him the Eagles' second-top scorer behind Chris Armstrong.

Indeed, his final goal of 1993/94 turned the last away fixture at Middlesbrough in Palace's favour and thereby helped to assure the club of the Division One title, so that Gareth fully earned the honour of holding aloft the Championship trophy before the last match of the season a week later. Gareth also carries the distinction of being the youngest Palace skipper to lead the club to a promotion, let alone to a Championship.

With Palace back in the Premier League, Gareth became the only player to appear in every Premiership game – indeed, in every fixture of 1994/95 and came close to leading us in a Wembley final because Palace produced a sequence of fine cup performances and were the only side to appear in the last four of both the major competitions. Unfortunately, Palace were edged out in the semi-finals, and, when Palace were relegated and Alan Smith left Selhurst Park, most Eagles fans realised that Gareth too would soon be on his way. He did so, but will always hold an honoured place in the Palace annals and in the hearts of all Palace fans, some of whom consider that he may yet return to our headquarters in an even more significant capacity one day.

SPARROW, Brian
Defender 1984-87

Appearances: 73
Goals: 2
Born: 24 June 1962, Bethnal Green
Previous clubs: Arsenal 1979, Wimbledon (loan) 1983, Gillingham (loan) 1984

Brian Sparrow was a pacy, perky left-back who loved to drive forward in support of the attack and also possessed a most useful long throw-in. He was one of Steve Coppell's first signings after the latter's appointment as the Palace manager, and proved to be a useful and popular member of the side that had to fight off the threat of possible relegation in 1984/85.

Injuries prevented Brian from contributing greatly during the following two seasons, but he is remembered by fans of the mid-1980s as a wholehearted, enthusiastic player who always gave his best to the Eagles and we were delighted when he returned to the club as the highly successful youth-team coach for 1995/96.

SPOTTISWOOD, Bob
Half-back 1909-15

Appearances: 189
Goals: 2
Born: 1885, Carlisle
Previous clubs: Carlisle United 1904, Croydon Common 1908
Subsequent League clubs: Clapton Orient 1919, Queens Park Rangers 1920

Bob Spottiswood was a strong and pacy right half-back. He quickly became a huge favourite with Palace's pre-First World War fans after he joined us in July 1909 and his fiercely determined performances in our colours were only brought to an end by the war. His appearance record was exemplary but Bob came to his peak as the First World War approached. In 1912/13 Palace finished fifth in the Southern League and our defensive record was not bettered by anyone, while 1913/14 was quite outstanding as Palace came cruelly close to winning the championship, only being denied on goal average by Swindon Town. Then, in the traumatic 1914/15 season, Bob was an absolute mainstay, and, with Horace Colclough, became a real pillar for the club as it had to leave its Crystal Palace headquarters and players had to move away to join the forces.

Bob's qualities were recognised by the Southern League authorities who selected him for one of their Inter-League games during 1912/13 and was awarded a Benefit by the Palace in 1914/15 along with his half-back colleagues Jimmy Hughes and Harry Hanger, though, in the confusion surrounding those times, it is uncertain whether the match was actually staged.

STEBBING, Gary
Midfield 1983-88

Appearances: 118
Goals: 3
Born: 11 August 1965, Croydon
Subsequent League clubs: Maidstone United 1989

Gary Stebbing was a stylish former England Youth international and sometime captain who joined the Palace straight from school in 1983 and played in a variety of midfield and defensive positions for us over a five-year span. His style was neat and composed and was therefore appreciated by our discerning fans but some of our supporters found it difficult to accept this refined talent among the hustle and bustle of midtable Second Division in the mid-1980s.

Come what may though, Gary is assured of a permanent place in Palace records because he became only our third player ever to appear in all the different numbered outfield shirts when he wore the number three jersey at Barnsley on 23 August 1986.

STEPHENSON, Alan
Defender 1961-68

Appearances: 185
Goals: 13
Born: 26 September 1944, Cheshunt

Subsequent League clubs: West Ham United 1968, Portsmouth 1972

Alan Stephenson was a tall, stylish, slimly built but strong centre half who played for the Palace with grace and power in the tough footballing days of the mid-1960s. Alan was dominating in the air and a solid and reliable tackler, so he was a perfect defender for a team marshalled by manager Dick Graham. He made a major contribution to Palace's progress, became our captain and earned England Under-23 honours.

It was 1963/64 when Alan forced his way into Palace's Third Division promotion team, playing alongside Brian Wood in an early dual-central defender's role. From then on, Alan developed into a distinguished centre half in the Second Division; he defended capably, led his team with authority and also scored useful goals, usually from aerial set pieces.

Alan himself always believed that his best game of all for the Palace was the fifth-round FA Cup tie against Nottingham Forest in February 1965 when the team beat the top-flight sophisticates 3-1. But, inevitably, Alan wanted to play in the First Division himself – he joined West Ham in March 1968 for a club-record fee of around £80,000. However, most agreeably, Alan has returned to Selhurst Park several times in recent years for various former players' reunions.

STEWART, Paul
Midfield 1994

Appearances: 18
Goals: 3
Born: 7 October 1964, Manchester
Previous clubs: Blackpool 1981,

Manchester City 1987, Tottenham
Hotspur 1988, Liverpool 1992
Subsequent League clubs:
   Wolverhampton Wanderers (loan) 1994,
   Burnley (loan) 1995, Sunderland 1995
International honours: 3 full caps for
   England

Paul Stewart is the second player who appears in this directory who was not, at one time or another, a Palace player – he only ever appeared for us on loan from Liverpool! He was brought to sharpen Palace's push for a top two place in Division One at a time when our momentum was beginning to fade, but he impressed immediately when playing up front alongside Chris Armstrong, with a superb first touch, immaculate control, and considerable 'presence'. Paul was without question the catalyst that ensured that the Eagles surged back to the top flight as the Division One Champions of 1993/94 and thus was hugely popular as well as a key figure at Selhurst Park at that time.

SUCKLING, Perry
Goalkeeper 1988-91

Appearances: 71
Born: 12 October 1965, Leyton
Previous clubs: Coventry City 1982,
   Manchester City 1986
Subsequent League clubs: West Ham
   United (loan) 1989, Brentford (loan)
   1991, Watford 1992, Doncaster Rovers
   1994

England Youth and Under-21 international goalkeeper Perry Suckling was signed by Steve Coppell to replace George Wood midway through the

Perry Suckling.

1987/88 season as Palace sought to remain in contact with the promotion race at the head of the Second Division.

Perry had actually been at the Palace as a thirteen-year-old schoolboy some nine years earlier, but he was delighted to return to us and proved a fine acquisition. Tall, handsome, brave and brilliantly spectacular, Perry immediately became a huge favourite at Selhurst Park. He had an excellent game on his debut against Huddersfield Town, making some important saves to enable Palace to come from behind to win and the Eagles only missed out on a play-off place on the final Saturday of the season. However, in the second half of 1988/89 Palace produced a superb run after Perry returned to the side following a long lay-off and we became clearly the best side in the division. Having clinched a play-off place, Perry inevitably came under a lot of pressure in those agonisingly exciting, two-legged affairs, but he coped wonderfully well, exuding confidence and making impressive, memorable saves in each of them to help the Palace into the First Division.

It is a shame that some football folk remember Perry simply as the 'keeper who let in nine goals at Anfield in Palace's top-flight game against Liverpool in September 1989, but, while there is no denying that, it would be a travesty to allow it to do more than cast a slight shadow across the reality, which was of an exceptionally fine goalkeeper who also, it will be recalled, subsequently returned to Palace's top-flight side and captained it at that level.

At his best Perry was certainly among Palace's top five all-time custodians and there are many Eagles fans of the late 1980s around at Selhurst Park who still absolutely idolise him.

SUMMERSBY, Roy
Midfield 1958-63

Appearances: 190
Goals: 60
Born: 19 March 1935, Lambeth
Previous clubs: Millwall 1952
Subsequent League clubs: Portsmouth 1963

Roy was a tough, chunky inside forward who joined the Palace from neighbours Millwall when the club was struggling to make an impact upon the Fourth Division leadership in its initial season.

Fast and clever, Roy was a typical inside man of his day: strong, industrious, and an accurate passer of the ball – but he was better than many, certainly at the club's level at that time. He had a hugely successful career with the Palace, was the ideal foil to the emerging talent of Johnny Byrne, and helped to make the club a respected Third Division side. While Roy's goalscoring feats were eclipsed by those of Byrne, present-day fans should understand that there were occasions when quite the reverse was true! For example Roy hit a hat-trick to rout Mansfield 4-1 at Selhurst Park in October 1960 with Johnny quite unable to get on the scoresheet and, at the climax of the promotion season, with Byrne now heavily shackled by opposing defences, Roy netted five times in the last four matches!

But if it is records that matter, then Roy has two great claims. First, he is one of a select few Palace men to have made over 100 consecutive appearances for the club immediately following his debut, with his run of 123 only ever beaten here by Johnny McNichol with 153. Then, Roy's 25 League goals in 1960/61 put him as runner-up to Byrne in that promotion season, but he remained only behind Byrne's figure of 30 for the highest number of strikes in a post-war League season of up to 46 games until Ian Wright (1988/89) and Andy Johnson (2003/04) both netted 27 in later promotion seasons. Also, his 59 League goals are still within the club's top eight since the Second World War, although those with higher tallies all had longer Palace careers than he did, and/or were out-and-out strikers.

SWINDLEHURST, Dave
Forward 1973-80

Appearances: 276
Goals: 81
Born: 6 January 1956, Edgeware
Subsequent League clubs: Derby County 1980, West Ham United 1983, Sunderland 1985, Wimbledon 1988, Colchester United 1988

Dave Swindlehurst (second from the left) nets for Palace against Notts County as we closed in on the (old) Second Division title in 1978/79.

Dave Swindlehurst was Palace's big, strong goalscorer as the club forced its way back to the top-flight limelight from the obscurity of the Third Division between 1974 and 1979. Brave and accurate in the air, Dave consistently proved his ability to find the net at all levels for the Palace and was our leading goalscorer for four seasons in the mid- to late 1970s. As befits a top striker, many of Dave's goals were crucial, either at the immediate time or in an historical context.

Thus, if his 14 goals in the 1978/79 Championship season was his biggest contribution, it did represent well over a quarter of our total of 51 in that season and included his late, low volley to ensure our victory over Burnley on the night the title was clinched. Equally, his more modest 10 goals in the 1976/77 promotion season included the one which opened the scoring in the all-important final match against fellow contenders Wrexham, and Dave had struck the winner against the Welshmen at Selhurst Park eight days earlier, to provide vital goals at significant times that, ultimately, earned the points which put Palace in front of Wrexham in the final table and enabled us to take the third promotion place.

For a long while Dave was second only to Johnny Byrne among Palace's post-war goalscorers though, of course, all but a handful of Budgie's goals were scored in the lower divisions.

TAMBLING, Bobby
Forward 1970-73

Appearances: 80
Goals: 20
Born: 18 September 1941, Storrington, Sussex

Previous clubs: Chelsea 1958
International honours: 3 full caps for
England

Palace boss Bert Head imported the vastly experienced goalscorer Bobby Tambling from Chelsea on loan in the midwinter of Palace's first season in the top flight, 1969/70. Tambling's arrival certainly provided a lift in morale for our club at a demanding time, even if he could not score and Palace did not win during that three-match spell. But Bobby enjoyed his month at Selhurst Park and so was keen to move to Palace with Alan Birchenall the following summer at a joint fee of £140,000.

During the two seasons after his arrival Bobby played regularly for our First Division side, though he inevitably found it much more difficult to score for Palace than he had for Chelsea. In fact his most important strikes for us were made on opponents' grounds, so that he is best remembered for the spectacular twenty-

Bobby Tambling.

yarder which defeated Manchester United at Old Trafford in October 1970, the penalty which ensured our victory at Arsenal in a League Cup replay a month later, and the brace he netted in the Anglo-Italian Cup to enable Palace to beat mighty Inter Milan in the San Siro Stadium in June 1971 and secure as prestigious a victory as any we have witnessed.

TAYLOR, Colin
Forward 1968-69

Appearances: 40
Goals: 10
Born: 24 August 1940, Stourbridge,
Worcestershire
Previous clubs: Walsall 1958, Newcastle
United 1963, Walsall 1964
Subsequent League clubs: Walsall 1969

Colin Taylor was a powerful, raiding outside left who spent precisely one season as a Palace player after coming forcibly to the attentions of all Palace patrons in January 1968 when he struck a blistering free-kick into our net during a third-round FA Cup-tie at Third Division Walsall to secure a replay for the Saddlers which they won on our ground. So impressed was Bert Head by Colin's awesome shooting that he signed the pacy, stocky winger the following summer and Colin became a key member of the Palace side which won promotion to the top flight in 1968/69. He was aptly nicknamed 'Cannonball' and with Mark Lazarus on the opposite flank, he helped to form one of Palace's most effective forward lines in the post-war era.

Colin returned to Walsall immediately after Palace's success, but our first FA Cup

Colin Taylor.

tie as a First Division side brought him back to Selhurst Park with his colleagues. Thankfully, though, on this occasion, we were not treated to another of his shooting exhibitions and Palace were able to edge through to the next round despite Colin's best efforts!

TAYLOR, Kevin
Midfield 1985-87

Appearances: 99
Goals: 15
Born: 22 January 1961, Wakefield, Yorkshire
Previous clubs: Sheffield Wednesday 1978, Derby County 1984
Subsequent League clubs: Scunthorpe United 1987

Kevin Taylor was a tough, stocky, tenacious midfield ball-winner who was secured for the Palace by Steve Coppell at a critical time in the manager's first season in charge. Palace were struggling,

pretty badly too, and greatly in need of Kevin's experience and sheer dogged hard work in the engine room of our side.

Nicknamed 'Ticker' because of his non-stop running, Kevin proved a thoroughly worthwhile asset to the Palace and provided real value for money, not just in the immediately ensuing dogfight in which relegation was staved off successfully, with several impressive victories over leading clubs secured, but also during the following two seasons when the Eagles were able to make serious challenges at the other end of the table.

Naturally, as Palace's fortunes revived, Kevin became a highly popular fellow among Palace supporters, so that many were disappointed when he and his wife requested a move back north in the summer of 1987 and he joined Scunthorpe early in the new season.

TAYLOR, Peter
Forward 1973-76

Appearances: 142
Goals: 39
Born: 3 January 1953, Rochford, Essex
Previous clubs: Southend United 1971
Subsequent League clubs: Tottenham Hotspur 1976, Orient 1980, Oldham Athletic 1983, Exeter City 1983, Maidstone United 1990
International honours: 4 full caps for England
Managerial appointments: Southend United 1993, England Under-21s 1996, Gillingham 1999, Leicester City 2000, Brighton & Hove Albion 2001, Hull City 2002, England Under-21s 2004

Peter Taylor was a fast, stocky goalscoring winger who was brought to the Palace as Malcolm Allison's best signing for the Eagles, and Palace fans who saw him play for us carry permanent memories of him marauding down the right flank, then cutting in and delivering a rasping left-footed drive or tantalising cross. Usually wearing number eleven despite operating largely on the right, Peter was speedy, with neat control. His shooting was accurate and his use of dead-ball situations was intelligent and effective. While he was with the Palace Peter gained 4 England Under-23 caps and scored in every game. He also won 4 full England caps while he was with us and netted on his first two appearances for the national side.

Peter was Palace's on-field inspiration and came very much to the attention of the country's football followers during our fabulous run to the FA Cup semi-finals in 1976. At Chelsea in the fifth round, he scored two exquisite goals to win the match while his strikes in earlier rounds had helped Palace dismiss Millwall in a replay and Scarborough.

Peter was obviously destined for stardom on a bigger stage and he joined Tottenham in September 1976, but a measure of his popularity at the Palace may be gained from the splendid reception he was accorded by our fans when he returned to Selhurst Park a full seventeen years later as the manager of Southend, and on subsequent less public visits in more senior capacities.

TAYLOR, Tony
Midfield/Defender 1968-74

Appearances: 231
Goals: 11

Born: 6 September 1946, Glasgow
Previous clubs: Kilmarnock 1962, Celtic 1964, Morton 1967
Subsequent League clubs: Southend United 1974, Swindon Town 1976, Bristol Rovers 1977, Portsmouth 1978, Kilmarnock 1978, Albion Rovers 1979, Northampton Town 1979

Bert Head brought many fine footballers to the Palace from Scotland, but none was of more value to the club than Tony Taylor. His hard-working, selfless style rarely caught the attention of the media, but Palace patrons of the late 1960s and early 1970s thoroughly appreciated his worth.

After joining the club in the autumn of 1968, Tony played in every remaining match of that wonderfully successful season. Palace then owed much to Tony's midfield contribution in the First Division, but he also played in a variety of positions, from attacking winger on his debut, to left-back. In fact he became known as Tony 'play me anywhere as long as you play me' Taylor! It may be the longest sobriquet in Palace annals, but it perfectly sums up this splendid servant of the club!

Thus, it is no surprise that Tony put in more First Division appearances for Palace between 1969 and 1973 than anyone except John Jackson and Mel Blyth, but many of our fans thought that he was at his best at left-back. Certainly, Tony played extremely well there after Peter Wall was injured for most of 1972/73 and in the first half of 1973/74, and it was from that position that he captained the Palace side.

THOMAS, Bob
Forward 1952-55

Appearances: 102
Goals: 33
Born: 2 August 1919, Stepney
Previous clubs: Brentford, Plymouth Argyle
   1946, Fulham 1947

Bob was a clever, industrious inside or centre forward who joined the Palace in September 1952 for what was a substantial fee for those days of £3,000. He was certainly one of manager Laurie Scott's best signings and was an immediate choice for our team for over two seasons, coming out as Palace's top League goalscorer in 1953/54 with 20 strikes from his 45 appearances.

Bob was a fine dribbler and showed deft ball control. He had a distinctive hunch-shouldered gait and was a neat as well as a strong header of the ball, but he fell out of favour when Cyril Spiers arrived as manager and introduced a policy of replacing the more experienced men with younger players.

THOMAS, Geoff
Midfield 1987-93

Appearances: 249
Goals: 35
Born: 5 August 1964, Manchester
Previous clubs: Rochdale 1982, Crewe
   Alexandra 1984
Subsequent League clubs:
   Wolverhampton Wanderers 1993,
   Nottingham Forest 1997, Barnsley 1999,
   Notts County 2001, Crewe Alexandra
   2001
International honours: 9 full caps for
   England

Geoff Thomas was Palace's inspirational, attacking midfield supremo and occasional central defender who skippered the club through the most successful years it has so far experienced.

Fair-haired and with a distinctive, upright stance, Geoff's powerful running and cultured style soon made him a firm favourite with Palace fans who voted him Player of the Year in his first season, 1987/88. Injuries reduced his availability in 1988/89 but he captained the Eagles throughout the following term upon the club's return to the top flight, also scoring some crucial goals in the tremendous run to the FA Cup final, where his Wembley performances impressed many neutral observers, but his dream, and that of all our fans, of receiving the trophy almost certainly rested upon an appalling refereeing decision in the replay when he was fouled at least five yards inside the Manchester United penalty area, only for the referee to award a free-kick outside the area by some distance!

Geoff continued to progress in the First Division throughout 1990/91 when, in company with Andy Gray, Palace's midfield repeatedly outplayed high-ranking opponents and we secured some tremendous results on our way to a final placing of third. None were better than the Eagles' victory at Liverpool, coming from behind and the winner secured by a Geoff Thomas header in front of the disbelieving Kop. He also netted Palace's opening goal in our 4-1 extra-time victory over Everton to secure the 1991 Zenith Data Systems Cup at Wembley and was awarded his first full England international cap in Turkey in May 1991.

With all these achievements, it was almost inevitable that Geoff should gain

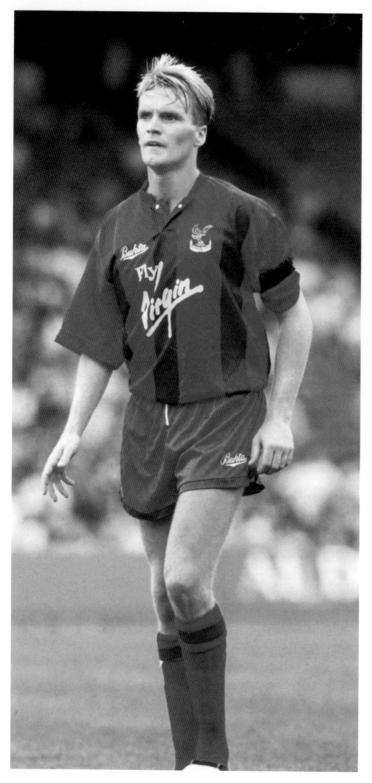

Geoff Thomas.

his second Player of the Year award while the fact that he earned it in Palace's best season ever is a clear demonstration of his immense value and contribution to Crystal Palace at that time.

THOMPSON, Garry
Forward 1990-91

Appearances: 22
Goals: 4
Born: 7 October 1959, Birmingham
Previous clubs: Coventry City 1977, West Bromwich Albion 1983, Sheffield Wednesday 1985, Aston Villa 1986, Watford 1988

Subsequent League clubs: Queens Park Rangers 1991, Cardiff City 1993, Northampton Town 1994, Bristol Rovers 1997

Garry was a strong, intelligent, and thoroughly experienced striker who joined the Palace on the transfer deadline day in the spring of 1990, to provide us with additional proven resources up front at a time when Ian Wright was out of action with a twice-broken leg.

Garry responded superbly, netting after only four minutes on his debut, to provide Palace with three invaluable top-flight points at the expense of Championship contenders and eventual

Garry Thompson.

runners-up Aston Villa, and then continued to render quality cover for our first-choice centre forwards in 1990/91 with a level of sophistication which delighted all Eagles fans.

THOMSON, Steven
Midfield 1995-2003

Appearances: 122
Goals: 4
Born: 23 January 1978, Glasgow
Subsequent League clubs: Peterborough
    United 2003

Scottish youth international defensive midfielder Steven Thomson was renowned at the Palace for his direct, no-nonsense style. Guaranteed to produce a hard-working performance, Steven possessed a biting tackle and a tenacity which were of enormous benefit to the Eagles during the difficulties we encountered in the late 1990s.

Although rarely a goalscorer, Steven netted Palace's second goal with a fabulous twenty-five-yard drive that flew past the bewildered Leicester goalkeeper to help Palace crush the prominent Premiership Filberts 3-0 on their own ground in a League Cup clash in November 2000.

Steven had been with Crystal Palace since joining us at seventeen years old and he was Palace's Young Player of the Year at the end of his first season.

THORN, Andy
Central defender 1989-94

Appearances: 168
Goals: 7

Born: 12 November 1966, Carshalton
Previous clubs: Wimbledon 1984,
    Newcastle United 1988
Subsequent League clubs: Wimbledon
    1994, Tranmere Rovers 1996

Andy Thorn was a proven top-flight centre half when Steve Coppell brought him to Selhurst Park in November 1989. It was a brilliant signing, for Andy immediately shored up Palace's rather leaky defence to help ensure First Division survival in 1989/90 while also assisting in the club's run to its first-ever FA Cup final. The following season, teamed up alongside his former Wimbledon colleague, Eric Young, Andy proceeded to secure the club's best ever defensive record in the top flight along with its highest finishing position of third in that top division.

Tough, unrelenting, obdurate and a fearsome opponent, Andy won 5 England Under-21 caps in his earlier years in the game. Upon joining the Palace he proved more than capable of subduing the nation's best strikers week after week and served as skipper in the absence of Geoff Thomas before doing so in his own right, thus earning the respect then admiration and gratitude of all Palace supporters, as a wholehearted footballer of the old breed who always gave of his best to his club whatever the circumstances.

It was therefore no surprise that Andy won the Player of the Year award in 1993 but he incurred a troublesome knee injury later that year and returned to Wimbledon in October 1994.

Andy Thorn.

TOWNSEND, Don
Defender 1962-64

Appearances: 82
Born: 17 September 1930, Swindon
Previous clubs: Charlton Athletic 1950

Don Townsend joined the Palace as a vastly experienced, polished left-back and he made that position his own for the two seasons after he arrived at Selhurst Park. Thus he was an integral feature of the Palace side that won promotion in 1963/64, taking the club back into the higher divisions of the Football League after an absence of thirty-nine years, and only being denied the Third Division Championship on goal average, following an aberration in the final match of the season.

Steady, utterly reliable, knowledgeable, an expert reader of the game, Don was everything a manager, a club or its fans could ever want from a full-back and his displays are remembered with pleasure by Palace supporters from the mid-1960s.

TURNER, Billy
Midfield 1925-36

Appearances: 302
Goals: 37
Born: 16 November 1901, Tipton,
    Staffordshire
Previous clubs: Bromsgrove

Billy Turner signed for Crystal Palace in the summer of 1925 as a skilled, tough little inside forward. He came into the Palace side at the start of 1925/26 and, injuries or illness apart, was a fixture there for the next eleven seasons, accumulating so many appearances that he still remains within the top-ten places in the club's all-time charts.

Billy rarely scored many goals himself, but everyone who saw him play for the Palace agreed that he helped to make hundreds of them for the club. There was also no doubt that right-winger Albert Harry played much better with Billy there beside him, and that our forwards could become really devastating if Billy was directing our attack.

Billy became known to Palace fans as 'Rubber' and his resilience and adaptability were certainly an unusual feature of the pre-war game: later in his career, Billy played in the wing half positions and then, towards the end, even as a full-back! Thus, in an age when players were never encouraged or expected to be adaptable, the only positions Billy did not fill for us at one time or another were those of goalkeeper, centre forward and centre half!

Billy was simply one of those players who win the hearts of football fans with their wholehearted commitment and full-blooded displays: as Palace manager Jack Tresadern once said of him: 'He's 100 per cent wherever you play him!'

UPHILL, Dennis
Forward 1960-62

Appearances: 74
Goals: 20
Born: 11 August 1931, Bath, Somerset
Previous clubs: Tottenham Hotspur 1949,
    Reading 1953, Coventry City 1955,
    Mansfield Town 1957, Watford 1959

Strong, burly and ungainly, yet possessing ball control that initially appeared surprising in such a hefty frame, Dennis Uphill was manager Arthur Rowe's most astute signing in his first season in charge at the Palace. Dennis was secured to ensure that the refined talents of Johnny Byrne and Roy Summersby were allowed to run free and not be thwarted by the heavy treatment that was beginning to be meted out to them by some of the more unscrupulous Fourth Division defenders, as Palace's progress under Mr Rowe's 'push and run' style gathered momentum with impressive victories.

Rugged and experienced, Dennis took a lot of the buffeting – although he received little praise for his role at the time – yet he was also a deft footballer. Thus, with him at the centre of our attack (and helped by two goals in his debut, against visiting Barrow (4-2), the first only ten minutes after the kick-off) Palace quickly regained top place in the Fourth Division, then went on to secure an impressive promotion at the end of the term.

It was a pleasure for Palace fans of the early sixties to meet Dennis again at a 2002 players' reunion at Selhurst Park.

VAESEN, Nico
Goalkeeper 2004

Appearances: 13
Born: 28 September 1969, Belgium
Previous clubs: CS Bruges 1993, Aalst
1995, Huddersfield Town 1998,
Birmingham City 2001

Present-day Palace fans understand perfectly well why an on-loan player who only made 13 appearances for our club has a place in this book. Those who come to this volume rather later will simply need to know that Nico Vaesen was a key member of the Palace side which beat Division One Champions-elect Norwich along with play-off rivals West Ham and Sunderland without so much as conceding a goal to take the Eagles into the 2004 play-offs, and then performed superbly in those nerve-shredding contests. Well as he did in the two-legged semi-final against Sunderland, at the Millennium Stadium, Cardiff, Nico simply broke the hearts of West Ham with outstanding saves from Bobby Zamora, Steve Lomas and Michael Carrick.

WALDRON, Ernie
Forward 1934-46

Appearances: 86
Goals: 32
Born: 3 June 1913, Birmingham
Subsequent League clubs: Aberdeen
1946

Ernie Waldron was a neat, composed, intuitive inside forward who played for Crystal Palace during the five seasons immediately prior to the Second World War, but did so largely as the understudy or deputy for rampant goalscorer Albert Dawes. Indeed, having joined the Palace in November 1934, he made his debut in our home game against Aldershot (3-0) at the end of December in place of Albert, had 'an impressive' opener and was involved in two of our goals.

But, because of Albert's prowess, and the avowed policy for those days of importing experienced players, Ernie's opportunities were limited, so that his best spell with us was the first two-thirds of 1937/38 prior to Albert's return from Luton Town. Ernie hit 14 goals in 23 League appearances at inside left that term, including a twenty-minute hat-trick against Reading (3-1) in September and he played in all our five FA Cup ties that term too. These included probably his best performance for Palace, in the FA Cup replay at Liverpool when some of the northern scribes thought he was the best forward on the field.

Most of Ernie's war was spent far from Selhurst Park. Certainly he delighted Aberdeen with his twinkling displays and soon after the resumption in August 1946 he joined The Dons and finished his career with them.

WALKER, George
Centre half 1936-38

Appearances: 111
Goals: 1
Born: 24 May 1909, Musselburgh, East
Lothian
Previous clubs: St Mirren, Notts County
Subsequent League clubs: Watford 1939
International honours: 4 full caps for
Scotland

George Walker, a tall, well-built, experienced centre half, was a Scottish international with a string of caps at various levels who joined the Palace early in the summer of 1936 for a fee of £500.

George made 41 splendid appearances for Palace in his first season with us and took over the captaincy from Fred Dawes in November. This was at Fred's suggestion and with the acclaim of all the playing staff, so it clearly indicates the charisma as well as the professional ability of our man.

George was indeed a first-rate skipper and a masterful centre half. He was a fine supplier of telling passes to his forwards while his confidence and authority in defence were magnificent. His career with the Palace ended abruptly when he incurred a nasty knee injury in the game at Watford on the last day of 1938 and he was unable to play again that season, so that there are still fans at Selhurst Park who will argue that that loss cost Palace the single promotion place to the Second Division for 1938/39, when we finished as runners-up to Newport County.

WALL, Peter
Full-back 1970-78

Appearances: 208
Goals: 4
Born: 13 September 1944, Shrewsbury
Previous clubs: Shrewsbury Town 1962, Wrexham 1965, Liverpool 1966

Peter Wall was a fast and clever full-back who added proven top-flight quality to Palace's defence after our inevitably difficult first season at that level. Palace's restructured defence, of which he was the only new member, kept six clean

Peter Wall.

sheets in the club's first eight matches of 1970/71 – our best such sequence during the initial First Division tenure of 1969-73.

An intelligent, neat and articulate player, Peter was a considerable asset, but in only his third match of 1972/73 he had the misfortune to break his leg in a tackle with his former Liverpool teammate Tommy Smith, and it was a year or more before he was able to play properly again. Ultimately though, Peter overcame this adversity in fine style and his later Palace career was highlighted by his regular appearances throughout 1975/76, in which he played in all eight FA Cup ties in the Eagles' historic run to the FA Cup semi-final, and he missed just four league matches, all because of injuries.

In the following two seasons Peter assisted Palace to promotion from the Third Division and was captain at times in the autumn of 1977 after the loss of Ian Evans.

WALLACE, Charlie
Forward 1905-07

Appearances: 68*

Goals: 15*

Born: Sunderland

Subsequent League clubs: Aston Villa
1907

International Honours: 3 full caps for
England

*Includes appearances and goals in Southern
League Second Division 1905/06*

Charlie Wallace was Palace's first ever out-side right. He was immensely talented and was to have a distinguished career with Aston Villa and England. Learning his craft at this early stage, he was exceptionally speedy and gained the nickname 'The Palace Flyer' for his runs down our touchline! Charlie featured with the Palace for our first two seasons. He was an exciting player, rarely missed a match and was a real favourite with the earliest Palace fans.

Like most of his contemporaries, Charlie's greatest match with Crystal Palace was when he featured in our sensational FA Cup victory at League Champions and Champions-elect Newcastle in January 1907 – but since Charlie came from Sunderland no doubt he enjoyed that triumph more than most!

WALLACE, Willie
Forward 1971-72

Appearances: 42

Goals: 6

Born: 23 June 1941, Kirkintilloch,
Dunbartonshire

Previous clubs: Raith Rovers 1959, Heart of Midlothian 1961, Celtic 1966

Subsequent League clubs: Dumbarton
1972

International honours: 7 full caps for
Scotland

Willie Wallace was a diminutive but supremely skilful Scottish international centre forward with an illustrious career at Hearts and Celtic behind him when he joined Crystal Palace with his compatriot John Hughes in the autumn of 1971, Bert Head having found it necessary to remodel his Palace team to remedy a disappointing and potentially perilous opening to 1971/72.

Willie was a craftsman and an artist, a throwback to the Scottish style of ingenious ball-playing which so characterised the game north of the border between the wars and was seen at its peak when the Tartan Army cheered its Wembley Wizards of 1928 as they thrashed England 5-1 at our then-recently opened national

Willie Wallace can't hide his disappointment during Palace's narrow defeat at Chelsea (1-2).

stadium. Willie's passing was immaculate, his control wonderful to watch, and he and to a lesser extent John Hughes, were able to sufficiently augment the efforts of another Scotsman, Gerry Queen, so that Palace eventually climbed clear of the danger zone at the foot of the First Division.

Willie's stay at the Palace was all too brief – almost exactly a year after he had joined us he was on his way back to his homeland to play for Dumbarton – but those of us who were able to watch his noble efforts with the Palace consider ourselves privileged to have done so.

WALSH, Ian
Forward 1976-82

Appearances: 133
Goals: 27
Born: 4 September 1958, St Davids, Pembrokeshire
Subsequent League clubs: Swansea City 1982, Barnsley 1984, Grimsby Town 1986, Cardiff City 1988
International honours: 18 full caps for Wales

Ian was a bright young striker who, after helping the Palace juniors to win the FA Youth Cup in 1977, forced his way into the League side and became a key member of our 1979 Second Division Championship line-ups, scoring eight invaluable goals to become our second-top scorer behind Dave Swindlehurst. Among Ian's several crucial strikes that season were Palace's single goal that accounted for his fellow countrymen, Wrexham, at Selhurst Park in early March, his wicked angled drive with less than two minutes to go which gave us both

points at Bristol Rovers on Easter Saturday, and of course the first one, an arrowed header into the top corner with fourteen minutes to go, in the decisive victory over Burnley which clinched the title in the final game of the season.

With the Eagles in the top flight, Ian became a regular choice for the full Welsh international squad and he is one of three Palace players to have gained 14 full caps for his country while with the club.

WATSON, Ben
Midfield 2003-

Appearances: 26
Goals: 1
Born: 9 July 1985, London

Ben was a thoroughly impressive seventeen-year-old Palace debutant in April 2003 but his progress has been restricted by a nasty groin strain which necessitated an operation in January 2004. Most Palace fans see a huge future for Ben at Selhurst Park but he deserves a place even in a retrospective book like this one because, despite limited senior appearances for the Eagles, his tremendous displays, when he has been available, have enthused everyone while clearly demonstrating the promise to help lift Palace on to even higher planes in the near future.

WATSON, 'Jock'
Defender 1949-51

Appearances: 63
Goals: 1
Born: 31 December 1917, Hamilton, Lanarkshire

Ben Watson.

Previous clubs: Fulham, Real Madrid 1948

Jock Watson was a strong, tall, loyal, lantern-jawed and experienced centre half whom Ronnie Rooke brought to Selhurst Park in August 1949, having previously been with him at Fulham. Jock was the pivot of our defence throughout 1949/50, missing only one game in Palace's best post-war season in the Third Division (South).

   After Rooke's retirement as a player, then ultimately his departure from the club, Jock took over the mantle of skipper for 1950/51, only to become surplus to the requirements of newly appointed managers Fred Dawes and Charlie Slade midway through the season following a dreadful, traumatic 1-6 home defeat by Champions-elect Nottingham Forest.

WERGE, Eddie
Midfield 1961-65

Appearances: 90
Goals: 7
Born: 9 September 1936, Sidcup, Kent
Previous clubs: Charlton Athletic 1955
Subsequent League clubs: Orient 1966

Eddie was a winger with a distinctive upright stance when he joined us for a £4,000 fee from neighbouring Charlton Athletic the summer after Palace's promotion to the Third Division, but he was an adaptable and therefore most useful fellow, and served the club in traditional manner on both our flanks as well as on both sides of midfield, so that he wore no fewer than seven different numbered jerseys during his time at Selhurst Park.

Hard-working Eddie was a clever footballer, but he was always ready to graft when the match or conditions demanded it. Thus he was among the few players who were able to meet the different requirements of both Arthur Rowe and Dick Graham, whose criteria were as contrasting as chalk and cheese. In fact, Eddie was involved in the latter's promotion-winning Palace side of 1963/64, then, after a spell in South Africa, rejoined his former Palace boss (along with not a few of his former Palace colleagues!) over at Orient's Brisbane Road stadium for a couple of seasons.

neat control and could shoot powerfully. Thus, two of his Palace goals are embedded in the club's folklore: when Palace opened their first ever Second Division campaign against favourites and eventual Champions Nottingham Forest, John scored a quite magnificent solo goal to complete our 4-1 victory and it was he who netted the opener in our amazing 6-0 rout of Everton at Goodison Park in the FA Cup first-round tie in January 1922 with a header before providing the cross from which John Conner put Palace three up midway through the second half.

WHIBLEY, John
Forward 1912-23

Appearances: 150
Goals: 27
Born: 1892, Sittingbourne, Kent
Previous clubs: Sittingbourne
Subsequent clubs: Sittingbourne

John Whibley was a quiet lad, tall and willowy, who hailed from Sittingbourne and starred for Crystal Palace either side of the First World War as a winger of quality, although it was after the end of the hostilities that he became our automatic choice at outside left and remained so for four seasons. Thus, his effectiveness and value can be measured by the fact that he retained his place on the Palace flank while aiding the club's progress from the Southern League, via the Third Division Championship and so to a place of relative dignity in the Second Division.

Even as a youngster before the war, John had proved a useful asset: his slight frame made him a tantalising opponent and he possessed scorching pace and

WHITE, Tom
Forward 1966-68

Appearances: 40
Goals: 14
Born: 12 August 1939, Musselburgh, East Lothian
Previous clubs: Raith Rovers 1959, St Mirren 1962, Heart of Midlothian 1963, Aberdeen 1965
Subsequent League clubs: Blackpool 1968, Bury 1970, Crewe Alexandra 1971

Tom White was a sturdy, powerful, balding but dynamic centre forward, with a deserved reputation as a fine goalscorer in Scottish football, who came to Selhurst Park in the 1966 close-season straight after Bert Head had taken over as our manager. Along with John McCormick, Tom was the first of many splendid signings made for the Palace by Mr Head from Scottish clubs, and he immediately demonstrated his talent for goals with a brace on his debut in the opening fixture of 1966/67 when Palace beat visiting Carlisle United 4-2 in tropical heat.

Perhaps the feature of Tom's game which showed him at his best was his heading ability: whether it was delivering an effort on target with power and precise accuracy, or the finesse of a neat knock-down or flick-on to a colleague, his aerial prowess was considerable, but a broken collarbone in only his seventh game reduced his effectiveness for us. Thus, in March 1968, after playing and scoring for Palace against Blackpool and thereby impressing 'Pool's manager, the marvellous Stan Mortensen, Tom joined the Seasiders ten days later to begin an involvement at Bloomfield Road which spanned several roles and many years.

WHITEHOUSE, Brian
Midfield 1963-66

Appearances: 92
Goals: 17
Born: 8 September 1935, West Bromwich
Previous clubs: West Bromwich Albion 1952, Norwich City 1960, Wrexham 1962
Subsequent League clubs: Charlton Athletic 1966, Leyton Orient 1966
Managerial appointments: West Bromwich Albion (caretaker) 1975

The statistical contribution of Brian Whitehouse to Crystal Palace may not have been among the heaviest in Palace's annals but he is certainly one of those footballers who brought something to the club that was out of all proportion to the contemporary expectations and can be recognised in retrospect to have been absolutely crucial at an important, even vital, time. He was, in truth, the catalyst which ensured that Palace's good, strong side of 1963/64, became a promotion-bound one.

Brian had previously been engaged in promotion campaigns with Norwich City and Wrexham: now he made it a trio with the Palace. It was during the closing stages of 1963/64, when many matches were hard-fought, close-run affairs, that he proved invaluable, scoring 6 goals in the last 9 matches to secure precious additional points, which took Palace to within a whisker of the Third Division Championship. He then became a regular member of our side which performed creditably in the Second Division during the ensuing two seasons and he captained the club for 1965/66.

Brian also served admirably in an unexpected role: twice he was called upon to deputise for an injured Palace goalkeeper – and, to his credit, he remained unbeaten on both occasions!

WHITTLE, Alan
Forward 1972-76

Appearances: 126
Goals: 26
Born: 10 March 1950, Liverpool
Previous clubs: Everton 1965
Subsequent League clubs: Orient 1976, Bournemouth 1980

Alan Whittle was a fast, tenacious, clever, blond, tousle-haired striker who joined the Palace at a time when manager Bert Head was desperately seeking scoring power to keep the club in the First Division in midwinter 1972/73, and his goalscoring debut must rank among the most magnificent such occasion in the history of the club, because he helped us to destroy Manchester United by five goals to nil, one of the matches which will live forever in the memories of those who saw us rout the Old Trafford outfit.

Regrettably for everyone connected with the Palace, Alan found it difficult to adjust to Second and then Third Division football, where his undoubted skills were given short shrift by our opponents and, although it was never doubted that he gave of his best, he was equally always a heavily marked man because of his pedigree. However, another goal from this former England schools and youth international will always stay with those Palace fans who were there to witness it, for it was his glorious strike which beat Sunderland at Roker Park to put Third Division Palace into the FA Cup semi-final for the first time.

Some of Alan's admirers from his playing days with the Palace were delighted to see him again at Selhurst Park in April 2003 at a reunion for our former players.

WHITWORTH, George
Forward 1921-25

Appearances: 118
Goals: 50
Born: 14 July 1896, Wellingborough, Northants
Previous clubs: Northampton Town 1913
Subsequent League clubs: Sheffield Wednesday 1925, Hull City 1925, South Shields 1928

George Whitworth was a brave, strong centre forward who had guested for Palace effectively during the First World War and joined the club in March 1922 when we needed a quality centre forward to replace Bert Menlove.

Upon his debut up at Bury, George equalised for Palace before the break, hit the bar soon after the interval, then set up Ben Bateman for the winner! Some debut! He then hit 17 League goals from 36 Second Division appearances in 1922/23, but it was after Tom Hoddinott joined the club in 1923 that Palace fans (sadly, all too briefly) saw Whitworth at his very best. Playing now at inside right, Whitworth was our top scorer with 16 goals, but he also combined with Tom so effectively that Palace had a comfortable Second Division season. He headed the scoring chart once more in 1924/25 when, but for an eye injury which kept him out for six games in the spring of 1925, he might have kept Palace in the Second Division. As it was he notched a late winner to despatch Chelsea on 1 April in the second match of his return but he joined Sheffield Wednesday before the season had ended.

George's 48 goals for Palace in the higher divisions, scored, frankly, when we were far from being a great side, were easily the club's best tally in the period 1921-25 and, at the time of writing have only been bettered by Mark Bright, Ian Wright, Clinton Morrison and Dougie Freedman.

WILDE, Jimmy
Half-back 1928-37

Appearances: 293
Goals: 6
Born: 24 September 1904, Lyndhurst, Hampshire

Jimmy Wilde was a Palace first-team regular for eight full seasons from 1928/29 and club captain for six of them. Tall, slim, elegant but totally dominating at centre half, he had earmarked the pivotal role for himself upon his debut when he managed to subdue even the great Peter Simpson as Palace beat Kettering Town in a testing first-round FA Cup tie in October 1928. Palace also embarked upon a seventeen-match unbeaten run in the Third Division (South) and from mid-table rose to become possible, then even likely, Champions, although we were pipped, on goal-average alone, at the climax by neighbouring Charlton.

Jimmy quickly became recognised as one of the most accomplished half-backs in our division and his displays won him the approval of the fans on many grounds besides Selhurst Park. He usually appeared at centre half, but, when the management or playing policy required it, he could provide constructive driving performances in both the wing half berths.

Even today, some seventy years later, there are Palace fans who still speak with huge admiration and approval of Jimmy Wilde.

WILLIAMS, 'Ginger'
Forward 1909-14

Appearances: 149
Goals: 58
Born: May 1884, Buckley, North Wales
Previous clubs: Birmingham City 1908
Subsequent League clubs: Millwall 1914
International honours: 2 full caps for
  Wales

James Williams was a stocky, well-built young Welshman who could fill any forward position but was at his best at inside right or centre forward. He played so well for the Palace that he gained 2 Welsh international caps in season 1911/12. Williams quickly became a great favourite

with the Palace fans who nicknamed him 'Ginger' on account of his mop of red hair.

Palace's best season during Ginger's four-and-a-half years with the club was his second one, 1910/11, when Palace were in contention for the runners-up spot until the final game, when we lost at Northampton and ended up finishing fourth. His career record with Palace of 57 Southern League goals is an impressive one and only Ted Smith scored more times before the First World War, while Ginger's other claim to fame at the Palace would be the five goals he scored in one of his earliest games for us, during the 6-0 rout of Southend at the Crystal Palace in September 1909 – and only Peter Simpson has ever bettered that goal tally in a single match in the Palace colours, which is some company to be in!

WILLIAMS, Paul
Forward 1992-95

Appearances: 53
Goals: 9
Born: 16 August 1965, London
Previous clubs: Charlton Athletic 1986, Brentford (loan) 1987, Sheffield Wednesday 1990
Subsequent League clubs: Sunderland (loan) 1995, Birmingham City (loan) 1995, Charlton Athletic 1995, Torquay United (loan) 1996

Paul Williams came to Selhurst Park in the transfer deal which took Mark Bright to Sheffield Wednesday. It was an intriguing transfer, because little more than two weeks earlier he had scored to rescue a point for the Owls in a 1-1 draw with the Palace at Selhurst Park and had revealed to us just what a talented, subtle player he could be.

Diminutive, but possessing supreme control, balance and the ability to flight the perfect pass, Paul's original task was to add some sophistication to Palace's direct style, but, while he undoubtedly did that, he could not manage a single goal for us in our fight against relegation and was beset by injuries that term.

However, Palace fans quickly appreciated his skills and he had a splendid first half of 1993/94, culminating in a run of 5 strikes from just 7 midwinter games, which helped the Eagles back to the top of the Division One table and set us on course for the Championship.

WOAN, Alan
Forward 1959-61

Appearances: 46
Goals: 23
Born: 8 February 1931, Liverpool
Previous clubs: Norwich City 1953, Northampton Town 1956
Subsequent League clubs: Aldershot 1961

Alan was a tough, sturdy inside forward who could be relied upon to contribute a regular supply of goals and he was bought to boost Palace's flagging strike ratio in the autumn of 1959. Hard-working and a classic goal-poacher, he netted in only his second game as Palace romped to a 4-0 success over visiting Rochdale, but it was in the opening match of 1960/61 that he put on his best display for us, scoring a hat-trick in Palace's 9-2 rout of hapless Accrington Stanley.

Alan contributed 13 goals from just 16 Fourth Division games towards Palace's

promotion at the end of 1960/61, but by that time he had moved on to Aldershot, for whom he demonstrated his ability against the Palace in the most emphatic manner with a goal in the 'Shots' 2-1 victory over us at the Recreation Ground in a rare Saturday evening fixture at the end of March.

WOOD, Brian
Defender 1961-67

Appearances: 152
Goals: 4
Born: 8 December 1940, Poole, Dorset
Previous clubs: West Bromwich Albion 1958
Subsequent League clubs: Orient 1966, Colchester United 1968, Workington Town 1970

Brian Wood was a strong, solid, ever-dependable centre half who became a thoroughly reliable pillar of the Palace defence through the early and mid-1960s.

Dick Graham had recommended Brian to former manager Arthur Rowe, and paired him with Alan Stephenson to form probably the first, and certainly one of the most effective, central defensive partnerships at the Palace. He made a huge, if often unacknowledged, contribution to the club's promotion to the Second Division in 1963/64 in which he missed just one match all season and when Palace's defensive record was only improved upon by one other club in that section.

Brian then had the misfortune to suffer a badly broken leg in a third-round FA Cup tie in January 1965 from which he never fully recovered, although he did play a few matches for Palace in the season which followed his nine-month lay-off.

Brian then left Palace to rejoin Dick Graham over at Orient and Palace fans were pleased for him as his career burgeoned again, while his many admirers at Selhurst Park have been delighted when he has returned to our headquarters for occasional former players' reunions.

WOOD, George
Goalkeeper 1983-88

Appearances: 221
Born: 26 September 1952, Douglas, Lanarkshire
Previous clubs: East Stirling 1970, Blackpool 1972, Everton 1977, Arsenal 1980
Subsequent League clubs: Cardiff City 1988, Hereford United 1990
International honours: 4 full caps for Scotland

Scottish international goalkeeper George Wood joined the Palace as one of Alan Mullery's best signings for the Eagles. He had been a top-class custodian and quickly demonstrated his skill to Palace patrons.

George was ever-present for nearly three seasons and became the club's second post-war goalkeeper to put together a run of 100 consecutive League games (John Jackson, inevitably, was the first) while those 100 appearances straight from his debut were the first achieved by a Palace player for over a quarter of a century. In fact, during George's four and a half seasons at Selhurst Park, he missed only three senior games and those

absences were forced upon him by the urgent need for surgery.

His best seasons with the Palace were his last two complete ones, when, under Steve Coppell, the Eagles finished fifth and sixth in the old Second Division, though probably his finest single game for Palace was in the second leg of a League Cup tie with Manchester United at Old Trafford in October 1985 when he matched the high standards of his counterpart Gary Bailey who was the Reds' man to do most to deny Palace any reward over the two legs.

A top-class goalkeeper is expected to be both courageous and consistent. George Wood, the gentle Scotsman in the Palace goal, provided both qualities in full measure while he was with the Eagles – and evidence of his popularity was clearly to be seen 'below stairs' when he returned to Selhurst Park with Cardiff City for a League Cup match in August 2000.

WOODGER, George
Forward 1905-10

Appearances: 177*
Goals: 47*
Born: 1884, Croydon
Subsequent League clubs: Oldham Athletic 1910, Tottenham Hotspur 1914
International honours: 1 full cap for England
Includes appearances and goals in Southern League Second Division 1905/06

George Woodger was an inside or centre forward of the highest quality who played for Crystal Palace in the club's earliest years and soon became the first Palace superstar in an age when today's media hype was unthinkable.

George Wood.

He was a local boy – in itself a rarity, for virtually all the Palace staff in the club's first few seasons were professionals from the north of England recruited by manager John Robson. It was soon apparent to everyone that George was a prodigy. He quickly became a permanent feature of Palace's Southern League line-ups, his poise and delicate ball-playing skills rapidly endearing him to supporters and earning him the quaint nickname 'Lady'.

George's best season with the Palace was 1907/08 when he was our top goalscorer with 13 Southern League strikes, missed just two games and assisted the club to fourth place in the table while also contributing a couple of FA Cup goals in the first-round defeat of Coventry. He also notched his first senior hat-trick in Palace's 4-1 victory over visiting Swindon Town in October.

George became Palace's captain for 1909/10, succeeding Wilfred Innerd, but by now his playing responsibility was more that of supplying ace strikers George Payne and Ginger Williams than of scoring goals himself. So successful was this arrangement that Palace scored 69 League goals and only a disappointing sequence in the closing few games prevented the side from claiming at least a top-three finish.

By this stage Woodger was a well-known and much appreciated performer. He was also, quite rightly, ambitious and it became clear to him and to all Palace fans that the only way he would gain the international recognition he craved would be for him to join a club in the more prestigious Football League. Thus, after weeks of frenzied speculation, George moved in September 1910 to Oldham, intriguingly making his Latics debut at nearby Woolwich against

Arsenal and he at last gained his coveted England cap against Ireland at Derby (2-1) the following February.

WOODHOUSE, Charlie
Centre forward 1910-11

Appearances: 45
Goals: 23
Born: unknown

Charlie Woodhouse was initially signed from Halesowen to replace club skipper George Woodger when the latter was transferred to Oldham in September 1910, but strong, powerful, rumbustious Charlie was a quite different type of centre forward to Woodger.

That said, he was as effective as he was unlike his predecessor. Charlie netted on his debut, played in every remaining Southern League match of 1910/11, and finished as our top scorer by some distance with 15 goals from his 33 outings.

However, early in 1911/12 Palace suffered 'a crushing blow' with the death of their new ace striker and a promising Palace career was brought to an abrupt untimely end. Charlie's was the first of several unfortunate deaths to hit Crystal Palace and he is buried in Beckenham Cemetery, adjacent to Birkbeck Station.

WOODRUFF, Bobby
Forward 1966-70

Appearances: 139
Goals: 48
Born: 9 November 1940, Highworth, Wiltshire
Previous clubs: Swindon Town 1958, Wolverhampton Wanderers 1964

Subsequent League clubs: Cardiff City
  1969, Newport County 1974

Bobby Woodruff was a prominent member of Palace's sides in the late 1960s. A chart of his appearances would show that he made full appearances for two seasons after coming to Selhurst Park, while only a broken collarbone prevented him from making an even more impressive contribution towards the club's promotion to the top flight in 1968/69.

Bobby had an excellent goalscoring record with the Palace and his 18 League goals in both 1966/67 and 1967/68 were not approached in the top divisions by a Palace player for two decades. In fact, Bobby was a double-edged weapon for Crystal Palace. Firstly, he was a magnificent header of the ball and graceful too, so that many of his goals were spectacular, picturesque affairs which stand in the memory to this day, while he also possessed that all-important talent for a striker of being in the right place to snap

Bobby Woodruff.

up any half-chance that came his way in the six-yard box. Thus, in the early spring of 1969 Bobby hit 5 goals in 6 games while his winner at leaders and Champions-elect Derby was what first kindled the hope and belief that Palace themselves could claim success that term.

Equally, Bobby possessed a prodigious long throw-in: it was the league's prototype for this ploy and Palace exploited it most successfully, for Bobby could reach the penalty spot without any difficulty.

For all these reasons it was a pleasure for everyone associated with Crystal Palace to see Bobby back at Selhurst Park at the 1968/69 players' reunion in March 2001.

WOODS, Charlie
Forward 1964-66

Appearances: 51
Goals: 5
Born: 18 March 1941, Whitehaven,
  Cumberland
Previous clubs: Newcastle United 1959,
  Bournemouth 1962
Subsequent League clubs: Ipswich Town
  1966, Watford 1970, Colchester United
  1971

Charlie was a dapper, tenacious outside right who had caught the discerning eye of Dick Graham. His speed, penetration and crosses proved a useful source of openings from which Palace goalscorers Cliff Holton, Peter Burridge and Keith Smith could benefit, thus ensuring that Palace acquitted themselves creditably in our first spell in the Second Division for forty years.

A feature of the latter years of Dick Graham's managerial tenure at Selhurst

Park was the 'numbers game' he played to confuse the opposition, so that while Charlie almost always operated on Palace's right flank he actually wore no fewer than nine different numbered jerseys in his time with us!

WRIGHT, Ian
Forward 1985-91

Appearances: 277
Goals: 117
Born: 3 November 1963, Woolwich
Previous clubs: Greenwich Borough
Subsequent League clubs: Arsenal 1991, West Ham United 1998, Celtic 1999, Burnley 2000
International honours: 33 full caps for England

Mercurial striker Ian Wright joined the Eagles in the summer of 1985. He quickly made his mark as a highly effective 'super-sub' in his initial season to finish as Palace's second-highest scorer with Phil Barber on 9 goals. When Mark Bright arrived the following year, the duo soon established a marvellously successful striking partnership and it was largely their goals which took the club to the promotion play-offs and a return to the top flight in 1989. Ian's tally of 27 League goals that season represents the club's record in the higher divisions while his career total of 92 is exactly equal to that of Mark Bright and the best in the top two sections in the entire Palace history.

One of Ian's best-remembered goals was made as a substitute in the FA Cup final of 1990. Palace were 1-2 in arrears when Steve Coppell brought Ian on after sixty-nine minutes. Within three minutes we were level with a goal to equal the finest the old stadium had ever seen. Ian had us in front in extra time too with a spectacular flying volley! But United had time to regroup, equalise to force a replay and take the trophy by a single goal.

Season 1990/91 was another eventful and successful season for Ian Wright. This became Palace's most successful season of all time, in which we finished third in the top flight while also winning the Full Members' Cup final at Wembley with a rampant 4-1 extra-time win over Everton. He also netted an absolutely unforgettable hat-trick within just eighteen minutes of the second half of Palace's penultimate match of the season, at Wimbledon. It was our first hat-trick on an away ground since 1963, easily our fastest at top level and demonstrated in emphatic, magnificent style that when he was on top form there was no more dangerous or exciting player than Ian in the entire Football or Premier League.

YARD, Ernie
Midfield 1965-66

Appearances: 40
Goals: 3
Born: 3 May 1941, Stranraer
Previous clubs: Kilmarnock 1961, Partick Thistle 1963, Bury 1963
Subsequent League clubs: Reading 1966

At the time Ernie Yard joined Crystal Palace he became the only Scotsman on our books, but he had done enough in the two League games between Bury and the Palace in 1964/65 to demonstrate that he would be a useful acquisition, because he had scored three times against us to assist the Shakers to a 'double' over us.

Ian Wright threatened Blackburn throughout the second leg of the Second Division play-off final, 3 June 1989. Phil Barber is in support.

Ernie had originally been a striker, but Dick Graham used him mainly as a wide, left-sided midfield player. He was busy, hardworking and versatile, just the sort of guy Dick valued greatly. He scored one of his three Palace goals upon his return to Gigg Lane in November 1965, to help Palace merit a 2-2 draw, but he did not feature highly in new manager Bert Head's plans and he left us for Reading in the autumn of 1966.

YOUNG, Eric
Central defender 1990-95

Appearances: 204
Goals: 17
Born: 25 March 1960, Singapore
Previous clubs: Brighton & Hove Albion 1982, Wimbledon 1987
Subsequent League clubs: Wolverhampton Wanderers 1995
International honours: 21 full caps for Wales

Eric Young was Palace's superb 6ft 3ins defender and club-record holder of 19 full international caps for a home country while on our books, a figure that is well above the reach of any past or present Palace star.

There was some criticism of the fee that Palace had to pay Wimbledon to secure Eric in the summer of 1990, but Steve Coppell's judgement proved completely reliable for Eric netted some important goals for the Eagles and was magnificent in our defence. Thus, it was while he was with the club that Palace achieved their highest-ever finish in the top flight and won the Full Members' Cup final, beating Everton 4-1 at Wembley.

Eric Young.

Fan Zhiyi.

In fact Eric netted on his Palace debut, although perhaps his best-remembered goal for us would be the one he scored to beat Liverpool at Selhurst Park in March 1992, and he was always a terror to his opponents in their own penalty areas. In defence, alongside his former Dons' colleague Andy Thorn, Eric always stood out: he would have done so anyway because of his superb physique but he did so also because of the headband that he wore (which caused the Palace fans to nickname him 'Ninja' after the similarly attired turtles that featured in a highly popular cartoon of those times).

Unusually Eric's international career with Wales burgeoned late, but once he had been selected he became a regular and key member of the Principality's side that so narrowly missed out on qualification for the 1994 World Cup finals.

ZHIYI, Fan
Defender 1998-2001

Appearances: 102
Goals: 6
Born: 22 January 1970, Shanghai, China
Previous clubs: Shanghai Shenua
Subsequent League clubs: Dundee 2001, Cardiff City 2002
International honours: 109 full international caps for China

Fan arrived at Selhurst Park with his compatriot Sun Jihai amidst a blaze of publicity in August 1998 because the duo were the first Chinese nationals to sign for a British League club. Sun only stayed at the Palace for the rest of 1998/99 but Fan progressed marvellously during the turbulent period for the club, and his contribution to the Eagles gained increasing appreciation from Palace supporters as the months passed. He was the captain of the Chinese national side and Asian Footballer of the Year in 1999, quickly becoming an asset to our cause and a favourite with all Palace followers.

For his first season Fan was usually deployed defensively in midfield but his two later terms saw him in commanding form at the centre of Palace's backline. Discerning supporters recognised that Palace's Division One survival in 1999/2000 was owed in no small part to Fan's partnership with Andy Linighan at a time when Palace came under a lot of pressure from opposing attacks.

His popularity at the Palace was also due to the evident fact that he was clearly delighted to be playing for our club and proud to be wearing the claret and blue. As such our supporters made him Player of the Year for 2000/01 and have followed his subsequent career with interest.

If you are interested in purchasing other books published by Tempus,
or in case you have difficulty finding any Tempus books in your local bookshop,
you can also place orders directly through our website

www.tempus-publishing.com